NATURAL LAW

–

AUSTRALIAN STYLE

A Study in Disputation focusing on the Work

of

Peter Singer, John Finnis and Tracey Rowland

"Let there be light". (Gen: 3: 10)
"Love is the fulfillment of the law." (Rom. 13: 10)

Dr. DONALD G. BOLAND

En Route Books and Media, LLC
Saint Louis, MO

ENROUTE
Make the time

En Route Books and Media, LLC
5705 Rhodes Avenue
St. Louis, MO 63109

Cover credit: Sebastian Mahfood

ISBN-13: 978-1-956715-49-1
Library of Congress Control Number: 2022938249

TO SAINT ANGELO RONCALLI

POPE JOHN XXIII

whose encyclical "Peace on Earth" (1963)

set out the natural rights of the human person

"Any well-regulated and productive association of men in society demands the acceptance of one fundamental principle: that each individual man is truly a person. His is a nature, that is, endowed with intelligence and free will. As such he has rights and duties, which together flow as a direct consequence from his nature."

Pope Saint John XXIII Encyclical *Pacem in terris* 1963 (n. 9).

"The Church's action in promoting human rights is therefore supported by rational reflection, in such a way that these rights can be presented to all people of good will, independently of any religious affiliation they may have."

Pope Benedict XVI: *Address to Pontifical Academy of Social Sciences. 04/05/2009*

"The defence of the environment and the fight against exclusion demand that we recognize a moral law written into human nature itself, one which includes the natural difference between man and woman, and absolute respect for life in all stages and dimensions."

Pope Francis: *Address to UN, Friday, September 25, 2015*

"Men look to seats of learning in their doubt,
But seats of learning have contracted out
Of natural law, and bid us do the same:
Truth has no rights that error may not claim;"

James McAuley: *A Letter to John Dryden,* Collected Poems 1936–1970

ACKNOWLEDGEMENTS

For much the same reasons, my debts to others in the writing of this book is the same as those acknowledged in my previous book *Economic Science and Saint Thomas Aquinas*. I simply repeat therefore what I have said there except for one important addition.

There is one person to whom I am most greatly indebted in the production of this work on Natural Law. That is my colleague Frank Calneggia, excerpts of whose essay I have included as Appendix A of the book. But his contribution has been much more than that. In fact, I must say that his cooperation in the production of this work has been so close and helpful that he deserves to be described as a collaborator in its production.

I have consulted his advice continuously throughout the writing of the book, and he has been a constant source of encouragement. I wish to thank him for that. The book would otherwise have been a long time coming and might not have seen the light of day at all.

What is in the excerpts of his essay here included as Appendix A is fully his own work, and any contribution of mine to it may be seen as indirect only as his contribution to mine is indirect.

I would not wish, however, for him to be held accountable for the errors and faults of the work, for which I must take full responsibility.

TABLE OF CONTENTS

PREFACE

As with my previous book "Economic Science and Saint Thomas Aquinas" this book has been the product of a lifetime's study of the works of Aristotle and St. Thomas Aquinas in an effort to make some sort of sense, not specifically in this case of matters economic, but more generally of the moral and legal aspects of modern social and political life.

In writing on the Natural Law, however, I encountered a peculiar problem, that of having to deal with a matter that seemed to straddle two separate disciplines, those of Ethics and Law. As studied today they seem to be quite unrelated. My study of law only intensified my interest in this regard. So I should explain how I have come to see the relationship. It appeared quite early that there was a deep problem in reconciling the legal positivist position adopted by the University of Sydney Law School (in this respect no different from most law schools in the English speaking world), especially in its more philosophical course on Jurisprudence, with the very notion of Natural Law that has been so fundamental to the ethico-political practical science which began with Aristotle and continued throughout the history of Western civilization right into our own times, if more and more disdained in the modern era.

The study of ethics, law and politics are intertwined in the Aristotelian and Scholastic traditions. There was, however, even in ancient Greek society a development that has had a deep and lasting effect on the study of law. This was the tendency for the knowledge of law to be separated out as belonging to an art necessary for a citizen to possess in the prosecution and defence of his rights in the courts of justice. This was closely allied to involvement in "practical" politics. This tendency was further strengthened when Roman rule came to dominate Greek culture.

Thus, the study of law developed early a certain independence from moral and political philosophy, and this was concreted in the creation of the Roman Civil Law tradition. It was closely allied with the art of Rhetoric, as is understandable, but there also developed along with it an expertise in linguistic and literary expression. We notice in Cicero, for instance, a connection between mastery in the Latin language, the art of rhetoric, the practice of law and engagement in Politics. The practical bent of the Roman mind seemed to mean the reversal of the philosophical relation between moral philosophy and law as a practical study. But more than that it meant in regard to the study of law its subordination, as it were, to the needs of succeeding in court proceedings.

This literary, legal, political connection carried through into the Christian era and is most evident in St. Augustine. As a teacher of rhetoric, he was training the legal practitioners of his day. Law had become a profession whereby one gained a living. The significance of all this is that the practice of law came to be seen more connected with a (liberal) art, such as rhetoric (the art of persuasion), than as part of a moral science. At the same time Politics came also to be seen rather as an art than a form of prudence. It is only the latter that carries with it a moral character.

After the fall of the Western part of the Roman Empire the study of Roman Law had a chequered career. But it did survive, thanks to the likes of Justinian and the move of the Law School at Rome to Ravenna (Bologna was its successor). Moreover, it later on formed the basis of nearly all other legal systems and law schools in Europe and England. For a fascinating account of this story see the article by Charles P. Sherman, Faculty of Law, Yale University: THE INDEBTEDNESS OF MODERN JURISPRUDENCE TO MEDIEVAL ITALIAN LAW in the Canadian Law Times VOL. XXXIII. OCTOBER, 1913. No. 10. Faculty Scholarship Series. Paper 4437. (digitalcommons.law.yale.edu)

But what we want to bring out here is an explanation for the separation of the study of law as it is found in Aristotle and St. Thomas Aquinas – focusing on the natural moral law – and the study of law as found in ancient and modern times, seen as falling within the context of a judicial system where the principal task is to persuade the judge and/or jury of the truth of one's version of the facts and the application of the law in one's favour. What this does is take the focus off the morality (justice) or otherwise of the law and puts it on the application of the law as it stands – that is to say the law as laid down (posited) by the government of the day.

Even in the modern study of law in which a subject called "Jurisprudence" is included there is a disconnection between law as it is studied and practised and the study of "Jurisprudence" (which from its very name should be interested in morality). The study of theories of law, including Natural Law, is made but it is felt not to serve any "practical" purpose. That it seems to me to be the reason why Natural Law is felt to be a foreign body in the law schools of today.

However, the point of what we are saying is not to deny a proper place for the study of law so focused on its concrete application to the cases before the courts, nor necessarily to criticise the development of a legal profession devoted to the conduct of such cases. It is only the taking of such a focus to the extent of disconnecting Positive Law from Natural Law, or more pointedly, of disconnecting the study of law from the study of Natural Law.

Perhaps a comparison will help bring out the point we wish to make. St. Thomas makes a distinction between military prudence and the arts of war. So too we may make a distinction between political prudence and the arts of politics; and also between jurisprudence and the arts of law. It is not suggested that many "determinations" dependent upon political and legal will only are not necessary for the implementation of law and justice. Of themselves they do not necessarily contain a moral judgment. What is required, though, is that they are not contrary to a moral law and a judgment of conscience.

To take the military example, the general is bound by the natural laws against murder and theft in regard to the conquest of an enemy. His prosecution of the war must always be in accord with justice to fellow human beings. But there are all sorts of tactical manoeuvres to be employed in order to prosecute a war successfully. Moral rectitude as such does not supply for these military arts and skills. Similarly, the advocate is bound by the natural laws against false witness and deceit. But within that moral ambit there are all sorts of rhetorical moves that can be employed to ensure success in one's case.

There is much then of positive legislative theory and judicial practice that is to be taken into account in a full treatment of human law. So too there are many rhetorical judgements to be taken into account in the prosecution and defence of a case. Considered by themselves these positive determinations may be simply the result of human will, but considered in the whole context of the application of the law as an ethico-political discipline they must amount also to an exercise of prudence. They determine the natural moral law to the concrete case. For, having to do with human conduct, every case will come under some general moral principle.

Where the legal positivist goes wrong is in disconnecting these legitimate arts, and the study they require, from their natural moral/prudential foundation. The problem arises when there is legal and political pressure to apply "the law" regardless of any moral considerations. The positivist lawyer will say: "law is public, your morality (even sense of justice) is private". The primary duty of the judge is seen to be to apply the law as it is laid down, regardless of his or her opinion as to its justice or injustice. (That serves well enough in a society whose laws are in fact based for the most part on natural morality and Natural Law but it breaks down under extreme conditions as is manifest in "legal systems" that are not so based, like those of Nazi German and Soviet Russian of the last century – the worry is that the West generally is itself fast "progressing" in that same immoral direction).

So it is that under present conditions the Natural Law is more suitably dealt with in Ethics and Politics as understood by Aristotle and Aquinas. Indeed, law as understood in modern law schools will be an impediment to the proper understanding of Natural Law and natural morality.

However, to concentrate upon the ethico-political philosophy of Aristotle (as developed by St. Thomas Aquinas) did not seem to me to address this problem of the actual divide between the study of Law and Ethics.

Then there appeared to be a way whereby this problem might be addressed, by taking the work of someone, who had attempted to bridge the gap from within, as it were, the study of law as so considered distinct and even separate from Ethics, and to build upon the deficiencies of his approach, in that he kept too close in my view to the modern positivist position. This is not to deny that his effort was a major step towards bridging the divide. But it left some important parts of the problem unresolved.

This person is John Finnis, who happens to be an Australian, who studied in the same Australian school of law as I had done, (in Adelaide rather than Sydney). The core of my book is a critique of his most celebrated work, "Natural Law and Natural Rights". But, fortuitously, there have also appeared the works of two other celebrated Australians, which can be related to the problem and, as I see it, a critique of their works can round off the treatment of it. These persons are Tracey Rowland and Peter Singer. Each represent two opposed extreme positions with regard to natural morality and the Natural Law as will be made clear.

This has determined the structure of my book and also the lack of a copious bibliography. The references are confined in the main to the works of Aristotle and St. Thomas Aquinas and the three works the object of my critiques.

The history of the study of Natural Law is, of course, not confined to Aristotle and Aquinas. Indeed, there was intense interest in it early in the modern era. Prominent figures in this regard are Hugo Grotius and Samuel Pufendorf. They and a host of others, including many members of what has been called "The Scottish Enlightenment", such as Adam Smith and Thomas Reid, drew upon the scholastic tradition of Natural Law in their moral and political philosophy. But their thinking could not fail to be affected by the general rejection of Metaphysics and preference for the new scientific method.

This led to the study falling into line with the two opposed schools that characterize modern thought generally, on the one hand, rationalism (modelled on the mathematical part of the modern scientific method) and, on the other, empiricism (modelled on the experimental part of the modern scientific method).

It was nonetheless a most influential discussion at an important time in modern history, as may be gleaned from these extracts from the entry in the *Stanford Encyclopedia of Philosophy* on "Pufendorf's Moral and Political Philosophy"*(First published Fri Sep 3, 2010; substantive revision Tue Nov 3, 2015)*: "The discourse of natural law became the *lingua franca* of 18th-century moral, political, and social (including economic) thought ... natural law thought also became part of the intellectual inheritance of the American Revolution and constitutionalism."

It incorporated much that was in the Aristotelian and Scholastic tradition with regard to Natural Law but, owing to the internal contradictions within it by reason of its futile attempt to apply the modern mixed method of science to practical/moral/political/legal matters, its influence only continues in the creation of modern International Law, related to but not to be identified with the "Law of Peoples" (*Ius gentium*).

I have not ventured to include this study of Natural Law in early modern times as it does not really add anything of moral/legal importance to that of Aristotle and Aquinas. It would anyway only complicate our discussion. I have also not ventured to include the study of Canon Law, which, for analogous reasons apparently, has developed as a separate study from Moral Theology.

The focus may appear to be narrow and negative, but I believe it is the best way to bring out the essence and importance of Natural Law for our times.

I would only add some explanation of the cover design of the book. It shows the Australian continent as background. But the photos superimposed are of the three universities where each of the Australians discussed began their academic careers, influenced no doubt by the prevailing positivist notion of law or relativist notion of ethics, going on to Oxford or Cambridge. The other photo is the Australian Federal Parliament, the principal law making body in Australia, though each of the states and territories have their own parliament, all parliaments bastions of positive law without any belief in the natural law as dealt with in my book.

NATURAL LAW - AUSTRALIAN STYLE

(A Study in Disputation focusing on the Work of Peter Singer, John Finnis and Tracey Rowland)

INTRODUCTION

It is rather striking that three of the leading figures in contemporary moral and legal philosophy are Australians. Two are qualified as lawyers and practicing Catholics, the third is a bioethicist and a non-religious Jew). The three are high profile academics. All specialize in Ethics. Rowland is a theologian. The two others we may describe as moral philosophers with specializations within that field, Singer in Bioethics, Finnis in Legal Philosophy. The two Catholics have written on Natural Law, one, John Finnis, quite extensively in connection with his specialty of legal philosophy, though this has branched out into Ethics generally.

So far as the study of Natural Law is concerned the central figure is John Finnis. Singer relates to it indirectly as adopting a position in Moral Philosophy that rejects Natural Law in any traditional sense, but takes a naturalist position in a utilitarian sense. Rowland adopts a position that downplays Natural Law as knowable by human reason or philosophy outside the theological order of grace.

The two Catholics try to bring their theories of Natural Law within the work of St. Thomas Aquinas. In our view they fail. We are concerned however to judge their efforts from a purely philosophical point of view and therefore are not directly concerned with sacred theology.

We might just note however that theology is often taken ambiguously today even by Catholic philosophers and theologians, confusing Sacred Theology and Natural Theology, simply because both are directly concerned with God and the divine influence on creation. This ambiguity is particularly evident in the case of Rowland who purports to be discussing matters of Sacred Theology in relation to Natural Law when what she may be opposing are atheistic positions at a philosophical level. The heavy modern ambiguity regarding the notion of reason is also in play here (which is a failure to accord to Metaphysics, of which Natural Theology is part, a place of honor in the field of reason and philosophy). This latter ambiguity is of especial influence, in two quite opposite ways, as we shall shortly endeavor to demonstrate, on the work of Singer and Finnis.

We do not deny the importance for Christians of applying the light of Faith to the better understanding of natural morality, and accordingly of the natural moral law. However, it is also important to avoid neglecting the light of our natural intelligence in such practical matters as the Natural Law (which St. Thomas insists is a participation in the Eternal Law).

Moreover, for the Catholic philosopher, grace and Faith (we use here the capital letter in order signal the difference of divine faith from human faith or opinion - another quite blatant ambiguity indulged in) enable one to see better the truths, both theoretical and practical, of reason.

There should be no apology for such reliance on natural reason, then, on the part of Catholics in their disputations upon fundamental philosophical matters with those not of the same Faith. To an objective observer it is the non-believer who is quite evidently in the weaker position from a rational point of view in such disputations. In the end he or she inevitably resorts to an absurd skeptical lack of position or to a stubborn refusal to acknowledge the need for ultimate explanations.

Rowland as we see her position on Natural Law is too much influenced by the distorted modern truncation of reason, and she beats a retreat from reason into Faith in order to explain the apparent failure to defend the Natural Law by Catholics philosophers/theologians. What she fails to appreciate properly is the extent to which all modern lawyers/philosophers (sadly including herself it seems) are captured by a distorted notion of reason. For anyone educated in modern schools, especially in the law schools of the West, it is almost impossible to avoid the effects of such distortion.

We could begin our discourse by disputing the position of Rowland from a Thomist point of view and then go on to consider the positions of Finnis and Singer. However, we feel it necessary to go back to basics and, drawing on St. Thomas's method of disputation, outline first the general principles or rules of disputation so that we may see clearly how one ought to proceed in disputing each of these positions on Natural Law.

I wish to emphasise one thing as to how this book, including the appendices, is to be read, which is that the criticisms made, even when phrased as if directed against the persons who have made the statements the subject of complaint, are to be taken strictly objectively. Thus, I wish to have applied to the critique within the book the same criterion of pure objectivity that St. Thomas recommends in any philosophical discussion. Particularly in regard to matters of moral principle discussed, comments and criticisms mean in no way to imply any subjective fault on the part of the makers of the erroneous statements.

Hence, in this regard I ask the reader to adopt for this book the same principle of interpretation underlying what Josef Pieper had to say about the moral defect of presumption that he saw as part of Reformation theology: "It is but proper to emphasise at this point what is surely obvious: that we are speaking here only of the objective erroneousness of the presumption that is part of Reformation theology. It would be ridiculous and absurd to raise or attempt to answer the question of subjective guilt." From his book entitled "Hope", Ch. 4. "Anticipation of Fulfillment (Presumption)

PART ONE

BACKGROUND

Chapter 1

The Search of a Common Ground in Disputed Questions

It is difficult to get people to agree on anything, even on most fundamental questions. Yet, one virtue that moralists talk about is being agreeable. Social life would become practically impossible if everyone was disagreeable.

There are all sorts of reasons for calling a meeting but the most important is to obtain a meeting of souls or minds. However, in questions to do with practical affairs this cannot come about without a meeting of hearts or wills. That is to say human association at all levels depends upon mutual love mutually known, Aristotle's masterful definition of friendship.

There are, however, three kinds of friendship according to Aristotle. The first and only lasting kind is where the love concerned is love of good will, willing good to the other. The other kinds are called friendship for the sake of something useful and/or pleasant, where without the first kind in place the love becomes a case of willing good to oneself only. Business partnerships are examples of the useful, though there can be all sorts of unions formed for some mutually useful purposes. Unnatural sexual unions are extreme examples of those for the sake of pleasure, though there are plenty of pleasurable natural unions, sexual and otherwise, that do not exclude genuine friendship.

Useful and pleasurable friendships are good, for both utility and pleasure are good. But they are only good in a qualified way and to retain their goodness need to be founded on the first kind of friendship, which is at the spiritual level of human life. In true marriage we have the three kinds of friendship marvelously harmonized. Sadly, those actively engaged in unnatural sexual unions, deceive themselves about love and friendship – for such unions may exist as useful and pleasurable but not being consistent with moral virtue they are incompatible with genuine love of goodwill.

Partnership is an appropriate word for useful friendships; loving union is used in a debased sense for unions based upon pleasure only, or on pleasure and utility only, as in unnatural sexual unions. A union based solely on mutual utility or pleasure will soon disintegrate, for such ends are ephemeral and changeable. Only the virtuous love of goodwill can sustain a union when its condition becomes unprofitable and unpleasant to one or other of the partners or lovers.

These considerations become relevant when discussing ethical theories. For, the notion of good sought, applied most to ends and the ultimate end or happiness, is a basic way of distinguishing the kinds of ethical theories that have been proposed from ancient times down to modern times, the eudemonist, utilitarian and hedonist. However, as we shall see, there are many permutations to be had in a full analysis of ethical theories.

It may be immediately noticed that genuine morality, for which reason called natural morality, has to involve the first kind, for it seeks what is good for its own sake, what is good *per se* not *secundum quid.* It is characterized by disinterestedness and is not spoiled by self-interestedness. Being disinterested is not the same as being uninterested. For it is of the very notion of love to be interested in the object. Self-interested means being interested in something simply because it is useful or pleasant to one's self. Taken without love of goodwill, willing true spiritual good to others as well as to oneself, makes the secondary kinds of love self-centred, or selfish in an immoral sense. Modern economic science mistakenly takes self-interest in this immoral sense. It is significant that the founders of modern economic science were very much imbued with a utilitarian ethics.

What should be noticed as well is that human love is of two kinds, corresponding to the two parts of human nature, the spiritual soul and the material body. Thus, we have man defined as rational animal. Love of goodwill necessarily belongs to the spiritual soul; love for the sake of utility and pleasure belongs naturally to the animal and bodily part but it is not absent from the spiritual. It is only when love of utility and pleasure is taken as opposed to love of goodwill that, as Aristotle noted, it can constitute the two alternative ethical theories of utilitarianism and hedonism.

The eudemonist theory of ethics is thus associated with the higher rational life and the other two, utilitarian and hedonist, with the lower animal life of man. The tendency of utilitarianism is to focus on material goods or wealth; the tendency of hedonism is to focus on goods of the body and thus on the pleasures of sex and food. It is clear that they are not legitimate goods only when opposed to the spiritual goods of the soul. We have to be careful, however, not to interpret all utility and pleasure in purely materialist and sensualist terms. There are genuine useful goods and pleasures of a spiritual order; they flow however from spiritual goods and ends. One other consideration is that the two material kinds of goods are often not clearly delineated and in the use of the corresponding notion of happiness it is difficult at times to classify an ethical theorist as hedonist or utilitarian.

Further complications enter the discussion when we include the supernatural order of morality. But we will deal with these in due course. This division is made here at the natural level of human nature and is but preparatory to our treatment of natural morality and the Natural Law, whereby we may already see why theories of Utilitarianism and Hedonism are deficient as theories of Ethics.

There is however a series of further distinctions that we wish to draw before coming directly to deal with the modern treatment of morality or Natural Law, and in particular that by Peter Singer, John Finnis and Tracey Rowland. These distinctions are required in our view in order to make it possible to find agreement upon the subject matter with which we are concerned.

First of all, we need to consider the possibility of agreement in regard to disputed questions in the two quite diverse fields of Faith and Reason. We are not talking here about human faith or opinion but divine faith or revealed truths. St. Thomas points out that we can only dispute with others if we all recognize the same principles or fundamental propositions. In matters of Faith then Catholics can only dispute with Jews about the truths revealed in the Old Testament. For, they do not accept the New Testament. However, we can dispute with heretics regarding matters of Faith in both scriptures.

So it is that disputation is limited to where there is some agreement to begin with. Aristotle had already noted that there is no point in discussions where the parties have no common ground. But St. Thomas points out that in matters of reason there is necessary agreement in principle, for human beings are defined by having natural reason. Hence, fundamentally there is common ground with all in a dispute in the field of reason.

This applies to those who would dispute this proposition itself, as where Heraclitus denied the first principle of reason, the law of non-contradiction. For, as Aristotle noted in this very regard: what a person says in not necessarily the same as what he thinks. It is impossible to think that something can be asserted and denied in the same breath. Thus,

Aristotle pointed out that, in order to refute a person who takes such an attitude, we simply need to get him to speak.

Radical skepticism is self-refuting. In every case where a fundamental proposition or first principle is denied we can employ the argument known as the *reductio ad absurdum.* There is moreover a use of reason in matters of faith above reason. Where someone challenges a truth known only because revealed by God we cannot prove it by reason, naturally enough, but we can show that there is no truth of reason that contradicts it. For, as St. Thomas points out, truth is integral and whole, all truth, both natural and supernatural, comes from God.

There is another consideration in regard to truths that are revealed and that is that some of them are in fact ones we could arrive at from the use of our human reason. Refer to Book 1 of St. Thomas's *Summa contra gentes.* That God is the first cause and last end of all creatures are two such truths. The most important moral obligations that men might fail to acknowledge by the use of their reason but which have been revealed in the ten commandments and other scriptural commands are other such truths. Accordingly, disputed questions in regard to these matters can be debated not only with those of the same faith but also with all from the point of view of reason.

When we come to consider the position of Tracey Rowland on the Natural Law we will see that there is some confusion by her in this respect. The mistakes of John Finnis and Peter Singer, however, are within the field of reason only and have to do with the truncated understanding of human nature and reason in modern thinking since Descartes, Hume and Kant. Part of Rowland's problem is that in opposing faith to reason she is locked into the same truncated notion of reason that the modern mind has inherited.

The question of Natural Law, or natural morality, comes into this mixed field of reason and faith. We are able then to dispute, and hopefully come to agreement, with others not only of our same Faith but with those who share our common nature as rational.

Those who refuse to listen to faith and/or reason may, of course, find something of interest in some useful occupation, such as making money, or in some pleasant pastime, such as watching the football. They may quite well, however, without realizing it be missing out on something not only more noble and fitting for us but also more useful and pleasant, namely, a better understanding of the way of salvation. The cultivation of cupidity and avarice, on the one hand, and pleasure and entertainment, on the other, we should notice are two ways in which the evil one can distract us from our true interests. Allied to these vices is falling into the philosophical errors of Utilitarianism and Hedonism. These practical philosophical errors will be found to be rooted in theoretical errors with regard to science and reason.

Our three Australian ethicists and moral lawyers are all caught up in this misconception of the natural moral law.

The basic reason for this is their weakness in Metaphysics. So let us complete our picture of the substitution of the Aristotelian view of theoretical science and wisdom by the modern view of science and the scientific method, which is to be looked at initially independently of practical science and wisdom. The new concept of Science can be seen as a combination of Mathematics and Natural Science, or Physics in Aristotle's language. This is a legitimate distinct order of science with its own mixed scientific method.

It is clear that it was the empirical notion of science, with its dominant inductive method, that was deficient in the pre-modern notion of science, which had developed, contrary to Aristotle's explicit definition of natural science, without the necessary empirical/material complement to the rational/formal approach. The previous overuse of the deductive method in the natural sciences then gave way to an intensive use of the inductive method.

Unfortunately, this came to be taken to the extreme of rejection of any formal analysis and so the formal distinctions necessary to understanding the higher levels of even physical or material being became lost. Such are the distinctions between the living form of being and the non-living, between the knowing form (consciousness) and the non-knowing, and most importantly between the non-rational form of knowledge (sense) and the rational (intellectual). This last marked the point where human knowledge moved from theoretical science taken in the strict sense (physics and mathematics) to science as wisdom (metaphysics).

The move back to a basically materialist view of reality therefore involved more than a loss of Metaphysics. It involved the notion of natural science taking on a reductionist interpretation, which inevitably could end only in a formless notion of physical nature more or less equivalent to Aristotle's notion of primary matter or potency. The progress of science so far as our knowledge of physical nature was concerned therefore was towards more and more unintelligibility, rather than intelligibility.

This materialist/reductionist progress of science was counter-balanced by an application of a formal/rational approach. However, this was not in terms of natural qualitative forms, but quantitative ones. That is to say the empirical element in science as described was combined with a mathematical/formal analysis. Fortuitously, this moved towards constituting a genuine order of medial science with its own mixed scientific method. Such was the success of this new scientific approach that the whole notion of science was transformed to conform to it.

It clearly is in principle self-contained as a legitimate order of science with a distinct scientific method. However, as envisaged it meant not only the exclusion of Metaphysics from the notion of science but also of formal/rational analysis of nature (including human nature) other than mathematical. This can be seen in the reduction of life and consciousness to their material elements when they are clearly new and higher forms of physical nature.

The exclusion of higher natural forms only reinforced the reductionist tendency in scientific explanation or "theory". For, quantitative forms flow from primary matter and are manifested in marking the geometric limits and numerical multiplication of qualitative forms. The colour red, for instance, considered as abstracted from the material individual qualities in which it is found is one in form (in the accident of quality) but by reason of quantity in individual bodies it is confined to a limited surface expansion and multiplied in any number of bodies.

St. Thomas outlines in his *De ente et essentiae* the various ways in which we consider the notion of body and its connection with the notion of quantity. All of these philosophical subtleties are lost on the modern reductive mind, for whom "body" has a univocal meaning equated with "matter", "mass" and the like as the most generic concept providing the content to quantitative relations. So formless has the notion of this content become that the mathematical side of this mixed science has all but taken over the notion of science.

However, we do not wish to deny some natural truth to the conclusions of modern science or to its theories. It is just that it is of the lowest order from a formal point of view. Nature devoid of so much intelligible distinction provides a convenient basis for many of the scientific dogmas of modern education, such as the propositions that man is but a speck in an ever expanding universe and that all reality can be accounted for by a materialist theory of Evolution.

When we come to the order of practical sciences, such as Ethics, Economics and Politics we will see there the influence of such a materialist/reductivist approach. Moreover, the notion of practical science is lost. For the modern notion of science is only theoretical; technology is regarded as applied science. Human nature is viewed as no more than a highly complex body explicable in terms only of material elements and physical processes. Even life and consciousness, as we have seen, are simply processes that perplex the scientists by their higher "immateriality" without them losing faith that "some day" all will be revealed by empirical investigations and mathematical analysis.

What has happened is that the prestige of modern physico-mathematical science with the success of its mixed scientific method has come to affect all study both theoretical and practical. In the practical ethico-political order this method has found its most congenial subject matter in Economic Science. This may be detected in the very language used by such as Peter Singer. By "practical ethics" he means no more than an application of ethics considered according to utilitarian ethical theory. His book "Practical Ethics" first of all consists in reducing human nature to the merely animal level (on the hedonist principle that happiness consists in the maximization of pleasure or rather the minimization of pain) and then he excludes the whole of sexual life (since his focus as a utilitarian is on utility rather than pleasure). His main focus, true to the tradition of Bentham, Adam Smith and J. S. Mill, is on the furtherance of human welfare in the sense of economic "interests" – an individualist ethics of self-interest (money-wise) that inevitably slides into a socialist solution of world poverty.

But we will consider this more fully below. Here we are only concerned to treat of the difference between pre-modern and modern approaches in terms of theoretical knowledge. The truncation of the notion of reason at this fundamental level has repercussions in the understanding of practical knowledge. But we first have to clarify the two levels of theoretical knowledge, or science as it refers to the physical and the metaphysical.

The more basic difference then is something that can be put in the simple terms of the difference between Physics (to which we may ally Mathematics as a associated science confined to the natural/material world) and Metaphysics (which still deals with the order of material reality but transcending its physical limitations).

Generally, then, the shift of mental focus that occurred at the beginning of the modern era was a falling back to the lower level of theoretical consideration of reality, to confine science to the investigation of material/bodily things and the meaning of nature to physical nature. Human nature being partly within this world was thus totally subjected to the same "science".

This was a return to the ancient beginnings of philosophy/science and necessarily meant the abandonment of the gains in natural wisdom made by Plato and the complete rejection of Aristotle's Metaphysics. However, there was, as we have indicated, more to this shift than a mere return to materialism. The key to the shift was in the new role Mathematics played in science. The pure science of Mathematics continued in its development and exercised an influence on philosophy much like that it had in Plato's philosophy. Indeed, Geometry and a belief in Metaphysics were for a time closely aligned (as in Spinoza).

But the real break occurred when Mathematics and Physics (Natural Science) became "married" in the medial science of physico-mathematics, focused initially on Astronomy. This gave science a special meaning that seemed to justify it ditching Metaphysics. The restoration of the empirical method in the physical side of the science also provided a good excuse to ridicule and reject previous natural science. Apart from Mathematics, then, the modern approach involved a complete rejection of previous theoretical knowledge, with which Aristotle was identified.

This turn of events has had an effect not only on those who were convinced that there was nothing good in the "old" and everything good in the "new", but also on those who, whilst having to admit the value of the new science, were committed to preserving what they saw as good in the old. This especially applied to the adherents of religion, which in the West (where the new science was triumphant) may be equated with Christianity, and particularly with Catholicism.

This was not just a case of preserving Faith and the truths of Revelation, that is to say the content of Sacred Theology, but also of preserving Reason and Metaphysics, of which the part called Natural Theology was for the greatest of the philosophers of ancient Greece (Socrates Plato and Aristotle) the most fundamental rational support of religion.

Thus, the prestige of the modern approach to science took its toll on the upholders of tradition, as its materialist and atheist presuppositions gained ascendancy. Not wishing to appear anti-science or anti-modern many were prepared to jettison the formal/rational part of natural science if Metaphysics could be saved.

Many surrendered the territory of Aristotelian Natural Philosophy (equated with Natural Science) to the modern empirical aspect of modern science. Natural Philosophy as distinct from Metaphysics disappeared. Some, even Thomists like Maritain, tried to preserve Natural Philosophy as a distinct part of philosophy but only by inventing an unnatural separation between it and "empiriological science", with a distinction made between mobile being as being and mobile being as mobile. This resulted, however, in effectively morphing Natural Philosophy into Metaphysics. For the consideration of any being as being, including mobile being, is metaphysical.

Thus, the study of the field of the physical was handed over to modern science as its exclusive province called Science. What was failed to be noted was that the difference between Natural Philosophy or Aristotelian Natural Science (with which Mathematics could be allied) and modern science lay in the emergence of a distinct new order of science (not unknown to Aristotle) that was not purely natural or mathematical but a composition of both, as masterfully detailed by St. Thomas. Apart from Metaphysics there are thus three kinds of theoretical science in the strict sense, namely, pure Mathematics, pure Natural Science (Natural Philosophy) and Physico-mathematical science.

Mixed up in the change to modern science is the correction of the neglect of the empirical side of natural science in the pre-modern (which correction is fully in accord with Aristotelian principles). It is this correction that has to be acknowledged and honoured. Unfortunately, the complexity of the change, with its positive and negative elements, led to both sides on the ensuing controversy going to erroneous extremes.

Up to date the supporters of modern science against pre-modern have had the ascendancy but that is now falling apart. That does not mean that the right solution is being proposed. It is rather a case of general confusion reigning. A true solution will require us going back to basics, the first step being recognition of the difference between a view of the world from a physical and metaphysical standpoint, and that the former is inferior to the latter, as the child is to the adult. This means a recovery of the range of reason, philosophy and science to the full extent to include wisdom. Otherwise, our educational institutions will continue to be manned by very learned men and women, but, strictly speaking, they can only be learned fools.

This is the situation from the standpoint of theoretical knowledge or science. But, as all other knowledge, including practical knowledge, depends on this kind of intellectual foundation. If the world of practical morals, economics and politics seems to be falling apart we do not have far to look for the root cause.

The division between Metaphysics and Physics, as theoretical knowledge, finds a kind of parallel with the "practical sciences" of Ethics and Technics. Practical science is not a study of nature or being generally, however, but a study of human doing. As St. Thomas explains, such science studies an order that is made, not found (by us). Natural Law, for instance, is not concerned with activities found in nature outside human nature but belongs to laws or judgments made within the human intellect.

Nonetheless, it depends upon the understanding we have of our human nature derived from our knowledge of nature outside us. So, practical human knowledge or science is not something arbitrarily devised (as Kant surmised). The division of the objects of theoretical knowledge into physical and metaphysical will therefore come into play in the practical sciences. This comes about because human nature is a composite of the "physical" (bodily) and the "metaphysical" (spiritual), being made up of a material body and a spiritual soul.

Thus, even though we could divide Ethics and Technics as the former concerned with the spiritual side and the latter with the material side of human nature and activity that would not bring out the intimate union between soul and body in man. The better division is into acts bearing principally on an internal order in our will and acts bearing on an order in external things. Then again, these acts of will bear upon an external order in so far as they control the bodily part of our nature, and relate to bodies and wills that are other than our own.

Disputations involving Faith and Reason

Before we proceed to consider specially the practical order of things let us sum up the basic theoretical order of our knowledge and discuss shortly how they relate to questions of Ethics and the Natural Law. Then to deal properly with the position of Tracey Rowland we need to return to the distinction between the truths of Faith and reason. Ethics or Moral Philosophy and, accordingly, the Natural Moral Law belong to the order of reason or philosophy (and science).

There are therefore two fields of study to be clearly distinguished in this regard, Faith and reason.

But we need to keep in mind also that there are two kinds of areas of Faith, or truths from Revelation, those that transcend the order of reason altogether, such as the doctrine of the Trinity, and those that do not, such as the existence of God as Creator and Lawgiver. The most basic practical truths of the Natural Law as revealed and confirmed in the Ten Commandments belong to the latter. It is clear that this part of Revelation does not change essentially the content of these laws. They are a merciful reinforcement of them towards our salvation.

However, Tracey Rowland's position is that our appreciation of these laws depends upon our belief in the Trinity. That is to confuse the orders of Faith and reason. The Ten Commandments are directly from God, but not explicitly from God as the Trinity. The Natural Law is from God, but as Creator and Universal Legislator of everything created. One does not have to have Faith in the Trinity to understand the morally binding force of a precept of the natural law such as the natural institution and right of property.

The divine origin of these moral laws we can know from reason, if for many it has to be assisted by Faith. Indeed, multitudes of secular societies operate according to these laws. Does one need to be a Christian to know that murder is naturally morally wrong? Does one need to be a Christian to believe in the existence of a divine being, absolutely transcending creation?

Does one need to be a theist to know that murder is wrong? The answer is explicitly, no, but, implicitly, yes. Can one disbelieve in the existence of God and be wise? No ("the fool says in his heart there is no God") It is here that another distinction comes into play, that between Natural Theology and Sacred Theology. Using such terms as "theological" and "theist" indiscriminately can obscure the distinction between Faith and reason in religious and moral matters.

The absorption of religion as such in the West into revealed religion, even in public opinion, is no doubt a consequence of the historical association of religion with the Catholic Church and Christendom. The rebellion against the authority of the Church was made to seem to be a rejection of religion and any moral authority itself. With this rejection of Catholicism went the gradual rejection of the traditional *mores* attaching to the civilization known as Christendom. Principal amongst these customary attachments was "Christian morality", which had come to be regarded almost as the most basic support of civilisation itself. Calling something "unchristian" was equated with calling it "immoral".

Thus, with the weakening of Christianity's hold on the modern mind went almost unconsciously a weakening of that of natural morality. The political and academic (secular educational) levels of society were a cause and effect in this regard. The doctrine of the separation of Church and State virtually meant the separation of government and public education from morality. "Free, compulsory and secular" was the catchcry for education by the end of the nineteenth century, by which time all Christian influence even by way of Protestantism had dissipated. Religion was effectively, if not officially, outlawed from "the public square". By association, this applied as it were subconsciously also to any notion of a natural morality.

Many Catholic academics and politicians generally went along with this, a prominent example in the USA being President Kennedy. In Australia similar positions have been adopted by some Catholic politicians, mistakenly thinking that this would not negatively impact on their decisions concerning grave moral matters, for which they may be held personally accountable, not just as Christians but also as responsible human beings.

This historical factual confusion, however, has to be carefully separated from the intellectual confusion of Faith and reason, especially in regard to morality. There is an overlap in the practical order of human behaviour; for salvation depends upon our being naturally just and virtuous as well as being theologically faithful and charitable. Faith has something to say about natural law, justice and rights but this is supplementary to what we ought to know, and do know, from reason. It is surprising that one well instructed in the Faith should be confused in this regard.

Thus, we have not only to avoid mixing up Faith and reason but also matters knowable both by Faith and reason and this in particular with regard to natural morality and the Natural Law. Tracey Rowland has mixed up the proper places of consideration of Natural Law, for she has made it dependent upon Faith in relation to what is totally above reason. Besides anything else that makes disputation about all morality by appeal to reason impossible.

She imagines it would strengthen the defence of Natural Law in disputation with the faithful to show that it issues from God as Triune. But, in this she is mistaken. For, as is manifest, our knowledge of the truths of natural morality does not depend on Faith in the Trinity, which only became explicit in Christ. The principles of the Natural Law are not essentially supernatural.

In regard to her argument on the Natural Law, therefore, Rowland fails to observe the fundamental rule of disputation in any question whether theoretical or practical, namely, that one must move from positions or principles that are proper to the matter in dispute and then only where those with whom one is in dispute accept or ought to accept these as common ground.

Disputations involving Reason alone

Let us move on then to consider the positions of Singer and Finnis. They do purport to confine themselves to the order of reason only, though Finnis is a Catholic. This will enable us to consider the place of reason in disputation about morality and the Natural Law. The modern treatment of them depends however most fundamentally upon the understanding of the range of reason, which, as noted above, has been gravely affected by the revolution in the conception of science that took place at the beginning of the modern era.

As we have put it, this "revolution" involved a reversion to a narrower notion of science, applied only to the particular theoretical sciences of Mathematics and Physics, eschewing Metaphysics. In Aristotelian terms this meant the putting of science above wisdom (which was relegated to opinion). In effect it meant a rejection of the reality of the spiritual and a return to materialism. It was only possible if the philosophy of Aristotle was disdained.

We have seen however that the change in the notion of science acquired a special feature that led to great technical or technological success. That was the flowering of the medial or mixed science of physico-mathematics, most familiar to Aristotle in Astronomy. Then again there was another significant feature that attached to the new notion of science. That was the flowering of the empirical spirit in the modern era. This focus on material cause in the study of physical nature, considered by Aristotle as essential to any genuine natural science, had been virtually lost after Aristotle.

Unfortunately, the lesser minds that followed simply took over his many necessarily tentative conclusions and generalisations. This was not helped by the shift of intellectual attention to matters of theological and spiritual interest. The development of natural science thus stalled for a long period. It has to be acknowledged however that it was coming to life again before the beginning of the modern era. Scholastics such as Roger Bacon and St. Albert (thereby called "the Great") are rightly regarded as forerunners of the empirical basis of modern science. St. Thomas also brought out the empirical side of the natural sciences and its emphasis by Aristotle. Long before the logical empiricists he insisted that physical science (not all science) had to be "terminated" (verified) in sense observation.

The general move then was backwards, or rather downwards, from the metaphysical to the physical. But in some respects it was forwards; for it was to a better physical science which brought along with it enormous material benefits. The loss, however, was enormous and of a higher human kind, even from a natural and rational point of view. It was spiritual and moral, the former leading to a loss of religious piety and the latter ushering in an era of personal immorality and political corruption, not to speak of nationalistic wars and economic oppression of the majority.

It is this truncated concept of reason that the modern philosopher has inherited and it has had a general effect, not only on the secular academic but also on the religious. For, like with morality, metaphysics was associated with religion, relegated to the area of faith as opinion. Any claim to certainty in regard to ultimate questions, to natural wisdom, was disdainfully dismissed as "unscientific". What this meant was that science was officially atheistic. Some claimed to be agnostic. However, knowledge limited to the material order must exclude any divine being. Hence, the logic of the way that modern science is taken drives the human mind to atheism. It may be appreciated that this tendency does not belong to science as such.

Once Metaphysics has been excluded from reason and science taken in the general sense, the whole spiritual order of reality has to be consigned the unscientific, i.e. to irrationality. Puffed up with his new found rational superiority the modern scientist/philosopher relegates religion, metaphysics and morality to the level of individual infancy and historical mythology, not taken in the good sense we have seen Aristotle took it, but in a sense contrary to reason.

The religious scientist is somewhat embarrassed by this attitude of many of his colleagues, but he has no answer to their criticisms. So, too, the theologians who have from their general education the same notion of the scope of reason and science and therefore cannot answer the argument of modern science fall back on Faith as the only refuge. This, however, involves them in a painful contradiction. For Faith is in the reason, and cannot "breathe", as Pope Benedict XVI put it, without reason. That it seems to us is the dilemma that those such as Tracey Rowland find themselves in with regard to the Natural Law.

This dilemma has come about because the modern notion of reason and science has pushed metaphysical questions into the order of Faith. Belief in God, or theism, which is a matter that can be determined in that part of Metaphysics called Natural Theology, has been treated as a matter of Faith. The modern secular philosopher equates that with human faith or opinion. The modern religious philosopher often accepts the scientific verdict but takes comfort in equating Faith with divine faith. Both have abandoned reason in its highest form.

Consequences of Modern Redefinition of Reason

All three positions on morality and Natural Law that we are considering are therefore flawed basically by the modern re-definition of reason, which is a truncation that Aristotle would have readily recognised. The modern philosophers of science have fallen for it. So it seems have some Catholic theologians.

So, too, have some Catholic philosophers, into which we may place Finnis in relation to his analysis of Natural Law, though we may have to qualify this in some respects. To understand this, however, we need to look at the history of modern philosophy. For, though the proponents of modern science leave no rational room for any thinking about things that are not material and accordingly cannot in principle accord any intellectual status to the discussion of things or activities that transcend the material order, some ingenious thinkers have found a way (or believe they have) to reach such a transcendental order of reality.

Kant is the classic example. But before that Descartes had devised a "proof" of the existence of a spiritual order of things. This effort to transcend the material order of things lasted for a while. But, it petered out and was replaced by Kant's transcendental philosophy. The clue to the understanding of modern philosophy as distinct from modern science, however, is Mathematics.

We have put the difference between pre-modern and modern science in terms of the dethronement of Metaphysics by Physics or Natural Science. But, there was more to it than that. Recall that the old Physics had a rational/formal character and the new Physics saw itself as replacing this with a purely empirical/material character. This was an inadequate basis for an ordered science. If it were the only part of the scientific method we could not organise our thinking in natural science. We would be confined to simply accumulating unrelated "facts" (information), as Hume concluded.

Aristotle's insistence on Natural Science having not only an empirical/material part but also a rational/formal part would not be denied. However, for reasons already adverted to, what replaced it was not a better use of natural forms but mathematical forms or formulas. The empirical "data" came to be organised mathematically. That slotted well into the identification of science with the mixed science of physico-mathematics, as explained above.

For, relatively speaking, mathematics is meta-physics. It does not depend upon empirical evidence. It prefers deduction to induction. Having lost the true notion of Metaphysics, the modern mathematically minded thought they found an adequate substitute for the rational part of physical science in the mathematical part of modern science. But there was here no true transcendence of the material and physical order of things.

Kant, having noted the failure of the Cartesian attempt to resurrect Metaphysics, and immersed in Newtonian physico-mathematics, ingeniously devised a philosophy based upon the combination of the rational/formal and the empirical/material parts of the objects of modern science. The *a priori* forms were inspired by the geometrical concepts of extension and the arithmetical concepts of number, put in the form of the notions of space and time. Kant then extended the notion of *a priori* forms to formal principles in natural science such as natural causality. These forms provided a rational order for things but they did not transcend the physical and sensible world, as Kant realised.

Kant thus became in the eyes of modern thinkers the philosopher of science supplanting Aristotle. In a way this is true but only because modern science, as mathematical/physical, does not transcend the material order of sense and imagination. We are concerned here only with theoretical knowledge. It is significant that Kant had to disconnect his analysis from the order of practical knowledge, for ethics necessarily involves the spiritual.

This "transcendental" move of Kant seemed to solidify the attempt to provide the rational form necessary for the empirical materials of the new science. It was basically a new kind of Physics. Descartes had tried to derive the formal part from the Metaphysics of the human spiritual soul (Thought) but this was incompatible with the fact that science was now conceived as purely within the physical order of things.

The "meta-physics" devised turned out to be little more than a use of Mathematics to supply a logical structure for thinking about physical nature. Leibniz's effort in this regard has come through in modern mathematical logic. This development of logic, which is a necessary instrument of all science, not just Mathematics, is a separate subject of study. We do not go into it here, as we are focusing on the principal theoretical sciences dealt with by Aristotle. We may note however that method and subject matter became inextricably confused in the subsequent development of the rational side of modern philosophy.

What we wish to bring out here, however, is the dual character of reason in modern science, which reflects the mixed nature of empirical/mathematical science. Though there is a genuine order of mixed or medial sciences, acknowledged by both Aristotle and St. Thomas, in its modern form it was and is in many ways an artificial union. Accordingly, there came into existence two opposed streams of modern philosophical systems, called Rationalism and Empiricism. The rationalist stems from Rene Descartes, refined by Immanuel Kant, the empiricist from Francis Bacon, refined by David Hume. Kant's intervention, however, transformed these streams into Idealism and Positivism.

Thus the shift of consideration of the range of reason from the metaphysical to the physical, which necessarily amounted to a shift from the spiritual to the material, did not result in a unified philosophical understanding of reality. The reason for this may be found in the substitution of purely quantitative forms for natural substantive ones in the vision of physical being. This made the unity in material nature something accidental, not substantial, with all the instability and unintelligibility that brought in its wake.

When we come to consider the practical moral order we see this duality reflected in opposed ethical theories and systems named "deontological" and "utilitarian". The latter is frankly tied to the physical or bodily side of human nature; the former, whilst trying to "transcend" this inevitably fails because of its lack of a metaphysical/rational foundation.

We do not propose to go into Kant's mental gymnastics in devising a Moral Philosophy that is both positivist and idealist. Because of the turn to a mixed science, with justified abandonment of the old non-empirical physics, the notion of science was faced with a strange union of two objects, one physical the other mathematical. Without a proper understanding of the union of form and matter, however, the union remained something mysterious or "magical". The spectacular success of the "experiment" only reinforced this feeling of scientific miracle. Philosophically, however, its two parts could not be reconciled and so there arose opposing philosophical explanations, reduced to basically two.

Implications for Practical Sciences

This brings us to the practical moral order, which is radicated in the metaphysical/spiritual reality of the human soul. The human spiritual soul it is to be remembered reflects in its powers of intellect and will the reality of the world in which it exists. That is why, despite Ethics or Morals being concerned with an order made within human acts flowing from reason and choice, the practical principles humans follow are founded in the very nature of reality (including our own), and are ultimately traceable to the divine source of that reality.

The move from metaphysics to physics we have noted in regard to modern theoretical science has the necessary effect of undermining that practical order and hence invalidating any Ethics. However, because of the bodily part of human nature the effects of human choices can be observed in the physical world (constituting a mystery for modern physicists), the modern mind endeavours to deal with these human and social "phenomena" is some way. These observable "data" provide the material upon which to build some sort of rational system along the lines of modern science.

It is in the end a futile exercise, for the effects of a spiritual reality and power cannot be detected even by Geiger counters. The rational forms devised are either mathematical in nature or partial pseudo-spiritual/ethical explanations about justice, free will etc. Without a full embrace of Metaphysics, which includes natural theology, there can be no intellectual basis for a science of human behaviour. It is the same story in the practical order of endless performances of much learning without wisdom.

This unfortunately, is the sad picture of modern academia, whose fractured notion of science descends upon the general community with particular influence on the political leaders, who pride themselves on following "best practice". As we see it, Tracey Rowland, John Finnis and Peter Singer are, by reason of their secular education, particularly powerful in Australia, academics caught up in this modern limited vision of science. Singer adopts the empirical side of it wholeheartedly with some queer sort of moral fervour. The two Catholic academics try to work around the atheistic implications of the empiricist element in modern science, Rowland by resort to Faith, Finnis by resort to a kind of rationalist interpretation of St. Thomas. Both therefore are vehemently opposed to the position of Singer. Yet, in our view, neither escapes completely from falling for the distorted notion of reason in modern thought by virtue of the lack of a philosophical preservation of Metaphysics.

However, this is a judgment upon their work at the most fundamental theoretical level of reason. It must be attended to first if there is to be any basis for discussion and disputation on their positions with regard to natural morality and Natural Law. It is nonetheless at a rather remote point of principle and we will go on to examine their particular positions from a closer viewpoint.

As noted, St. Thomas explains that Ethics studies not an order we find (it is not a theoretical science) but an order we "make" (it is a practical science). The order is made in our will, or rather in the acts of our will (from which result habits in the will and in other powers under the will). This order governs all our human behaviour, both spiritual and bodily, at the level of reason. Human nature is constituted of a spiritual soul (substantial form) and a material body (substantial matter). So it is that ethical science or moral philosophy covers our spiritual and bodily activities, which means that Ethics involves two levels of reality, what we may call the metaphysical and the physical.

So it is that in the practical order human reason takes its theoretical foundation from Metaphysics and Physics (in the Aristotelian sense), connected with which latter are mathematical-like features. The virtue of justice, for instance, where it is bears upon relations between individuals in respect of external material goods, draws upon notions of equality that are quantitative. This does not make the formal moral consideration physical or mathematical, but nonetheless one cannot leave out altogether the bodily and material order of things.

Insofar as these relations are materially in the physico-mathematical order of human knowledge we will find that modern science may find a way of applying its scientific method and devising a theoretical "explanation" of the human social behaviour concerned. This largely accounts for the modern science of Economics, which was first practical study to take on the new scientific method. Such studies are not to be regarded as altogether useless but they do not rise above a material complement to Ethics/Politics. If they eschew the supervision of the true moral/political philosophy/science they can only become subject to political ideologies, such as radical Socialism or liberal Capitalism in modern times.

The point we make however is that the effect upon practical thinking and living in modern times of the shift from the metaphysical to the physical is that the spiritual aspect of Ethics/Politics has been lost. The modern attempts to deal with human social life therefore have to focus on the bodily side of human life. Though there is a moral dimension at that level the position is analogous to that of theoretical science without wisdom, namely, that of a practical science without practical wisdom, or the virtue of prudence. For this there has been substituted, as we shall see, art as technique.

Thus, another factor comes into play. Just as Ethics is principally the practical extension of Metaphysics so Technics is in the main the practical extension of Physico-Mathematics. For all "practical" purposes, the modern study of moral questions tends to be "applied" in technical terms (mainly of bio-technology). This is strikingly evident in medico-ethical questions. The newly invented science of Bioethics, though it should be simply treated as a department of Ethics or Moral Philosophy, has quickly been reduced to a theory of human behaviour at the level of mere animals, something explicitly endorsed by the leading Australian bio-ethicist of the day, Peter Singer. Such is the prestige of the scientific method so applied that the most horrific proposals advocated by him, in the name of Bioethics, are given serious consideration by suitably dumbed down governments and populace.

But here again we must observe the flow through of the split within modern thought in philosophy and science. Modern science is not simply empirical (concerned with material causality) but such mixed with what is mathematical but called rational (concerned with formal causality). Not able to reconcile these two apparently opposed characteristics modern philosophers have tended to be divided into two schools of thought, Empiricism and Rationalism. The "rationalism" is inspired by the mathematical character of the mixed science.

Though the early modern philosopher of science wished to reject any notion of "forms" or formal causality, with which they associated (Aristotelian) Metaphysics, they were faced with the obvious formal character of Mathematics as an intrinsic part of their notion of science. Indeed, Mathematical forms or formulas constituted in the eyes of such as Galileo the most important part of Natural Science.

Rationalism, derived from the mathematical part of the modern physico-mathematics, has the characteristic features of *a priori* reasoning, deductive proof, etc. This contrasted with the features of the empirical side of the science of *a posteriori* reasoning, inductive proof etc. It is to be noted that both parts involved reasoning in Aristotelian terms. So the term "rational" was one contrived from a partial view of reasoning. Kant distorted the picture further by transporting the terms *a priori* and *a posteriori* to the act of judgment from the act of reasoning.

What we had however was a division of thought, equated with all philosophy and science, within the physical or material order of things. But the shift from the metaphysical (all being) to the physical (material or mobile being) was the general basis of modern thought. It was the compound nature of material substance as substantial form and primary matter (just as well described as primary form and substantial matter) that was not understood and distorted into a formless substance ("matter") under an accidental form (quantity). This combination, though false as applied to the substance of bodies, nonetheless could work scientifically (physico-mathematically) limited to bodily reality.

The wrench from Metaphysics, however, took some time to be effected. Descartes, more a mathematician than a physicist (natural scientist), attempted to give metaphysical import to his "thinking" (modelled on the "clear and distinct" character of mathematical reasoning) and constructed a system of thought that he believed transcended the sensible order of nature. Since the spiritual nature of the human intellect is dependent (for its object) on the sensible world of our experience this project was bound to fail. Nevertheless, for a period the mixed up Mathematical/Metaphysical project continued, particularly through Leibniz, until Kant.

Kant dismissed Metaphysics, but he distorted the picture even further. His philosophical contortions, however, seemed to fit nicely the union of mathematics and empirics that had been canonised by Isaac Newton and called Physics. Metaphysics was now safely out of the scientific picture yet there remained a need for formal causality as well as material. Kant shifted the formal order of things into the mind only, where it necessarily took on the character of logical being. Thus was consolidated the modern union between Mathematics and Logic (incipient in Leibniz).

Kant had therefore developed an ingenious way of sidelining Metaphysics as the science of real being whilst retaining a science that is as extensive as Metaphysics, but confined to the mind. Universality is a mark of rational thought.

Kant made use of this in his moral philosophy, whereby he was able to disconnect Ethics from Metaphysics (and hence reality), but endow its practical logic with the necessary universality.

It may be appreciated that Kant's philosophy, both theoretical and practical, is designedly without substance, for he was convinced of the futility of Metaphysics, which he identified with the efforts of the Cartesians, and at the same time he made it as faithful to the state of modern science as he could, for he was fully persuaded of the truth of Science, which he identified with Newtonian Physics.

His work therefore is an attempt to retain formal causality in the science of the physical world after Hume had argued for a pure empiricism. It does not restore Aristotle's concept of natural forms and thus leaves even the science of nature (natural philosophy) in an inadequate state. This, however, is the way modern science is.

When we turn to practical science and Ethics (Moral Philosophy) Kant's rationalism (formalism) founders for the same basic reason – a lack of metaphysical or real foundation. But, he dresses Ethics up with many of the properties that it would have IF it had such a foundation. His moral philosophy and therefore notion of Natural Law, says some particular good things, but suffers from the lack of moral substance (objective goodness). According to Kant, only the human will is absolutely good. That made all law like divine positive law.

What is forgotten in the consideration of morality is that the good is but a transcendental mode of being, only distinct from it by a logical or mental relation (to desire). To give it a status independent of being, and therefore to attempt to make Ethics or morality stand apart from Metaphysics, is to empty it of natural content, which was Max Scheler's criticism of Kant.

Though there can be no morality without free will, in the creature this freedom is not absolute. It is subject to the (free) will of its Creator, who as St. Thomas explains, governs everything in accordance with their natures. That is to say, the created free will is made to fulfil freely (and responsibly) the potentialities of its spiritual substance or being. It can recognise God's will for it in the nature of that which it is (a human person). But the spiritual faculty by which the person knows what it should do is his or her intellect. The natural inclinations of human nature are known by the human intellect (reason) and find expression in the first principles that are propositions of the practical reason. That is what the human will freely follows to its natural end, the perfect good or happiness where its freedom comes to full fruition. The very first practical principle, synderesis, is based on the nature of the will itself as the appetite for good understood: "seek good, shun evil".

The specific goods or moral values to which the natural inclinations are inclined are not known separately. For, the natural desires for them are included in the notions of the things that are good (as ends). Human (bodily) life, for instance is the good that is the end sought by the natural desire for self-preservation. Murder is the act that frustrates that natural inclination. The continuance, or life, of the human being as a member of the human species is the good sought by the natural desire for mating and reproduction. Adultery is the act that frustrates that natural inclination, because this natural inclination in human beings rationally demands certain conditions that require the institution of marriage.

The subduing of the earth, that is things below man, is the good sought by the natural desire to make use of external goods required for human life and well being. Theft is the act that frustrates that natural inclination, because the achievement of this good or end rationally demands certain conditions that require the institution of property; and so on with the other natural inclinations listed by St. Thomas, which can be related to the Ten Commandments.

These primary goods with their logical relations to the natural desires for them are the objective basis of the first principles of practical reason. And the human (free) will is directed to them through the reason. Human reason, therefore, though it commands the will (morally) itself depends on the being of the goods that it knows and desires. It is in this way that Metaphysics founds Ethics. Kant and others who would disconnect Morals from Metaphysics (as Finnis tends to do) turn human reason and will into creators of the goodness of things, which is God's prerogative.

That is where the fundamental fault of Kant lies. Human reason is made independent of created reality and that makes human free will absolute. Kant thus consolidates the liberalism that may be traced to the beginning of the modern era, evident in Rousseau. Its roots lie in the rationalism of the Cartesians, in so far as this disconnected the outside world from our reason; realistically our reason and will should be the humble recipients of the being and goodness of things put there by the Creator.

Modern rationalism (formalism) can be seen as a tortured attempt to supply for the natural forms that had been evacuated from natural science with the rejection of Aristotle. At times this rejection was confused with the rejection of Metaphysics and the rationalism took the form of a pseudo-metaphysics. Hume frankly accepted the absence of any natural forms and opted for a pure empiricism/materialism (to which corresponded sensism/pheno-malism).

Kant took up the challenge and no better apparent defence has been found since. Hence, there is his continuing influence. But Kant not only defended the theoretical value of modern science (*a la* Newton). He completed the picture by applying his solution to the practical moral order. His moral philosophy, or system of ethics, thus provides the most favoured rationalist alternative to an empiricist based ethics, as in utilitarianism/hedonism. Its connection with political liberalism may be noted from its absolutizing of human free will.

Modern purported systems of Ethics focus, as is to be expected, upon the part of Ethics to do with the physical side of human nature. But here we see reflected the opposition noted in regard to theoretical science. The pre-occupation is with the morality "of the body", and accordingly mainly presenting as Utilitarianism or Hedonism, as mirroring an empiricist viewpoint.

However, this is opposed by the rationalist approach, mirroring the rationalist viewpoint in the field of modern theoretical science, as explained above. Since Kant, it follows much the same line as he did. However, Kantianism is not the only form that Rationalism might take. Rationalism is an attempt to supply for the lack of a formal/rational side in physical or natural science that is other than purely mathematical. It takes its inspiration however from the mathematical side of modern science.

In the practical order of Morals it is difficult to avoid the metaphysical side of human life and accordingly this formalism sometimes surreptitiously imports metaphysical considerations, though locating them in the human mind and mixing up metaphysical notions with general logical ones, giving priority to human reason over reality.

Reason and Will in Natural Law

Before embarking on our particular analyses and critiques, however, we will set out something that pertains to the consideration of Natural Law that is generally overlooked by all parties. From the standpoint of natural reason and will only, law is not merely a matter of reason, nor is it only a matter of will. The former might be called "intellectualism" or "rationalism", the second "positivism" or "voluntarism". Law consists in commands or ordinances of reason, and accordingly is in the reason, but St. Thomas explains that an act of will is presupposed, and that will provides the motive cause and reason the formal cause. Being and essence are the objects of intellect only; whereas good and happiness are the objects of intellect as moved by will. Apart from the very first act of understanding good, acts of will therefore both precede and follow the acts of knowledge of intellect, before as love, after as joy.

The focus in the consideration of Natural Law is on the part played by intellect and reason, but we should not overlook the part played by will. The very first practical principle: "seek good, shun evil" expresses the very natural inclination of the will to good understood. It simply says follow your desires for what is really good.

This rational command however is complicated by the fact that human knowledge, especially in practical affairs, necessarily brings in the lower animal levels of knowledge and appetite. So reason has to work with sense knowledge and will has to work with sense appetite or "passion". Descartes downgraded the part of sense, and consequently of passion in the explanation of the principles of human behavior. Hume, on the other hand, downgraded the part of reason and consequently equated the motive principle of will with "passion".

Kant attempted an artificial compromise. He followed the Cartesian lead in divorcing reason from sense, but in the practical order he divorced reason from will, making will a law unto itself. In the discussion of Natural Law, therefore, we have a doubly or triply complex problem, of keeping together all the powers of human nature, knowledge and appetite, intellect and sense. Socrates maintained morality was a matter of knowledge only, presumably intellectual knowledge. Hume maintained it was a matter of appetite, equating it with sensuality.

Aristotle held that it was a matter of both knowledge and appetite, including reason and sense and will and sense appetite, but with sense knowledge and sense appetite subordinated to intellectual knowledge (human reason) and intellectual appetite (free will), and reason and will so coordinated that they were both prior and posterior according to diverse orders of causality.

St. Thomas brought this out most clearly with the appropriate distinctions and, moving to the supernatural level of morality, of law and love, avoided the partial explanations and hence extreme errors at both the natural and supernatural levels of consideration of Natural Law. When dealing with law specifically he concentrated on the connection with reason, bringing it down to the concrete in the act of conscience and the virtue of prudence.

The superior role of will comes out in the other virtues, especially justice, which is from a love of the end or the common good, whilst prudence is about means. Law and love are therefore wonderfully tied together in the full understanding of the Natural Law.

Chapter 2

Some Preliminary Observations Regarding Finnis and Singer

John Finnis

Though Finnis has been accused by some of being Kantian, it is rather his tendency to rationalism within the modern internal rationalism/empiricism disputation that is the worry. Because in every error there is some partial truth one can find in St. Thomas apparent support for Empiricism and Rationalism. Though a lawyer thoroughly imbued in the modern secular academic climate, Finnis, as a Catholic, has found, he believes, something in St. Thomas's work on law that may be used to counter the dominant empiricist/positivist bias in current legal/ethical debate.

We will examine his position more closely below. Here we comment only on the definition of law that he uses (NLNR Part 2, x. 6) and compare it with that of St. Thomas, which is given first:

> "ordinance of reason [formal]
> for the common good of a community [final]
> promulgated [quasi-material]
> by the one who has the care of that community".
> [efficient]

We have divided it into four parts to show it fulfils the requirements of a perfect definition that contains the four principles corresponding to the four causes, noted in brackets. It should be noted that if any one of these principles or elements of the definition is left out the subject matter cannot be called a law according to its true definition. We might note at this stage that Natural Law is not made by human authority, even though it refers to principles (naturally) formed in the human mind. Strictly speaking, political governments are makers only of positive law. What else is included in human law is but the provision of the necessary concrete conditions for the application of the Natural Law. The definition of law as purely positive is different from Natural Law by reason of the difference in efficient cause. The positive lawmaker is bound to operate within the Natural Law, but the Natural Law remains necessarily too general for particular implementation. The command "do not murder" requires for instance a positive sanction to be operative in a particular social context.

Finnis evidently has in mind man-made laws. It is from this order of law that modern legal philosophers take their notion of law. It is to be noted that the authority of the human legislator/caretaker is to enact laws (of his or her own reason and will) in the manner of "determinations" that are by definition not contrary to the natural law. The nature of the laws of peoples (*ius gentium*) will be discussed later.

Though they have to be legislated these positive determinations partake of the Natural Law, as explained by St. Thomas.

Finnis's definition of law, summarised with abbreviated comment in brackets, is as follows:

> Rules [formal but vacuous]
> Made in accordance with regulated legal rules [redundant]
> By a determinate and effective authority (constituted by legal rules?) [efficient]
> For a "complete community" [redundant]
> Buttressed by sanctions [consequential]
> Directed to reasonably resolving problems etc. [consequential]
> For the common good of the community. [final]

Notice straight off that no reference is made to promulgation, which in human terms means publication to the people subject to the law. That is a serious omission. Are the citizens to be subject to secret degrees made "in cabinet"? Sanctions are needed only where the subjects are not disposed to obey the (reasonable) laws. Rules are but the same as laws, an obvious mere reduplication; no direct reference is made to reason in the making of laws. The governing authority is constituted by rules – made by whom?

On top of that Finnis says that his definition is not meant to exclude calling laws those rules that do not have all the requirements of his definition. That is quite nonsensical like saying that the definition of man does not need to include rational, or that law need not include "for the common good". But it is clear that it is to accommodate regimes where the only component of the definition is the efficient cause – the commands of a "determinate and effective authority" that is not constituted by legal rules above itself. Reason and justice are not intrinsic to the laws so made. The definition is perfect positivism; it comes down to equating the form of law to the arbitrary will of the legislator (as in the modern theory of English law, justified as the will of a majority in Parliament assembled).

Finnis it seems wants to save the notion of law as applied to what Aristotle and St. Thomas called corruptions of law, and St. Thomas calls "a species of violence". Yet he appeals to Aristotle and St. Thomas in doing so. In one respect his book NLNR may be viewed as an attempt to counter the classical assertion of St. Augustine and St. Thomas that "an unjust law is not law". It may be seen at once that this proposition is self-evident from the definition given by St. Thomas. For justice is but the practical equivalent of reason in regard to human social behaviour.

But Finnis mounts an argument that such an assertion has to take into account the use of analogous language specifically relied upon by both Aristotle and St. Thomas in related contexts, such as the discussion of friendship, citizenship, constitutional government and so on. On the face of it, it is a strong argument, for there can be found in Aristotle the analogous use of words that Finnis relies upon. But we shall see that his error stems from a failure to note the distinction between analogy applied to the use of words and analogy applied to concepts and things.

For instance, we may refer to someone as a false friend, as we may refer to an unjust law, which phrases are composed of contradictory concepts. Aristotle would say that the word "friend" is used in such cases in a secondary manner. Finnis would put it that the focal meaning of friend is the genuine one, but there is in Aristotle nothing against using it in the secondary sense. So too we do not necessarily exclude the notion of law from an unjust law. What is wrong with this analysis of language we will take up more fully later.

What it does, however, is provide a rational(ist) defence of positivist legal philosophy. That Finnis should do this may be explained from the fact that modern positivist legal philosophy, in which he has been schooled and which is the very atmosphere most English speaking lawyers breathe, resists religiously any necessary connection between law and justice considered as a moral quality. Indeed, they tend to put more importance in the notion of law upon the ability of the legislative authority to use force to effect its will, the very essence of "a species of violence".

This does not mean that Finnis is intentionally a positivist legal philosopher. He would vehemently deny that conclusion. But it does mean that his reasoning or philosophical position in this regard supports the proposition that positive law contrary to natural law can still be regarded as valid law. Unlike the pure positivist he wishes to preserve the notion of law for both natural law and anti-natural positive law if he gives priority in meaning to the natural law.

In this however he falls into a contradiction because of the use of words, which use is indeed a common usage, where something that is not what the name really signifies is called by the same name because of some deceptive appearance, as in referring to fool's gold as gold, or to a fallacious argument as an argument and so on. An unjust law is of this sort of nominal analogy.

Aristotle's explanation of the use of words in such an "analogous" way has to be carefully analysed. However, we do grant that a superficial reading of Aristotle can seem to support what Finnis argues for. One good service that Finnis's work may be said to perform is to draw attention to a confusion in the doctrine of analogy that has not been clearly exposed in the literature. The tendency has been to mix up the analogy of names (words) with the analogy of concepts taken from the real. The concept of law as defined by St. Thomas is a good example of the latter, for there are all kinds of law, from the eternal law to human positive law. All of them fit analogously into the real definition.

Peter Singer

Let us move on now to the position of Peter Singer. He is included not just because he is Australian but to give a complete conspectus of the ways in which the modern truncated notion of reason and science can lead to error in regard to the understanding of Natural Law. The first is the resort of supernaturalism, which we have associated with Tracey Rowland, the second is the development of a kind of rationalism, which we have associated with John Finnis and the third is based upon empiricism, which we associate with Peter Singer.

This last is the most blatant rejection of natural morality and Natural Law and it makes no attempt to defend natural morality in any way, as the other two do. An empiricist-based philosophy most clearly rejects the very possibility of there being any natural form or nature specific to human being (which Singer nonsensically labels "speciesism") and consequently any distinct concept of human nature so as to found any real ethics. Its materialism or formless physicalism prohibits any distinctive system of rules or laws for human beings. Indeed, to be consistent it should go all the way with Hume, who denied giving any rational status to any knowledge beyond sense impressions, i.e. to unrelated, and hence unregulated, phenomena.

It is impossible to maintain such a position of pure empiricism – its only function is to corrode thought as Hume found – and so inevitably those who subscribe to such a theoretical position put forward some sort of explanation in terms of formal cause though it will not be a natural one. The empiricists do not eschew reason; it is impossible to do so and continue to think. They just limit it to formal logic. They just draw nonsensical conclusions from their absurdly inadequate premises.

The opposition between rationalism and empiricism is never purely taken; it generally consists in the rationalist proposing some formal cause of intelligibility that is asserted without evidence, like Kant did, and the empiricist denying any but material/sense causes but nonetheless having to acknowledge reason in logical relations. As explained above the modern truncated notion of reason when applied to the practical order of ethics becomes utilitarianism/hedonism.

The philosophical basis of the utilitarianism of Peter Singer is the English empiricism of Locke. Singer has however none of the common sense restraint against going to extremes that characterises this early English Philosopher, particularly when dealing with moral matters. Wherever he got his desire to make (formal) logic his god, Singer lets the logical implications of the physicalist/evolutionist view of modern science and the corresponding animalist view of human nature have free and full rein.

His is a brutal bioethics, not necessarily issuing from a brutal sentiment – he no doubt has inherited the gentle temperament of his Jewish forebears – but from a combination of theoretically treating not just some but all human beings at the sub-human level of animals, arbitrarily assigning to some a lack of personhood (on a borrowed Lockean deficient definition), and then following out the iron logic of his premises to their horrific conclusions. It is a good example we believe of how one's philosophic/scientific education can drive one to adopt an immoral position against all one's better instincts.

However, for the reasons adverted to above, though his philosophical position is empiricist/materialist based, converting to a crass utilitarianism in practical terms, it partakes of a kind of rationalism/formalism. Singer's position puts one in mind rather of the logical positivists, though not so much immersed in mathematical logic as they were.

His position on Natural Law has to be of a concept of animal nature no higher than that of the chimpanzee. He has, however, to find something distinctly rational to base ethics on and this is that level of human concrete thinking where intellect and animal judgment coalesce in what is called in Thomist psychology the cogitative power. This is reason operating in co-operation with sense as it necessarily has to in order to deal with the material environment in which we live. It supplies in the human being for instinct in the brute animal.

The focus of this operation of the human mind is mainly practical and it is an essential part of prudence. The empiricist/utilitarian, however, cannot distinguish it from animal instinct. Singer's concept of reason or rationality is locked into the actual decisions of practical living and so he denies such rationality, his Lockean test of personhood, to the human person before, not the power of reason – which "rational" signifies - but the use of reason, which the human being only comes to gradually.

These are our preliminary observations on the distinctive positions of the three Australians with regard to natural morality and the Natural Law. It was necessary to assess their basic philosophical assumptions in order to find some common ground upon which to dispute their positions.

PART TWO

ON ROWLAND

Chapter 3

Plan of Critique of Works of Rowland, Finnis and Singer

So we can now go on to a closer examination of the three "ethicians". What we propose to do is take the work of each that represents their definitive statements of their positions on morality, of which Natural Law is the key rational component, and compare and contrast them with what we see as the right position to be taken.

The procedure in this work that we will follow is to take the one work of each author that is most as representative of the position we ascribe to them and base our exposition of their erroneousness upon what is contained in these books, whilst at the same time expounding as best we can the true position to be taken to which we hold St. Thomas's thought on the questions concerned conforms.

For Rowland we select her essay: "Natural Law: from Neo-Thomism to Nuptial Mysticism". For Singer we select his work "Practical Ethics" and for Finnis his "Natural Law and Natural Rights". Both of these latter two, though a number of years old, have recently been republished and so may be said to represent their present basic positions. We will use the more recent editions.

We wish to make one thing perfectly clear, however, before we proceed. Throughout this examination of these three works we will be referring to "Singer", "Finnis" and "Rowland". This is a shorthand way of referring to the particular book we are examining. It is not meant to be any more than a reference to what is said in the book itself and is not intended to refer to the thought of the authors except as disclosed in the book we are examining. The thoughts expressed on the matters discussed may be qualified and possibly retracted in their other works.

It is not even the object of this examination to try to determine what the authors' intent is in what they say. They may not have intended that what is said in some particular respect be taken the way we have taken it. We can only deal with what they say and the meaning of this so far as can be determined from the ordinary usage of such words, or, where relevant in the case of Rowland and Finnis, the meaning ordinarily to be taken in Thomist philosophy and theology. (If they define words in a special way in their books we will take account of that). They may vehemently dispute the implications we have drawn from what is said, and assert that they would never have adopted such an implied position. We can only counter this by contending that the implications are there. It is in this regard only that we are prepared to argue for what we say.

Any apparently general comments are, therefore, to be strictly applied only to the works in question. There is no intention to assess the authors' general philosophy or theology. Indeed, if we feel constrained to concentrate on certain erroneous positions taken by them, this is not meant to deny that there is in their work some things that may be worthy of praise. Moreover, there is no suggestion that all the authors discussed are any but seekers after the truth, who have for one reason or another fallen into what we regard as error, if in the case of Singer grave error. Moreover, as Aristotle said long ago: we should be grateful for any genuine intellectual effort too, despite its faults.

Thus, the one thing we wish to emphasize above all as regards how this our book is to be read is that the criticisms made, even when phrased as if directed against the persons who have made the statements the subject of complaint, are to be taken strictly objectively. We wish to have applied to our critique the same criterion of pure objectivity that St. Thomas recommends in any philosophical discussion. Particularly in regard to matters of moral principle discussed, our comments and criticisms mean in no way to imply any subjective guilt on the part of the makers of the erroneous statements.

Hence, in this regard we ask the reader to adopt for our book the same principle of interpretation underlying what Josef Pieper had to say about the moral defect of presumption that he saw as part of Reformation theology: "It is but proper to emphasize at this point what is surely obvious: that we are speaking here only of the objective erroneousness of the presumption that is part of Reformation theology. It would be ridiculous and absurd to raise or attempt to answer the question of subjective guilt." From his book entitled "Hope", Ch. 4. "Anticipation of Fulfillment (Presumption)"

Finally, what may be noticed as one reads this book of ours, with reference to the work of Finnis and Rowland, the criticisms made are directed for the most part against the assumptions and arguments in much of the work of modern Catholic theologians and philosophers at the present time, in so far as it manifests the anti-Aristotelian (and hence anti-philosophical or anti-metaphysical) bias that has been such a large part of Western intellectual life since the beginning of the modern era. The work of St. Thomas and those Thomists ("neo-Thomists") who most faithfully follow through with this Aristotelian aspect of his philosophy and in his theology suffers on this account more than any other, even, sadly, from some highly influential theologians and philosophers. Finnis and Rowland, if for opposite reasons, in our view, are unfortunately caught up in a current of thinking that takes reason and science in an anti-Aristotelian way.

Treatment of Work of Tracey Rowland

Let us, however, move to the particular tasks of evaluating each of the three positions under discussion and dispute. We will treat of Rowland first, for it is necessary to clear the ground as it were of supernatural considerations in the treatment of natural morality and the Natural Law. The task here is simply to point up an error with regard to the relation between Faith and Reason in the practical order of human behavior. It is of course a dispute that pertains only to those who accept the truths of Faith.

We are not saying of course that what has been revealed is irrelevant to the consideration of the Natural Moral Law. The error consists in Rowland saying that natural reason has no sufficient power of itself to know the practical necessity of the precepts of the Natural Law, which would logically exempt those not of the Faith from moral responsibility. St. Paul however says they have no excuse.

This point has not been expressed any better than by the previous Pope Benedict XVI:

> "There is no doubt that we are living in a moment of extraordinary development in the human capacity to decipher the rules and structures of matter, and in the consequent dominion of man over nature. We all see the great advantages of this progress and we see more and more clearly the threat of destruction of nature by what we do.
>
> There is another less visible danger, but no less disturbing: the method that permits us to know ever more deeply the rational structures of matter makes us ever less capable of perceiving the source of this

rationality, creative Reason. The capacity to see the laws of material being makes us incapable of seeing the ethical message contained in being, a message that tradition calls *lex naturalis*, natural moral law.

This word for many today is almost incomprehensible due to a concept of nature that is no longer metaphysical, but only empirical. The fact that nature, being itself, is no longer a transparent moral message creates a sense of disorientation that renders the choices of daily life precarious and uncertain. Naturally, the disorientation strikes the younger generations in a particular way, who must in this context find the fundamental choices for their life.

It is precisely in the light of this contestation that all the urgency of the necessity to reflect upon the theme of natural law and to rediscover its truth common to all men appears. The said law, to which the Apostle Paul refers (cf. Rom 2: 14-15), is written on the heart of man and is consequently, even today, accessible.

This law has as its first and general principle, "to do good and to avoid evil". This is a truth which by its very evidence immediately imposes itself on everyone. From it flows the other more particular principles that regulate ethical justice on the rights and duties of everyone."

(Address of His Holiness Benedict XVI To The Participants In The International Congress On Natural Moral Law, Clementine Hall, Monday, 12 February 2007)

The problem with understanding the clear rationality of the Natural Moral Law is to do with the taking of the notion of "natural" in its narrow physical sense, together with the modern effort to delve deeper into the quantitative structure of matter so as to gain greater dominion over physical processes. It is this near obsession that makes us incapable, as his Holiness stated, of seeing the metaphysical and moral order that is contained in the understanding of being and goodness itself.

St. Thomas had pointed out that, though as Aristotle said, the word "natural" is first taken from the physical order of things material, it is applied in Metaphysics to the essences of all being, as naming the capacity for existence itself. In his *De ente et essentia* he notes that taken so fundamentally it means the same as essence, not as it is considered relatively to existence but as relative to action or operation.

Hence, we speak of the natures of spiritual beings and even of the nature of the divine being. Thus, it basically means the same as essence, whether referring to material or spiritual beings. This metaphysical insight into the natures of things has been lost and as his holiness further highlights: "This word ["nature"] for many today is almost incomprehensible due to a concept of nature that is no longer metaphysical, but only empirical."

Rowland has in another place referred to the pope calling the concept of natural law a "blunt instrument". But all that he meant was: "The fact that nature, being itself, is no longer a transparent moral message creates a sense of disorientation ...". In this address he spells out clearly the importance of the concept, and indeed "the urgency of the necessity to reflect upon the theme of natural law and to rediscover its truth common to all men ...". As to its being knowable to human reason without Faith, he clearly indicates this, quoting St. Paul's famous statement: "The said law, to which the Apostle Paul refers (cf. Rom 2: 14-15), is written on the heart of man and is consequently, even today, accessible."

This is all that the "Neo-thomists", "of the strict observance", such as Garrigou-Lagrange, were saying. Yet, Rowland takes up the criticism against them of de Lubac, who accused them of having a closed concept of nature. Quite evidently, he and his followers, and the "postmodern Augustinian Thomists", have fallen into the all too common modern mistake of having a concept of "nature" and "natural" that is "no longer metaphysical but only empirical". Even an Aristotelian concept of nature confined to the physical order is not able to be the recipient of grace. The modern materialist oriented empiricist concept is even more closed because it is matter that closes a being to the reception of grace and the supernatural.

But a concept of nature that is metaphysical and thus can accommodate the spiritual is open to grace. That is the point of obediential potency. Otherwise, how could the human soul and the angels be raised to the supernatural level of the divine nature? De Lubac and Co., it seems, are among the disorientated in the discussion of Nature and Grace. Their exaltation of grace is to be applauded but not their use of a debased notion of nature.

This is apparently what has affected Rowland's concept of Natural Law. We argue, too, that both Finnis and Singer fail to appreciate the metaphysical dimension of morality (which does not deny the physical side of human nature). Singer, of course, is mired in empiricism. Finnis, as we shall see, flirts with positivism. In this respect it is worth quoting the pope from later in his address:

> "In today's ethics and philosophy of Law, petitions of juridical positivism are widespread. As a result, legislation often becomes only a compromise between different interests: seeking to transform private interests or wishes into law that conflict with the duties deriving from social responsibility.
>
> In this situation it is opportune to recall that every juridical methodology, be it on the local or international level, ultimately draws its legitimacy

> from its rooting in the natural law, in the ethical message inscribed in the actual human being.
>
> Natural law is, definitively, the only valid bulwark against the arbitrary power or the deception of ideological manipulation. The knowledge of this law inscribed on the heart of man increases with the progress of the moral conscience."

It can be demonstrated then that the concept of nature and natural in modern thought is fundamentally flawed. Like de Lubac, Rowland, no doubt feels this inadequacy in the attempts of many to defend Catholic Faith and Morals. Unfortunately, she has felt the need to dispense with reason and nature and found natural morality and law on Faith (of no question a better foundation, but not excluding that of reason). She does not seem to be aware of how much this approach is at odds with the repeated declarations on the matter by the Magisterium, including that of Pope Benedict XVI. We have it on Faith that knowledge of the Natural Moral Law belongs to reason's own resources.

Should anybody be in any doubt with regard to this we have appended as Appendix A, with his permission, an excerpt from our colleague Frank Calneggia's book: *Assertions and Refutations: An Assessment of Dr. Tracey Rowland's Natural Law: From Neo Thomism to Nuptial Mysticism.* (En Route Books & Media, 2022) This is a most thoroughgoing critique of Rowland's work on this subject almost line for line with copious quotations from the popes including the one from Pope Benedict XVI we have highlighted above.

Preliminary Comments on Work of Singer

We will develop the criticism of the modern concept of reason in our examination and critique of the positions of John Finnis and Peter Singer. Singer's position is clear-cut in this regard, whereas Finnis's is a bit more complicated. We should therefore move to consider the position of Peter Singer, where as indicated we will use his book "Practical Ethics" as the expression of his position.

First of all, we should comment on the title of his book. As may be clear from what has been already said it is of the very notion of Ethics to be practical. It covers all human behavior in so far as it is human (rational and free). So, why the redundancy in his title, if not to suggest that what he will treat of is that part of human life and behavior that he thinks is important or "relevant" for us to be concerned with? This becomes clear when he explicitly excludes any moral question to do with sex or religion. There are apparently no ethical limits to consider - one way to dispense with questions of immorality or injustice where sexual activities or religious practices are concerned.

This truncation of the object of Ethics and selective treatment of ethical questions are obviously connected with his arbitrary assumption of the utilitarian theory of Ethics (he makes some effort to defend it). Utilitarianism stands between the other two main theories of Hedonism and Eudemonism. It distances itself from the latter by its theoretical base in physicalism – man is no better than an animal. It is close to hedonism, as may be seen in the common definition of happiness in terms of pleasure and pain. But it affects to have a more rational criterion of good than base sensual pleasures – man is evidently a higher sort of animal that can reason about his interests.

But the anti-spiritual bias prevails and the relevant interests are decidedly materialistic. What best realizes utility for the utilitarian are material goods or wealth, which in a social context is measured or reckoned in terms of money. It is here that there is such a close affinity between utilitarian philosophy and economic science.

Though Singer spends the first part of his book discussing the morality of killing where he cannot rise above considering human beings as animals – a quasi-hedonistic treatment (suffering being the negative criterion) - the latter part is focused on the morality of world poverty and the exploitation of the environment. Here his ethics does treat man as more than a brute animal, and counters the brutality of the conclusions of the first part of his book. Indeed Singer's book, as it develops, becomes two books.

In the first he is the champion of animal nature against "speciesism", which for him is the ethically arrogant human animal attitude of superiority. This leads him logically to espouse all sorts of horrific positions, which frankly are a denial of the crime of murder in the case of certain individual human beings. His idea of suffering as the criterion of morality in this context in effect puts him squarely in the camp of hedonism. For suffering is plainly defined in animal terms only (pain).

No doubt he was influenced in this regard by the likes of Bentham, who thought of happiness in terms of sense pleasure and pain, rather like the Cyrenaics, who crudely equated them with immediate sensual pleasures and pains. The later Utilitarians, such as J. S. Mill, however, like Epicurus, defined pleasure and pain more rationally and brought in higher levels of human happiness. Nonetheless, the Utilitarians manifestly tie the notion of happiness to the material interests of man, that is to say mainly material welfare or a sufficiency of wealth or money.

It is this more "rational" (economic) notion of human good or happiness that comes to the fore in the second part of Singer's book. In this part the first part seems like an aberration, a case of a mind gone mad with logically applying a gross animalistic notion of pleasure and pain to human nature, so as to justify "putting down" anyone that is suffering "too much", or causing healthy adults to suffer in witnessing such distress.

Few other utilitarian ethical theorists, if any, have gone to the same extent as Singer in this "animal liberation" ethics – hence his notoriety. But he is in congenial company in championing the cause of the poor and a tortured environment. Unfortunately, not having the slightest clue of distributive justice as explained clearly by St. Thomas, the utilitarian school of social ethics can see in radical Socialism the only solution to what is a worldwide situation of the greatest mal-distribution of wealth (blindly acquiesced in by "mainstream economists" who are schooled in the ethico-political theory of Liberal Capitalism). Without subscribing to Socialism, Singer can do no more than bring the full force of utilitarian moral condemnation upon the present state of world affairs.

Taken overall, however, his book "Practical Ethics" is a poorly digested meal of raw hedonism with horrifying conclusions with regard to human life and mistaken utilitarianism with regard to human welfare. There is no hope whatsoever of being able to correct the gross distributive injustice weighing on humanity by the help of an ethical theory that does not understand the spiritual/moral concept of justice. And such a concept of justice cannot be conceived except within an ethics that takes into account the moral law based in the human intellect's understanding of reality and nature.

Neither a hedonist nor a utilitarian theory of ethics can accommodate a true notion of Natural Law. For law has to do with ordering means to the true end of human nature. In these alternative ethics, provided one acts for an increase of pleasure or "utility" (or a decrease of pain or "disutility") one does what one wills. There may be a pseudo-rationality in reckoning so that one maximizes pleasure (or wealth) or minimizes pain (or poverty) but the ends fall infinitely short of the proper dignity of human nature. Singer's "Practical Ethics" should be renamed "Impractical Ethics".

Preliminary Comments on Work of Finnis

Let us move on, however, to consider the position of John Finnis. Here what we find we have to deal with is an Ethics that takes Natural Law into account, and indeed identifies it correctly with the work of human practical reason. Unfortunately, as we propose to show, he distorts its connection with human theoretical reason and its dependence upon nature and reality – reminiscent of Kant, though not to be taken simply as Kantian.

For one thing Kant dispensed with the intelligibility of theoretical reason altogether with regard to reality and nature. Finnis does not deny the value of theoretical knowledge or its dependence on reality. He simply disconnects practical reason from theoretical reason where the knowledge of the natural law is concerned, making its self evidence independent of theoretical reason and accordingly of reality and nature outside reason. He uses here an illegitimate distinction between epistemology and ontology that we will come to shortly.

For another thing Kant founded morality and law upon human will alone, making it independent altogether of the human intellect. Even though he might refer to practical reason it has no necessary regulation of the will, which is conceived as totally autonomous. Finnis does not make human will the ultimate and sole source of the moral law. Rather he gives this function to the human intellect as practical reason. But according to him we do not need to go behind such practical reason to found our knowledge of the Natural Moral Law. The principles of the natural law as principles of human practical reason stand without the need of anything else.

Let us say that he has taken their self evidence too much to heart. Propositions can be self-evident and yet be subordinate to higher principles that are more self evident, as is the case for instance with the theoretical proposition that the whole is greater than any of its parts. St. Thomas points out that this first principle would not be able to be held with certainty if the principle of non-contradiction were not held first as certain. Indeed, the principle of non-contradiction underpins all other principles, theoretical and practical.

For Finnis the human practical intellect grasps certain fundamental goods and these become the basis of the moral order. They are "self-evident", absolutely taken, not needing any more fundamental knowledge or source of intelligibility outside the human practical reason. What this overlooks is the fact that the practical intellect is not to be taken in isolation from its position in the human soul, It is not other than the intellect, which as the power of knowledge is essentially dependent upon being conformed to the forms of nature and reality. It is this same intellect that orders human behavior to its natural end, which it therefore does in dependence upon the state of the real world in which we live.

Criticisms of Finnis, by such as Ralph McInerny, have therefore substance. But Finnis attempts to counter them by distinctions he draws from Aristotle and St. Thomas. He tries to justify the absolute independence of the first practical principles of the human intellect by making a distinction between what he understands is the epistemological order of things and the ontological. Thus he says that while we can say that the practical principles are dependent ontologically, i.e. in the order of reality and nature, they are not so dependent epistemologically, i.e. in the order of our knowledge. He points also to the fact that natural powers, for instance, are defined through relation to acts and acts through objects. Good is the concept of being considered relatively to desire. It is the object of desire, so we need to know good before the natural desires of our nature.

We should consider these two points separately, and the absolute before the relative. First, Finnis misuses the distinction between ontology and epistemology. Both are to do with knowledge, which may be seen in their etymologies. Ontology (*ontos logos*) is the knowledge of being; epistemology (*episteme logos*) is the knowledge of knowledge. In the order of knowledge epistemology has no real priority over ontology. Knowledge is a form of being, not vice versa. If we do not understand being first we cannot understand knowledge.

Epistemology has only a methodological priority. It is a dialectical defence of our knowledge of being. Finnis has fallen for the modern mistake of supposing that knowledge has some priority over being. Being is the absolutely first concept of the human mind; therefore every other knowledge, theoretical or practical, supposes knowledge of being. Putting this in terms of judgments of principles, the principle of non-contradiction is the absolutely first judgment we have to make; therefore every practical principle supposes knowledge of the principle of non-contradiction. Such first concept and principle give us an immediate knowledge of the nature of reality.

But more to the point here, metaphysics is a knowledge that is prior to moral knowledge. Practical principles cannot be absolutely independent of metaphysical principles (they are as it were but contractions of same). And it is the theoretical knowledge of Metaphysics (as Ontology) that immediately discloses to us the nature of reality.

Coming then to the concept of good, not as understood metaphysically or ontologically as being considered relatively to desire or appetite, but as the end or final cause of human will and action, it is the first reason or principle why the will moves and founds the first principle of all (moral) human behavior as the principle of synderesis ("seek good, shun evil"). Relatively, then good is the first concept and synderesis is the first principle of human action. Contra Finnis, this first practical principle is prior to the seven particular goods and practical principles he has listed (with adjustment later) despite their self-evidence. Moreover, these practical principles presuppose the principle of non-contradiction, which simply reflects the nature of reality.

Not only has Finnis put knowledge before being, he has put the relative before the absolute. He has fallen into the second of the two fundamental holes of modern thought, idealist scepticism regarding our theoretical knowledge and absolute relativism regarding our practical knowledge. One might expect some serious consequences in the conclusions come to. Like Kant he has tried unsuccessfully to climb out of such holes, though he is only concerned with the second.

Unlike Kant he has attempted to accommodate the thought of Aristotle and St. Thomas to this dilemma. The weakness is in the starting points. Both Kant and Finnis eschew Metaphysics as the absolute starting point of all practical human knowledge. Kant moves from Physics, or Mathematical Physics; Finnis moves from Legal Philosophy, or more generally, Ethics. Their thought is as it were suspended in the mind without support of reality. Kant manufactures a rational/logical order based on pure human will; Finnis makes it depend upon pure human reason.

Like every error there is some truth in what they say, and we could even grant that there is more truth in Finnis's position than in Kant's; but let us put it that in the practical order Kant's Ethics is a quarter truth, Finnis's is a half truth. In terms of his treatment of the Natural Law we might allegorize by saying that, like Athena being born from the head of Zeus, Natural Law comes newborn out of the head of man.

This results in disconnecting the moral order from the natural order of goodness and makes it as it were a rational order constructed in a mind suspended from reality. In fact, Finnis does not like the name "Natural Law" and no doubt would prefer to replace it with something like "Rational Law". There is reason in the name "Natural Law", for human reason reflects the natural order, and indeed as St. Thomas says is but a participation of the eternal law in the author of nature.

The half truth that is in Finnis's fundamental position cannot save him from slipping back into positivism in his philosophy of law. That might be expected given his positivist academic background. But here again he believes he has found a justification in Aristotle and St. Thomas for holding that in some sense an unjust law is a valid law. For positivism does not consist in positing positive law but such a law divorced from natural law. It should be noted that an unjust law is a positive law that is in direct conflict with the natural law, such as the laws of Nazi Germany for the extermination of the Jewish race, which contradict the moral prohibition of the killing of innocent human beings. That is a case of positive law sinning by commission; but it can also sin by omission where the law fails to protect the innocent, as in regard to abortion, or where it is complicit in a system of gross maldistribution of resources or common goods. Positivism holds that positive law has its own validity in human reason, right or wrong, which is argued for in various ways by modern legal philosophers such as Austin, Kelsen and Hart (Finnis's mentor at Oxford).

Finnis attempts to get around this unjust character of positive law by drawing on the doctrine of analogy that is to be found in Aristotle's discussion of the meanings of words. The doctrine of analogy is much contested even within strict Thomist circles. The disputes arise in our view from a difficulty of reconciling statements in both Aristotle and St. Thomas on the subject. The problem with interpreting Aristotle of course is that he was "inventing" the language that was needed to describe logic and accordingly there is a crossover in some respects in his use of the notion of analogy. The problem with the interpretation of what St. Thomas had to say on analogy was that he did not provide a separate treatise on analogy itself but simply applied the notion in the context of the various questions he was considering. In different contexts he did provide a sort of mini exposition of analogy, as he did with many other philosophical matters arising in the course of his theological works. But even in these there is a variation of approach that causes puzzles for his interpreters.

We see an important distinction to be made between what we might call the analogy of names (that cover both real being and mental being) and the analogy of concepts (that cover only real being). The former we may characterize as nominal analogy and the latter as real analogy. We should straightaway notice that Metaphysics is primarily interested in real analogies, but Logic has a use for nominal analogies.

Our contention in regard to Finnis is that he has mixed up the two (he is not alone). His weakness is therefore found to be in both Metaphysics and Logic. We have already discussed above the contrast between Finnis's definition of law and that of St. Thomas where the matter of analogy was also discussed.

Now Aristotle used the notion of analogy in his Metaphysics to extend the meaning of being not only to real being outside the mind but also to mental being, by which is meant being that is constructed in the mind for the mind's purposes, such as negations, privations and purely logical relations. Thus non-being or nothing may be (indeed needs to be) thought of in terms of being. Here Aristotle says that they are not being in the primary sense but in a secondary sense.

Aristotle had already excluded the "being of the proposition", to which these mental beings correspond, from the principal object of study of Metaphysics. The principal object of Metaphysics is being that really exists outside the mind. Now in the study of such reality there is much use for analogy. So the principal use of analogy regards what we have referred to as real analogies, such as the analogy of being as referring first to substance and second to accidents.

St. Thomas has given the real definition of law, in terms of its four causes. We may speak of analogy here but that will pertain to the differences in the nature of the causes, divine law, human law, eternal law, natural law. Finnis wishes to apply it to positive law, but with a twist. Positive law can be true law according to the real definition. But it has to fulfill all the elements of the definition. This it cannot do if it is not an ordinance of reason rightly understood. And it will not be such an ordinance of reason if it conflicts with what is law in a more primary sense, which means it does not conform to natural justice.

So too we may speak of real analogy in the case of friendship, which is defined as mutual love mutually known. This love may be the love of goodwill, of utility and of pleasure. But the latter two cannot fulfill the definition really if they conflict with the first. We can express this as them then being not true friends but apparent friends only.

But what if we speak of a false friend? Is that to be taken to be a friend by analogy? Not really: but we have used the word "friend" so it amounts to analogy verbally or nominally. It is thus that we may use words in phrases such as invalid proof, a square circle, where the adjective contradicts the noun, or the predicate contradicts the subject. This is what Aristotle was doing in referring to nothing as something thought about as being. It is the same sort of nominal analogy where we name something as a particular thing from a superficial appearance, such as in the expression "fools' gold". Is it gold; not really, but called so by the similarity of its colour to real gold.

Now Finnis, using the authority of Aristotle, believes he has found a way to justify an unjust law being regarded analogously as a true law, if only in a secondary sense. It may even qualify as a valid law. For it is validly called a law. Plainly, Finnis is playing here the sophistical trick of using analogy ambiguously. But, precisely because of the modern weakness in Logic, he and a multitude of his readers appear to be oblivious to the deception. Positivism is noteworthy for its affinity with sophistry.

To cover the ambiguity (and sophistry) Finnis (no doubt unwittingly) substitutes the phrases "central case" and "focal meaning" for the primary meaning so that he can allow that law in the primary sense means law as fully defined by St. Thomas. Nonetheless positive law (in the bad sense) can be called law in a secondary sense, implying it is a good or real sense. At the same time it allows the legal positivist to not take too seriously St. Thomas's dictum (reiterating St. Augustine) that "an unjust law is no law at all" but rather "a species of violence". Violence or force is then introduced into the notion of law as an essential element (when it is but a property contingent upon having to govern those who have no respect for the law). A law-abiding citizen does not need the threat of coercion.

Conveniently for unjust regimes, the positivist legal philosophers use this concept of law as a species of violence to justify the force needed by the few to make the majority comply with unjust laws (e.g. of "property" that has been misappropriated on a grand scale by force or fraud). Then we have what St. Augustine described in chapter 4 of Book 4 of his "City of God":

"Justice being taken away, then, what are kingdoms but great robberies? For what are robberies themselves, but little kingdoms? The band itself is made up of men; it is ruled by the authority of a prince, it is knit together by the pact of the confederacy; the booty is divided by the law agreed on. If, by the admittance of abandoned men, this evil increases to such a degree that it holds places, fixes abodes, takes possession of cities, and subdues peoples, it assumes the more plainly the name of a kingdom, because the reality is now manifestly conferred on it, not by the removal of covetousness, but by the addition of impunity."

For, once entrenched, an unjust regime, whether it is openly tyrannical or clandestinely oligarchical, masquerading as democratic, does enforce its own unjust laws with impunity. Significantly, the positivism of modern legal philosophers makes the power of coercion an essential element, if not the defining difference of their definition of law.

This is what Finnis is allowing in arguing that law without justice may by analogy be called law in some real if secondary sense. The "device", which Finnis explicitly attributes to Aristotle, enables all sorts of justification for unjust regimes, no matter how horrific. Undoubtedly, this logical defence of positivism is not what Finnis would have intended. He sees himself as defending Natural Law, with some necessary adjustment of St. Thomas's definition. The compromising result comes about from the lack of a proper understanding of Aristotle's Metaphysics and Logic.

Finnis makes use of what St. Thomas says about law under a tyrannical regime as if he would allow it to be law in some real sense. But let us look at what St. Thomas says in distinguishing between law simply taken and law taken in a certain respect (I-II, 92, 1):

> "For if the intention of the lawgiver is fixed on true good, which is the common good regulated according to Divine justice, it follows that the effect of the law is to make men good simply. If, however, the intention of the lawgiver is fixed on that which is not simply good, but useful or pleasurable to himself, or in opposition to Divine justice; then the law does not make men good simply, but in respect to that particular government. In this way good is found even in things that are bad of themselves: thus a man is called a good robber, because he works in a way that is adapted to his end."

Finnis thinks that calling someone a good thief is sufficient to qualify him as in some real way good, as a thief. But, St. Thomas points to the use of the word "good" here "as found in things that are bad in themselves". It is obviously a case of an analogy of name only. Laws of unjust regimes are really bad – even so far as being opposed to divine justice! How can they claim any obedience in the subjects?

What is perhaps mixed up here is that nothing is without some good element, even the devil. With regard to evil governments (of one, few or many) there may be cause not to try to overthrow it because it has at least some sort of unity if enforced. The same conditions apply as with the just war; it is only justified if it is not likely to produce some worse result. To overthrow a tyrant, say Hitler, one would have to consider this minimal good before doing so. As St. Thomas says elsewhere it may be more prudent in some situations to await the demise of the tyrant. But that in no way legitimizes the unjust laws enforced.

Finnis, like many a sincere positivist lawyer, seems unaware of the viciousness of the legality that they are endorsing. There are of course degrees of injustice, as a regime like Soviet Russia was based upon open violence. Other bad regimes such as oligarchies may eschew over time such means as torture and murder, but still maintain a system of injustice in the form of a gross mal-distribution of wealth by deceitful propaganda and compulsory "education". Modern legal philosophers under Liberal Capitalist politico-economic systems do not look all that closely into these forms of unjust laws.

His having a foot in both camps, of the naturalists and the positivists, the scholastics and the analytical philosophers, no doubt explains Finnis's acceptance as a distinguished scholar on law and morality by both Oxford and Notre Dame – a Fellow of the British Academy, no less. His heart may be with the Catholic University that wishes to follow St. Thomas, but his head is not clear of the influence of the British University that wishes to defend the status quo.

But we do not wish to question his academic integrity, nor his religious sincerity. We simply claim that his work is a product of the confusion of the times, which, where the study of St. Thomas on law is concerned, flows from a failure to be grounded in Metaphysics when attempting to explain his philosophy of law and morality.

To sum up at this stage, Finnis's NLNR is a mixture of some good insights built upon faulty foundations. Its treatment is unnecessarily long-winded and piece meal. It cannot be otherwise given its faulty foundations. However, so far our observations have been of a general nature, mainly to do with the fundamentals of the matters treated by the authors concerned. We now turn to a more detailed look at the contents of the books under examination of Peter Singer and John Finnis.

PART THREE

ON SINGER

Chapter 4

Summary Critique of Singer

Singer calls his theory of Ethics a form of Utilitarianism. This it is in some respects but it is rather a hybrid of different kinds of erroneous ethical theories, not to speak of flawed arguments. The theoretical basis of thought of most thinkers "educated" in modern thought falls into the two streams that flow from the rationalism of Rene Descartes, as transendentalized later by Immanuel Kant, and/or the empiricist experimentalism of Francis Bacon, as extended to its logical absurdity by David Hume. Singer belongs squarely within the empiricist stream from which the practical theory of ethical utilitarianism developed. However, as we shall observe more closely, he constructs his own peculiar eclectic theory of morality. He is affected no doubt unconsciously by the conversion of empiricism after Kant into positivism, where modern thinkers, unable to ignore the rising rational force of mathematical logic (suitably mechanised) in modern science, have modified the total dependence of empiricism upon sense experience and made room for some kind of reasoning (suitably truncated).

From an Aristotelian point of view both modern rationalism and empiricism are founded upon forms of reasoning, the first imitating the method of Mathematics in favouring *a priori* reasoning and deduction, the second focusing on the method of empirical science in leaning towards *a posteriori* reasoning and induction. Both are flawed in that they attempt to understand and reason about reality without Metaphysics. Both logical methods are appropriately dealt with in the modern mixed scientific method, but without a proper metaphysical foundation modern science loses touch with truth and flounders in a sea of shifting hypotheses. The attempt to provide some sort of philosophical basis resulted in the two errors of Rationalism and Empiricism both of which fall into a profound scepticism.

The unnatural limitation of the range of reason translates in the practical moral sphere of thinking, after a series of gymnastic mental manoeuvres, into the two opposed modern theories of Ethics of Utilitarianism and Kantianism. The key figure, here again, is David Hume. This development in modern thought in its turn consists in a loss of touch with moral goodness and a fall into relativism.

Thinking in moral matters is complicated by the fact that it is not simply a question of reason but also of will. Put more fundamentally, it is not purely to do with knowledge (as is the case with theoretical sciences) but also with appetite. The full explanation of moral theory (as with moral activity) therefore is to be found in two sources, and it is a matter of some difficulty to determine the relevant priority at any particular point in the process of thinking and behaving. For instance, Aristotle apparently hesitated over whether choice was a matter of reason or will. What we can say at this stage, however, is that it is not a case of reason or knowledge only, or will or appetite only. Hume famously put "passion" as the primary source of morality. However, his "slave" of passion (reason) gradually became more dominant as Utilitarianism developed from Bentham and Mill.

In dealing with Ethics we have to appreciate that there are two sets of opposition in regard to human nature that have to be sorted out. The first is between knowledge and appetite, the second is between the rational part of human nature and the animal. On the side of knowledge we have to note the difference between reason and sense; on the side of appetite we have to note the difference between will and sensuality. The problem with Hume's language is that passion is generally associated with the sensual side of human nature, which Hume inevitably falls into, given his understanding of human psychology.

One needs to note that for the modern mind (as was the case with ancient theories of Ethics after Aristotle) reason does not extend beyond the physical world. This does not mean that human nature is equated with brute animal nature, as happens with gross hedonistic theories of ethics, but that the range of reason is not conceived as extending to the purely spiritual and above. Reason, as exercised by human beings, is seen as concerned with the bodily and animal side of things only, which is to be seen in theoretical terms in the sciences of nature. What is rejected or lost is the capacity for knowing in terms of Metaphysics.

Following this anti-metaphysical line of thinking, reasoning about practical matters, such as Ethics and Politics, will confine itself to the practical aspects of human life and behaviour that have to do with bodily and worldly goods (hence the obsessive modern focus on bodily health and welfare economics). Where this descends to the level of brute animal appetites this becomes Hedonism; but where it endeavours to account for some rational control of human behaviour regarding our temporal interests this becomes Utilitarianism.

Kantian ethics tries to break out of the physical confines of this view of human life by endeavouring to construct a practical ethical theory that transcends materialism but he does this without any theoretical support (Metaphysics). This results in a state of mind of "what if", or of being required to behave "as if", hardly a satisfactory basis for human action upon which hangs eternal happiness. However, this line of thinking belongs more to the discussion of the work of John Finnis to which we will come later.

Peter Singer is in the modern philosophical tradition of Empiricism/ Utilitarianism, which has its roots in Hume. Although Hume put "passion" as the primary source of morality, he was more fundamentally enamoured of the experimental method as exhibited by Isaac Newton. Thus he said that he wished to do for the study or man or human nature what Newton had done for the study of nature. Hence, he did not eschew the use of reason in moral and political science but adapted it to the empirical or experimental approach of modern science. Not being all that interested in Mathematics he did not attach much importance to its part in the modern scientific method.

It is this notion of reason based upon experience, or "experiment", that was taken up by the school of Utilitarianism founded by Jeremy Bentham and James Mill, the father of J. S. Mill (We should notice the close connection between this ethical theory and modern economic science). It may be appreciated from what we have said above that this notion of reason not only excludes wisdom, or Metaphysics, but it is also further weakened by being reduced to explanations in terms only of material causes and bodily effects so that the notion of goods does not rise above those that engender physical pleasure, or that reside in the utility of material goods or wealth.

This weakness in the use of reason comes out most starkly in Singer's first definitive statement on Ethics right at the beginning of his book "Practical Ethics":

> The notion of living according to ethical standards is tied up with the notion of defending the way one is living, of giving a reason for it, of justifying it. Thus people may do all kinds of things we regard as wrong, yet still be living according to ethical stand-

> ards, if they are prepared to defend and justify what they do. We may find the justification inadequate, and may hold that the actions are wrong, but the attempt at justification, whether successful or not, is sufficient to bring the person's conduct within the domain of the ethical as opposed to the non-ethical. When, on the other hand, people cannot put forward any justification for what they do, we may reject their claim to be living according to ethical standards, even if what they do is in accordance with conventional moral principles. (p. 10)

There could hardly be more useless notions of morality and reason in regard to human behaviour than these. We are to regard persons as living up to ethical or moral standards regardless of their behaviour provided they are prepared to offer some excuse or justification for it (what can Singer mean by "successful or not" in this regard?). Hitler was thinking ethically, Stalin was acting morally because they rationalised their thoughts and actions. The child's excuse for stealing from the shop makes his theft an act done according to an ethical reason; the lunatic who thinks he is lord of the universe and murders indiscriminately is morally motivated – because he has a "standard" of behaviour, a mad reason for doing what he does.

The weakness in the very notion of reason may be glaringly seen when applied to theoretical matters, like Geometry. Singer does not know the distinction between good and bad reasoning let alone between true and false conclusions. Applying Singer's test in Geometry, any justification, any rationalisation, no matter how faulty or false, qualifies one's thinking as being according to the "standards" of geometrical thinking. Singer has got himself thoroughly confused here. Is it any wonder that his thinking goes seriously astray on a number of fundamental issues?

How is it possible that Singer could build a theory of Ethics on such a nonsensical basis? Well, he just doesn't. His next (logical?) step, immediately following, is to jump to a quite arbitrary limitation on the kind of justification, not note to do with whether it is nonsensical or not:

> "We can go further. If we are to accept that a person is living according to ethical standards, the justification must be of a certain kind. For instance, a justification in terms of self-interest alone will not do." (Ibid)

However, what has he done here? He has introduced a qualification that logically does not exclude Hitler's "ethical" standards of mass murder provided he does not justify them out of self-interest. We can accept that such a person is thinking according to ethical standards if he justifies it as being for the sake of the purity of the German race, or indeed for the perceived good of humanity generally.

Notice, however, the mental shift that is occurring here. In modern terms Singer has opted for social utilitarianism as opposed to individual utilitarianism. Put in modern economic language he has opted for Socialism over Capitalism – the official liberal capitalist explanation of the motivation of economic man is self-interest; whereas the socialist poses as being purely altruistic. Ordinarily, however, we tend to associate the unethical with self-interested thinking. Singer taps into this natural sense of ethics and thus creates an atmosphere of being morally serious. But, he has only translated his confused notions to the social sphere.

In the process Singer has introduced an arbitrary restriction on the notion of ethical. He will connect this with the characters of universality and objectivity. For the social viewpoint seems to avoid the particular and "subjective" interests of individuals. This does not mean that "community standards" are necessarily to be trusted. Whole societies can go bad, as recent history manifests. But the social standpoint or social ethics is a higher vantage point. It focuses on the questions of justice to one's fellow human beings, a noble aim if not the whole of ethics. This enables Singer to treat personal and even family ethics as "not relevant". On top of that he can exclude religious matters from the discussion. Sexual promiscuity too he can ignore as not sufficiently "important" to warrant serious ethical discussion "today". It is not difficult to see where his popularity comes from.

He thus represents this other-oriented character of the object of ethics as somehow equivalent to the "universal" standpoint evident historically in the consideration of moral matters, most evident in the Judeo-Christian tradition, but also adopted by Kant and even by precursors of the English Utilitarianism. Inconsistently, he does not include the more recent socio-political standpoints of German Nazism and Soviet Communism. Are not these attempts to rationalize one's social ethics (if most now would consider them unsuccessful)?

Universality and objectivity in morals are impossible without a foundation in Natural Moral Law. But such a notion is completely foreign to Singer's basic definitions of Law and Ethics. Hence, his "more plausible" practical theory turns out to be pure positivism in Law and pure relativism in Ethics. But there is more to Singer's collapsing rationalism/empiricism than this.

As mentioned above, Singer's theory is in fact two, one that he applies to matters of what we might term social justice today and the other that he applies to the more serious ethical issues of life and death of individuals. In the latter he lapses into a crass hedonism, erasing the distinction between human and animal life, and measuring the value of both in terms of pleasure and pain, or in his equivocal terms, interests and suffering. He tries to camouflage the erasure by using the language of "interests", which more appropriately belongs to the second part of his book, for the "interests" of brute animals (with which in this part he equates those of humans) are plainly in the area of sense knowledge, desires and aversions.

But before we come to the particular positions taken by Singer in this regard we need to finish with his process of reasoning about the nature of ethics. One would think that, insisting upon the properties of universality and objectivity of the ethical standpoint, he would want to attach them to his own theory of ethics. But no, the more basic modern philosophical position of skepticism that underlies the whole of modern and his philosophy comes to the fore. His respect for other viewpoints, extending to the lunatic and malevolent, as being equally "rational", and hence in an acceptable sense "ethical", causes him to hesitate so as not to become too "dogmatic".

Upon such a presupposition there can be no certainly preferable ethical standard, no human behavior, none that we as human beings find naturally repulsive. We may try to bring others around to our point of view but ultimately conviction is a sign of something wrong with our reason – for there is no such thing as truth, especially in regard to ethical questions. Judgment should be taken to mean suspension of judgment. That is of the very nature of "critical thinking".

Thus, saving his own soul, he draws back somewhat from committing himself to the evil conclusions he is about to propound as quite ethical and moral. He is only proposing one theory of ethics. The reader is to decide for himself (or herself). Thus he concludes this preliminary discussion of the nature of Ethics:

> "In this way readers will be able to come to their own conclusions about the relative merits of utilitarian and non-utilitarian approaches, and about the whole issue of the role of reason and argument in ethics." (p. 15)

What a civilised way to deal with matters of life and death! Is this not something we should provide for young minds to reflect on as they begin to deal with the problems of deciding what philosophy to live by?

Singer is not however withdrawing altogether from advocating that his readers should give serious consideration to the "ethical" conclusions that he will present in his book.

> "The universal aspect of ethics, I suggest, does provide a persuasive, although not conclusive, reason for taking a broadly utilitarian position." (p. 12)

The behaviour he will advocate and the reasons for same that he will defend may be unethical and irrational by any sane standards of morality but they do clearly come within his notions of ethical standards and moral behaviour, for they accommodate the thinking and activity of the foolish.

Singer proceeds then to "apply" his utilitarian ethical theory to particular cases, but only to those considered important to the modern mind, like fighting against social injustice and exploitation of natural resources. In the first part of his book, however, Singer has to prepare the ground for equating human life with that of the brute animal. Here his loose notion of reason will provide some useful sophistry, ignorant as he is of the distinction between deliberate human and merely spontaneous animal actions. But we may dismiss any conclusions he might wish to draw from his quite obviously foolish notion of reason. All it can tell us Shakespeare attributes to our unfortunately common condition in his "Macbeth":

> "*And all our yesterdays have lighted fools*
> *The way to dusty death. Out, out, brief candle!*
> *Life's but a walking shadow, a poor player*
> *That struts and frets his hour upon the stage*
> *And then is heard no more. It is a tale*
> *Told by an idiot, full of sound and fury,*
> *Signifying nothing.*"

That part of Ethics that relates to one's dealing with others (our neighbours) brings into focus the question of equality or justice. This simply means that each person (or thing) should be accorded what is due to him (or it) – a notion apparently foreign to Singer. The ethical problem then becomes how to determine what is due or owing to the subject concerned. It is quite evident that the question of justice does not have relevance between human beings and those things below them, including brute animals, for the existence of human beings depends upon being able to use the resources of nature even to the extent of eating. This does not mean misusing such things. Their relative goodness to us should be limited to what we really need, and their goodness otherwise as creatures is to be acknowledged and respected.

The notion of property confirms this so that such resources become what are due to human individuals. Singer tries to use the fact of injustice against other human beings in this regard to argue against property in anything below man, or at least those things that can be said to have interests – which comes from knowledge and desire for goods required for their well being. His argument would prevent anyone from owning animals.

He uses the word "exploit" which means to mistreat animals. But this is another subtle equivocation used to support his thesis. Most people do not mistreat the things they own. Then Singer shifts the notion of equality from what is due to what is desired (what someone or something is interested in) regardless of whether it is owed. The burglar is interested in others' property. So the notion of "interest" gets the same treatment as that of "reason", totally out of any control by reality. Singer's preferences, which he derives from modern mostly depraved custom, become the criteria of importance and relevance.

This is all done under the cover of a supposed "*persuasive, although not conclusive, reason for taking a broadly utilitarian position*". Thus he proceeds to assert:

> "I have argued that the only defensible basis for the principle of equality is equal consideration of interests, and I have also suggested that the most important human interests - such as the interest in avoiding pain, in developing one's abilities, in satisfying basic needs for food and shelter, in enjoying warm personal relationships, in being free to pursue one's projects without interference, and many others - are not affected by differences in intelligence." (p. 31)

How does he define "interest"? It is in fact the desirable side of good. Interest is but the expression of one's desire for something considered good. One would think that Singer would be careful to ensure only real goods would be relevant. But, like his notion of reason, his notion of interests lacks all relation to truth and what really benefits the person interested. The equal consideration of interests comes to mean that all interests are equal, well or ill founded, useful or harmful, provided the person is "interested".

To counter this nonsensical notion Singer concentrates upon what he thinks are interests that all would agree are important, such as to avoid suffering. This will enable him to extend the consideration of interests to brute animals. But even here his thinking is all awry. Animals' interests include undergoing suffering and pain. In human beings, that will be called courage, a highly acclaimed virtue. Animals fight to protect their territory, female animals fight to protect their young, even if it leads to death. They do not shrink from the suffering involved; they see it as in their interest to undergo pain in such circumstances.

Singer's utilitarian ethic in so far as it seeks to treat suffering as absolutely against a person's interest is an ethic of cowards. Certainly, suffering is not an ultimate end, but it is an integral part of life, including animal life. His focus is on the comfortable life of undiluted pleasure, avoiding situations that involve suffering. It is an ethic for the effete.

But his notion of interests is more nonsensical than this. Every "interest" is to be treated as equally valid. "*I have argued that the only defensible basis for the principle of equality is equal consideration of interests* ..." He has no way of discriminating between one interest and another. To do that one needs an objective scale of goods, something that is set out in the Natural Moral Law. So not only do interests that attach to brute animals rate the same as interests that attach to human beings as truly rational, but also interests that are not truly rational (such as in pornography) rate the same.

"Interest", so conceived, is, as a teacher of mine described other concepts, a "dirt box" concept. Every kind of rubbish is thrown into it. That is Singer's "defensible basis" for the principle of equality. His subsequent chapters in which he "applies" this ethic may be consigned to the same dirt box. It is full of the setting up of straw-man arguments and demolishing them.

Were it not for the horrific conclusions he draws in the first part of his book his ethical theory would not be worth condemning. It is no wonder that his book has been treated with moral revulsion in the country that has recent experience of the thinking upon which it is based. Singer is puzzled, because he sees himself as only engaged in an academic exercise of following through the logical implications of a "*broadly utilitarian position*". The more liberal nations of Western society, who do not have the same wrenching experience, are quite happy to regard his theory as one that "*can be applied consistently and convincingly to all the practical cases*". (from Preface)

However, as noted, the book is in two parts. The first part is a relapse to a crass hedonism of pleasure and pain as being the measure of human ethical conduct, with the focus on the negative side. If we looked for an ancient parallel we would find it in the Cyrenaics. The second part returns to the more classical utilitarianism, though with the focus not on the positive aspect of temporal welfare but on the negative aspect of poverty. An ancient parallel in this regard would be Epicureanism. The more immediate precursors of Singer however are the English social utilitarians, such as John Stuart Mill, though he goes back to Locke and Hume for grounding of ethics in empiricist psychology.

"Interest" here focuses on the human reliance upon material wealth (socially measured in money). There is no doubt that there is much suffering even in the "rich nations" owing to grave injustices in the distribution of wealth. So social utilitarianism, in attempting to equalise the possession and enjoyment of wealth within society, does work to counter such injustice. What is not understood is the position of the institution of private property in modern economies. Both liberal capitalist and radical socialist politico-economic philosophies misunderstand and misrepresent its natural law basis.

It is neither an absolute right, as the liberal capitalist holds, nor does it necessarily work injustice, as the radical socialist argues. It is a natural and necessary social institution, but it is subordinate to the universal destination of the earth's goods for all. It is meant to serve the possession and enjoyment of material goods of all mankind, so that rightly used all can have all the wealth necessary for a full human life on earth. The fact that this does not occur - and on such a large scale - is owing to the abuse of the institution committed or condoned by those in government.

Historically, those in power have used it to misappropriate for themselves and their few favourites the greater part of the wealth produced in a nation. As a consequence, the majority are deprived of their rightful share of property and are forced to serve as workers for the owners. Particularly in modern times this has resulted in a great gulf between the rich, who do not have to work, called capitalists, and the poor people who have to work, called indeed workers.

Naturally and rationally, the right of property is necessary because human beings live not so much by what they find but by what they produce. The production of wealth, however, can only be done by individuals, or small groups, who require exclusive possession of land and other materials. This right of property is not for their exclusive benefit but is meant to serve the interests of all. This comes about through the social process of exchange, where production and consumption come together. In order for this to operate properly, there needs to be a system of justice put in place and protected by the government. Unfortunately, more often than not, those in government are either the perpetrators of unjust distribution or beholden to those who are its beneficiaries.

Sadly, the modern state resembles more than anything else the robber kingdoms described by St. Augustine:

> "Justice being taken away, then, what are kingdoms but great robberies? For what are robberies themselves, but little kingdoms? The band itself is made up of men; it is ruled by the authority of a

> prince, it is knit together by the pact of the confederacy; the booty is divided by the law agreed on. If, by the admittance of abandoned men, this evil increases to such a degree that it holds places, fixes abodes, takes possession of cities, and subdues peoples, it assumes the more plainly the name of a kingdom, because the reality is now manifestly conferred on it, not by the removal of covetousness, but by the addition of impunity."

It is this impunity that passes for "law and order", to protect the property of the few. Bentham and the early utilitarians had some insight into this gross inequality. The depth of it explains the modern interest in equality that Singer alludes to. But there is no true understanding of the cause of the inequality. Social utilitarianism slides into Socialism in politico-economic thinking, railing against the institution of property itself, attempting to correct the injustice by taxation and other means to be employed by the very government that is at the root of the problem by reason of its failure in justice or complicity in injustice.

Singer latches onto the "interests" that need to be equalised. But, like all liberals, whether capitalist or socialist, he fails to see the elephant in the room, and timidly suggests that the unjust rich contribute a minor portion of their spoils to the relief of the poor and starving. The rich do not mind his moral strictures, for they can shift the obligation on to the community as a whole. Not surprisingly, it is the poor who end up coming to the aid of the poor.

However, Singer is on stronger ground when pointing out the inequality of interests in this respect and the urgent need to redress it. We are more concerned with the weakness of his basic position. Utilitarianism, whether individual or social, is a flawed ethical theory in putting the ultimate end of human conduct in a notion of good as animal pleasure or material utility, a kind of "interest" that in itself is unworthy of human striving, not because it is not good but because it is only good when serving the good pertaining to the highest part of human nature, which is spiritual not material.

Chapter 5

On the Person

We do not see the need to go further into the detail of Singer's argumentation but will make some comment upon the most egregiously nonsensical distinction he makes between being human and being a person. This he needs to do when he is considering the morality of killing. For not even Locke, from whom he takes his definition of person, was prepared to definitively depart from the universal ethical position in civilized nations that the killing of a human being is murder.

But Singer is so prepared to depart from the clear equation given in all standard dictionaries of a person with a human being. This common dictionary notion of person is even extended to the human body. In Christian theology the human body is considered as so sacred as to be referred to as the temple of the Holy Spirit. It is no wonder that Singer's revision of the definition of person is seen with such widespread revulsion not only by Christians but also by civilized people generally.

Singer makes a quibble at the start by saying that the meaning of "to kill" is not even specially related to human life. For we see nothing wrong in killing plants and animals.

He is apparently not averse to ignoring the moral context when it serves for making a facetious point. For as a moral prohibition it is obvious that to kill relates to killing of a human being. Others in the discussion with Singer (as critics) concede that: "the separation of the concept *person* and that of human is neither a novel nor a spurious distinction." ("Not a Modest Proposal: Peter Singer and the Definition of Person" by John Hymers – K U Leuven: "Ethical Perspectives 6 (1999) 2, p. 126) They do this however by bringing in the theological discussion of the distinction between divine nature and divine persons.

That again is to take the matter totally out of context in the opposite direction to which we will advert shortly. The classical philosophical definition of Boethius: "individual substance of rational nature", quite plainly is meant to be taken with reference to human beings. However, St. Thomas does explain that the word "rational", which strictly speaking defines human nature, is to be taken in so far as it refers to the spiritual intellectual part of human nature. Accordingly, being an individual substance of spiritual nature (which holds for the human being with a spiritual soul) is what constitutes the difference between a non-person individual substance (such as a tree) and a person. It is simply the difference between the spiritual and material so far as natures are concerned. Hence, pure intelligences or angels are also persons.

Not only being "rational" but also being possessed of free will is a mark of the life of a person. This is what the modern liberalist inclined thinker tends to focus on. Indeed, Rousseau and Kant have placed this notion as fundamental to their moral and social philosophy. Kant puts it that the person should not be regarded as in any way as a means, but as an end, existing purely for his own sake. With this goes the notion of autonomy, which means self-rule, a notion that we can see is at the basis of Aristotle's *Ethics* and *Politics*.

So it is that there has been some progress in modern times in the appreciation of the dignity of the human person, precisely because there has been progress in the insistence on linking freedom of the person with all humanity. This is obviously something that Singer and other utilitarians have had to contend with, when they are in effect reverting to a previously held "ethical" position of regarding some humans at least as non-persons. Indeed, we have recent experience of such a brutal view of human beings that one considers sub-human, in Nazi Germany. It is no wonder that Singer has had such an unwelcome reception in Germany.

The other way in which Singer arrives at such a repulsive "ethical" position is in taking up Locke's activist definition of person. This is standard empiricist practice. Having lost any concept of substance ("that of which we know not what" according to Locke) all our knowledge is reduced to the impressions received from the activities of things, such as their sensible qualities, and whatever it is that we retain within our knowledge ("Mind") flowing from these sensible impressions (then called "ideas"). All intellectual knowledge thus becomes reduced to sense knowledge whether of the external senses, "impressions", or of their "reflections" in the internal senses, the images that are now called "ideas". In such a solution to the problem of "understanding", abstract concepts (with Descartes as the villain) are ridiculed by the English empiricists, first partly by Berkeley, and then totally by Hume.

Locke had started the process, by dispensing with the concept of substance. Thus a tree ought not to be thought of as a substance but only as a collection of impressions to which we give some sort of unity, difficult to explain. With Hume this notion of unity in our speaking about the one tree becomes impossible to explain "from reason". Admittedly, Hume says all this empiricist reasoning only goes on "in the club" and dissipates once we go outside into the real world. But we philosophers belonging to the Empiricist Club must stick by its rules and not allow anything to be talked about that is not "rationally" defensible.

So, two things follow with regard to Singer's definition of person from this empiricist presupposition. Firstly, despite his putting of "autonomous being" in his notion of person, the notion of autonomy disappears with the dispensing with the notion of individual substance. For if we reduce a thing, such as one tree, to the bundle of impressions we receive from it, not only the notion of self-rule disappears but also does that of self-existence or substance. Self-rule strictly speaking belongs only to human beings, but it may be illegitimately stretched, as Singer does, to higher animals. But autonomy presupposes individual substantiality.

For, sense impressions only record, if even these external realities were admitted into the idealistic empiricist world, such accidental features as size and shape of the trunk, the green of the leaves of the tree, their rustling sounds and so on. Only an intellect can penetrate to the substance of things, including persons. In dispensing with substance (thought of as only abstract, which is only true initially) empiricism disposes of intellectuality, i.e. rationality. Singer's inclusion of "autonomy" in his definition of person is a contradiction no doubt forced upon him by Kantian and other influences.

The second thing that follows is that the difference between human knowledge and desire on the one hand and animal knowledge and desire is wiped out, making the attempt to distinguish between person and human superfluous. For the basic principle of utilitarianism of Bentham, Mill and others is that the measure of good and evil is the attainment or otherwise of pleasure and pain, and these are plainly understood by Singer in sensualist terms. This is not an uncommon interpretation of the ethical theory but very few, like Singer, are prepared to follow the logic to its inhuman conclusions.

Singer even expresses this criterion in terms of "sentience", which he identifies as the capacity for suffering. "Singer in fact praises Bentham for his recognition that we ought not to base our treatment of animals on the fact that they have reason, but rather on the question of whether or not they suffer." (Hymers)

> "The capacity for suffering [is] the vital characteristic that entitles a being to equal consideration … the capacity for suffering and enjoying things is a prerequisite for having interests at all, a condition that must be satisfied before we can speak of interests in a meaningful way … if a being suffers there is no moral justification for refusing to take that suffering into consideration … if a being is not capable of suffering, or of experiencing enjoyment or happiness, there is nothing to be taken into account. This is why the limit of sentience … is the only defensible boundary of concern for the interests of others." (*Practical Ethics*, p.50 – quoted by Hymers)

Thus, in the end, the interests of persons may have to give way to that of non-persons. It all depends upon the calculation of consequences (utility). That would justify, in some circumstances, not only abortion and infanticide, the killing of non-persons, but also euthanasia, the killing of persons.

However, in equating some animals with human beings so as to argue that they may both be persons, Singer is no doubt falling in with the modern loss of the ability to make the fine distinctions developed to a high degree by the Scholastics and especially by St. Thomas, when it comes to the psychology of humans and other animals.

St. Thomas makes the general point that in regard to the levels of being of natural bodies the highest of the lower touches the lowest of the higher, even where one is moving from one distinct form of being to another, such as from plant to animal. So true is this that it is often difficult to diagnose whether a particular thing is plant or animal, even though there is an infinite gap between a thing without sense knowledge (the lowest of which is touch) and a thing with knowledge.

So, too, human being in its lowest evidence, at the beginning of human life, is so close to animal life that for a long time scientists were not able to tell when human life began. Aristotle, for instance, proposed a staged process whereby the embryo was first plant-like, then animal-like and only after some months in the womb something of human form. With advance in science, however, it is now possible to identify the humanity of the embryo, produced by humans, as human from the start. Even if there are some problems with identification right at the stage of fertilization of the ovum, it is sufficiently scientifically proven as to warrant us treating the foetus in the woman as human from conception.

That means philosophically that the new being brought into existence is a new individual substance of human or rational nature. That is enough to say that it is a person. However, if we have to wait till this individual human substance develops the necessary organs for it to function properly as a rational being then this occurs over time, as part of the process of growth, not of generation. Things only grow to become more of what they are. If they are persons at the beginning their growth is in personhood.

What the empiricist John Locke and Peter Singer demand however is that we do not treat the subject as a person until he or she is capable immediately of exercising his highest functions of reason and will. Singer puts his definition into four characteristics, the fourth "autonomous being" we have already discussed. The other three are: "(1) a rational and self conscious being aware of itself as an extended body existing over an extended period of time; (2) a desiring and plan making being, and (3) a being that desires to continue living". Even if this were applicable to humans and some higher animals this active condition could be delayed and interrupted for all sorts of reasons, so as to require them to delay and even interrupt calling what is in an individual substance of rational nature a person.

This leads to all the nonsensical conclusions that they have derived from their original empiricist/activist assumptions. Persons injured in an accident and left in a coma have to be treated as no longer persons. Persons at the end of their lives and no longer able to look forward to life without suffering are to be "put down" like a dog, even though they may be prepared to endure courageously the suffering for some noble reason. It is said that the circumstances of Beethoven's birth were such that today he would have been thought not worth keeping alive. The utilitarian criterion of happiness is not only arrogant but also ignorant.

Even comparing an adult higher animal such as a chimpanzee with an adult human being one has to keep in mind the principle of St. Thomas about the closeness of the two levels of being, so far as observation of activity is concerned. The higher animal has three internal senses, called imagination, memory and another that is not well recognised, called by the Scholastics, the estimative sense. We know it commonly as "instinct". It is a power to judge the concrete situation in which the animal finds itself, as e.g. of distance in terms of avoiding obstacles or of danger in terms of alien bodies. The animal needs this natural power of judgment to negotiate the course of its life. It will be noted that the power is quasi-infallible, rarely making mistakes, and species determined, every one of the species having it in the same determinate way.

Now the human being is distinguished in knowledge from the brute animal, even the most "intelligent", by its capacity to have concepts that abstract from the concrete situation of here and now, and so to make judgments that also transcend the limits of the here and now, The human person's judgments are not naturally determined to one specific kind of course of action. His judgments are in principle universal. His power of reasoning shares in this universality and thus transcends the capacity of animal memory that can profit from concrete experiences of the there and then.

This demonstrates that the human being is of such a higher level of being as to transcend the bodily limits of merely animal being. Aristotle uses this intellectual quality of human knowledge to prove the spirituality of the human form or soul. However, St. Thomas points out that in between this purely spiritual understanding in human knowledge and the still material and temporal manner of mere animal knowledge there is a level of knowledge in man whereby the two are shared so that in the three higher internal senses the human being is able to operate in an even higher fashion because of the influence of the human intellect.

Thus, for instance, we have an imagination like the dog, which dreams in its sleep, and we have a memory that simply retains what has been experienced in the past; and also we have a power of judging our concrete situation in the here and now. But curiously enough as merely animal powers in us they are inferior to the brute animal. For our judgment of distance and danger is not quasi-infallible; our imagination is weak, and our memory fails. On the other hand, we can use these powers in a higher way to what brute animals can. We have a creative imagination that serves us as artists; we have a way of recollecting the past by deliberately searching for something we have forgotten (called reminiscence – a valuable tool for the story-teller) and we have a way of judging in the concrete that is not bound to automatic repetition of human actions even in the same situations. This last is called the cogitative power.

One can understand how these two quite different uses of the same internal senses can be confused (and are routinely so confused by empiricists/utilitarians) so that the activities of human beings, in regard to their everyday needs, are thought to be the same as higher animals, like chimpanzees. Yet the ontological gulf is infinite if one thinks in terms of substance.

That is one kind of error made in regard to the understanding of the human being as a person. Of recent times there has arisen another error, not resulting in a degradation of the notion of the human person, but in an unwarranted elevation, to the divine no less. Indeed, the attempt has been made to explain the notion of person, as applicable to human beings, by reference to the notion of person as not to be taken from individual substance but to be taken from the purely relative character of the definition of person applying to the divine persons in God, i.e. to the Trinity. That is to say it is proposed to put the essence of person in relation not substance.

There are some highly regarded modern theologians who have proposed this theory of the person, including Hans von Balthasar and Pope Benedict XVI before he was pope. Since it has theological ramifications we do not propose to say much about it here, wanting only to comment upon its philosophical implications so far as the concept of the person is concerned.

It is a side issue so far as the discussion of Singer is concerned. But it is relevant to the discussion of Tracey Rowland's notion of the Natural Law. For in effect she makes our understanding of the Natural Moral Law dependent upon belief in the Trinity, in the same way that von Balthasar and Ratzinger make our understanding of the person as such dependent upon our notion of it in the Trinity. Grace does raise us to the level of the divine, but that is to do with the supernatural order of human life. The notion of person first belongs to the order of natural knowledge at its highest in the metaphysical.

St. Thomas shows the way to relate our metaphysical understanding of the person as individual substance of rational nature to our theological explanation of the person. In the (spiritual) creature there can be only one person in one individual substance. In God though it is revealed that there are three persons in the one individual God. What we have to try to explain is how is it possible for there to be three persons in the one substance. The answer given by St. Thomas and all theologians is that the multiplicity of persons in God is not from any absolute difference but from relative oppositions within the one divine essence or substance. Absolutely speaking there can be only one God. The defining difference of a divine person then is in purely relative opposition to the others.

St. Thomas explains how this may be understood (to the extent that we are capable here below) by reference to the way a specific difference is added to a generic notion. Thus, we can say that man is truly animal, but only considered generically. It is necessary to add the specific difference of rational to determine definitively what is man. So, explains St. Thomas, we may see a divine person as being a person generically like a created person in that he is truly a divine individual substance, i.e. is God. But further than that he has an added specific difference in so far as he is relatively opposed to the other two divine persons. Thus the Father is relatively opposed to the Son and the Holy Spirit, the Son is relatively opposed to the Father and the Holy Spirit, and the Holy Spirit is relatively opposed to the Father and the Son. The full definition of the person of the Holy Spirit therefore is individual substance (God) with such purely relative opposition within the one Godhead.

There is no need to make the notion of the person even in the Trinity exclusive of the notion of individual substance. Still less is there any cause to make the notion of person itself, as in human persons, simply constituted by relativity to others. That is not only to mix the supernatural order of reality with the natural but also to misunderstand the natural order in respect of the person.

The notion of real relation outside of God is not within substance but outside it between two things. It is true that we use the word "relative" in all sorts of ways in speaking of the entitative and essential parts of principles of composite things, as in referring to the union of act and potency, form and matter and soul and body. St. Thomas points out that we are constrained to speak so, but we are not to think there exists real relations within created substances, joining them as it were. Form and matter are so proportioned to one another that they together constitute the same composite substance. It is the composite that exists, not its components.

However, we will leave the more detailed discussion of these matters to the theologians. The main point here is that the person as something pertaining to human beings and created spiritual beings ought to be clearly distinguished from individual substances below man and persons above the angels. Singer makes the former mistake. Rowland does not make the latter mistake directly in her essay "Natural Law: from Neo-thomism to Nuptial Mysticism", but she is most probably influenced in this regard by the insertion by von Balthasar and Ratzinger of the theology of grace into the philosophy of the person.

PART FOUR

ON FINNIS

Chapter 6

Overview

We have already discussed two serious errors in Finnis's theory of Natural Law, which has come to be known as the New Natural Law. The first is to do with the nature of first practical concepts and principles. The second is to do with the meaning of law itself and the related notion of an unjust law.

In regard to the first Finnis proposed that there are seven basic goods, which in relation to our knowledge of the Natural Law stand absolutely independent of any other concepts and of each other. That means that we do not need to underpin them with metaphysical concepts, such as being. We do not need to take into consideration that the principles of the Natural Law have to be expressed as well in propositions, the most fundamental of which is that of synderesis, which is based on the very nature of being as relative to the intellectual appetite (will); seek good, shun evil.

Finnis gives these primary goods the quality of self-evidence. But self-evident more properly applies to propositions (first judgments of principle) not to concepts such as knowledge. He slides the concepts of these basic values or basic goods into propositions by stating for example that knowledge is a basic good. That he claims is an underived self-evident truth. This he maintains is not a moral principle. If so then he is expressing it as a theoretical truth – which it is - but it does not follow (as he asserts) that it is worthy of pursuit, for that pertains only to knowledge as a practical notion.

Such a general theoretical notion of knowledge or truth is not relevant to morality, for there is plenty of knowledge that is not necessary to salvation and therefore worthy of pursuit in this life. This too general notion of knowledge comes out in his calling it curiosity, which can be the vice of idle curiosity, seeking knowledge simply for the sake of knowing regardless of its relevance to progress in virtue. That does not exclude studies as a matter of interest, provided they are consistent with progress in virtue.

The notion of knowledge propounded by Finnis is not a basic good to be pursued. The notion of good in ethics is expressed in the first practical principle or most universal law of morality, good is to be done and pursued, and evil is to be avoided. That is good as related to our ultimate end or happiness. Moreover, the basic good of knowledge relevant to morality and to the Natural Law is derived from the stated principle of synderesis.

But let us elaborate a little upon St. Thomas's analysis of self-evidence. He notes three meanings of self-evident, which apply to propositions rather than concepts. Self-evidence he explains lies in the very nature of the terms (subject and predicate) of the proposition. The one cannot stand without the other. Thus any necessary proposition, such as that man is rational, or indeed that man is animal, is self-evident regardless of whether it is known or not. That is the first and most fundamental meaning.

However, "evident" refers to knowledge and so self-evident is taken more especially in relation to our knowledge of the truth of the proposition. Some truths St. Thomas points out are known by all from the very fact that no one of intellectual capacity does not know the meanings of the terms involved. This is the second meaning of self-evident. This pertains to basic terms used, such as being and non-being, thing and nothing, one and many, whole and part, true and false, good and evil, substance and accident, potency and act. For, one cannot be in touch with reality (i.e. have a functioning intellect or reason) without an understanding of being and those concepts that follow immediately upon it.

Thus, the principle of non-contradiction is but a proposition expressed in the most fundamental terms of being and non-being. It is true that many today say that a radical intellectual scepticism is not only possible but also a necessary feature of "critical thinking". But we may apply to them Aristotle's comment upon Heraclitus's denial of the principle of non-contradiction: "what a person says is not necessarily what he thinks". Such verbal contestation in an argument is the typical ploy of the sophists, putting on their opponents the onus of "proof" in respect of first principles as if they were conclusions.

These basic propositions are metaphysical principles that underlie all human knowledge. They are known as soon as one's intellect or reason begins to function. It should be noted, however, that they are theoretical knowledge, simply had for its own sake. Practical knowledge adds the ordination of human knowledge to action. In that order good is the first concept. But it is good relative to what is necessary for human happiness, or in the order of grace to human salvation.

The understanding of good therefore is twofold, firstly metaphysical as a general mode of being and secondly as the final cause of human behaviour. Will, as the appetite for good understood, moves the intelligent agent to pursue the good so understood, and ultimately to the concrete ultimate end (happiness). This pursuit however has to be directed though concrete acts to that end. Setting of direction belongs not to will (or choice) but to intellect and reason. Thus we have to make room in practical and moral matters for both reason and will. The first principles of practical reason are in the reason, and are there as commands or ordinances, but, as St. Thomas clearly asserts, a prior act of the will is presupposed. There is no law, and hence Natural Law, without a superior will moving the subject to obey it. That is what is sensed in our consciousness of the Natural Law (conscience), even though it is expressed as an ordinance within our own reason.

What we are directly concerned here with, though, is the question of priority of the concept of good in our understanding. Finnis detects the relative priority of good in the order of ethical concepts but overlooks the absolute priority of being in regard to metaphysical concepts, including that of the good. Practical knowledge is dependent upon theoretical, and in particular the ethical on the metaphysical.

There is an order, also, among self-evident principles as known by us. This becomes clearer when we consider the third meaning of self-evident mentioned by St. Thomas. That is what is self-evident only to the wise (or we might adapt this to modern language as self-evident to the scientist). Notice that the wise only discern what is already self-evident in the first sense. They see better the evidence that is from the things, which for us humans consists in their essential natures and necessary properties, as considered without their contingent conditions attaching to their individual material existence.

Such intellectual knowledge has to be first universal from the very nature of abstraction from the material individuals. But in the context of a discussion of evidence we are speaking of some (universal) proposition being universally known. That only applies to the second meaning of self-evident. And then we are only speaking of principles not conclusions. Not all metaphysical knowledge is universally known. For Metaphysics, as (the highest) science, consists not only of absolutely first principles but also of secondary principles and conclusions.

Thus, there is a certain order in human knowledge of what is in reality self-evident "in itself". There is what is immediately evident to all, such as the absolutely first principle of non-contradiction. Then there are a number of first principles that are not deduced as conclusions from this first principles but their denial can be reduced to its denial (*reductio ad absurdum*). The first practical principle of synderesis is such but in its relation to other practical first principles it is similar to the principle of non-contradiction in that it does not tell us what is good. Then there are conclusions that can be reasoned to from such essential principles. Such reasoning consists in a certain contraction of the universality of the more basic propositions.

There is an order also here, some practical conclusions being so close to the first principles as to be looked upon as secondary principles and commonly adopted in laws by civilized communities, adapting them to the particular conditions of a nation by positive laws. In regard to practical propositions or laws St. Thomas notes that such is the character of what has come to be called the Law of Nations (*Ius gentium*). Two of these necessary conclusions are what we call the institutions of marriage and property.

We might note at this point that Finnis has included marriage among the seven basic goods, thereby including it among the first principles of practical reason. But it more properly belongs to the secondary principles as explained. It is derived from a more basic principle that St. Thomas describes as pertaining to man according to that nature that he has in common with other animals, namely, sexual intercourse and the rearing of offspring. (that the natural law of marriage does not bind all human beings to reproduce comes from it being a law upon man in general rather than in particular individuals) It may be noted that unnatural sexual intercourse that is deliberately contrary to the possibility of offspring is not only against the natural order of man as rational (in the institution of marriage) but more seriously is against the natural order of man as animal, and indeed as a living thing. St. Thomas characterises it as "proximate to homicide". (SCG, III, 128)

Neither is the institution of private property a first principle of the Natural Law, but it is derived from the universal destination of all goods. From reason it is clear that both marriage and property have to be instituted so that these more primary ends may be rationally fitted to the conditions of human nature.

However, the main point of criticism of Finnis's understanding of what is primary in the make up of the Natural Law is that he reads their self-evidence as giving them absolute independence from metaphysical concepts and principles. This is owing to a weakness in Metaphysics and in the understanding of Aristotelian logic. Though of lesser import he further exaggerates this independence by denying any order of goodness among the seven primary goods themselves. Murder is obviously a more serious moral offence than unfriendliness, or, according to his later list, than adultery. In later writings Finnis focuses on the immorality of homosexual acts as contrary to marriage, but they have an even more fundamental immorality than that.

But when we come to the list of basic goods (converted into basic practical principles by stating simply that each is a basic good) the reason for the disconnection of these goods taken generally or theoretically (as pre-moral) from the moral order becomes evident. The basic goods (or first practical principles) that are relevant to morality are not as conceived by Finnis. The knowledge to be pursued is not to be equated with curiosity - which may as we have seen be superfluous knowledge or even harmful to the path to salvation - but is knowledge that is necessary for ultimate happiness.

The same applies to the other basic goods Finnis lists: Life, Play, Aesthetic experience, Sociability, Practical reasonableness, and Religion except that the last two contain a moral reference already. Indeed, Finnis separates out the sixth good and lists under it nine basic requirements: The ordering of our pursuit of goods generally; A coherent plan of life; No arbitrary preference among values; No arbitrary preference among persons; Open-mindedness and commitment to one's projects; The relevance of consequences;

Respect for every basic value; The advancement of the common good of the community; Follow one's conscience.

Finnis gives practical reasonableness a separate listing because he is uses it to render the other goods moral. As such they are only "pre-moral". This can only mean that they are being considered theoretically, as aspects of being, not practically, as aspects of action. The use of practical reason, however, (if we exclude the technical reason) necessarily involves moral reasoning.

It is convenient to set out St. Thomas's analysis of the Natural Law as it relates to the natural inclinations of human nature. St. Thomas refers the first natural inclination to that of man as a substance to preserve his existence and to the second natural inclination of man as animal to reproduce his own kind. The third order of goods that human beings naturally desire is that which pertains to man as rational. That is where Finnis should have fitted knowledge. There is of course sense knowledge, which belongs to man as animal, but it is a good subordinate to intellectual knowledge.

St. Thomas's analysis is not meant to be complete but illustrative only. For instance, the inclination to reproduce is not peculiar to animals but belongs to plants as well, if the mode of sexual reproduction is most evident in animals. There is also one important natural inclination that is as fundamental as the preservation of life itself; that is the inclination in higher beings to make use of things below them. For animals depend on plants and plants on minerals to sustain life. Human beings obviously depend on plants and brute animals for food and clothing and on lower levels of material being for shelter and materials in regard to all sorts of things. Though the human intellect is spiritual and not dependent upon a bodily organ as a subject in which to exist and operate it nevertheless depends on the whole bodily world or physical universal for the objects/forms upon which to "feed" (inform) itself. This natural inclination is important in the analysis of the moral law of property, involving as it does the universal destination of all goods below man to all human persons and the need for distributive justice in the allocation (as property) to individuals of a due proportion of such common goods external to man.

Finnis has mixed up the relation between theoretical and practical knowledge and the relation between the natural desires or inclinations and the natural or basic goods to which they are essentially related. One cannot think of natural goods, as natural ends, without reference to the natural desires or inclinations towards them. One can therefore read them through natural desires. Thus St. Thomas says: "Wherefore according to the order of natural inclinations, is the order of the precepts of the natural law." This is how he orders the precepts and this is what makes the natural moral law natural.

Special mention should be made of sociability. Society, though a natural good (Aristotle: "man is by nature social"), is not a basic good even in the proper sense. There are in fact two natural societies, the family and civil society (Aristotle is referring to civil society). Both are rational institutions, called natural as pertaining to the *Ius gentium*. The animal urge to love the opposite sex in the first case and one's own kind in the second are the natural bases of them but both inclinations are transformed when raised to the human level and both need to be brought into existence by human agreement or convention. Finnis's notion of "friendliness" confuses the two aspects of human association, animal and rational. It may be noted that Hume and utilitarians do the same with the notion of benevolence. We are speaking here of the natural order. The supernatural order of charity transcends both the natural and rational orders of love and friendliness.

Religion is placed by St. Thomas in the third order of natural inclinations (and therefore of natural goods). Thus he says: "Thirdly, there is in man an inclination to good, according to the nature of his reason, which nature is proper to him: thus man has a natural inclination to know the truth about God, and to live in society: and in this respect, whatever pertains to this inclination belongs to the natural law; for instance, to shun ignorance, to avoid offending those among whom one has to live, and other such things regarding the above inclination."

This order of natural inclination of man as rational, however, is altogether different from the other two. For the notion of natural in respect of the lower inclinations is tied to the animal and bodily side of human nature. That is not to say that reason does not become involved as is clear from the doctrine of *ius gentium*, where in man these goods acquire a spiritual character. Thus in regard to marriage it is not enough to consider the natural orientation of sexual union to reproduction of the species but one must also consider the spiritual level of such union, which indeed is superior, directly connected as it is with the spiritual souls involved. However, though pertaining to the lower animal part of human nature reproduction of offspring is still an essential component of the union as a whole. That is why the total dissociation of sexual intercourse from procreation remains not only irrational but also unnatural.

St. Thomas's quite summary exposition, however, leaves a number of questions unanswered. What distinguishes man from the lower animals is that he has a spiritual soul, and therefore intellectual knowledge and free will. But this does not distinguish him from the angel. What distinguishes man from the angel is that his intellectual knowledge has to be completed by reasoning. Thus he is properly defined as rational. The primary natural inclinations belonging to the first and second orders stated by St. Thomas are to goods that are understood without reasoning, but simply and immediately understood as pertaining to the animal level of his being. They are the objects of the first two acts of human intellect, apprehension and judgment, which are the human intellect acting like a pure spirit.

Now there are higher goods that are understood in the same way, "intuitively", as those that pertain to the lower level of human nature, and these pertain to the purely spiritual order of human being. Such are unity, truth and beauty as transcendental modes of being. But human intellectual knowledge needs to be completed by reasoning. The goods in this regard are understood completely and desired through science and wisdom, theoretical and practical. Society in the two meanings adverted to above belong to this part of the order of rational goods.

Yet we can say that man has a natural desire to obtain these truths. It is to be remembered that they come within the first meaning of self evident given by St. Thomas; they are only known however by the "wise" (meaning scientist in the sense that includes wisdom) – which is the third meaning. The natural law (as necessary conclusions) pertaining to them is not immediately known by all but requires some process of reasoning (if some are so close to natural principles that they are virtually commonly known). In regard to practical moral matters, therefore, they include firstly those proximate conclusions that are contained in the *ius gentium*, which are knowable readily by all nations, but also all necessary conclusions obtainable by scientific proof properly considered. The modern notion of scientific proof is flawed, by treating certain principles, whether theoretical as in physics mathematics or metaphysics, or practical as in personal, domestic and political ethics as hypothetical.

St. Thomas does not make distinctions here between metaphysical principles immediately or naturally known and conclusions rationally derived from them, but classes them all as related to human nature as rational. The truth about God depends on reasoning. That is to say we have to prove the existence of God as the cause of being. But to an intellect not affected by sin this would be the most evident conclusion of all. For all people have a desire to know the causes of things, and in an ultimate way. There is a sense then in which we can say that we have a natural inclination or desire to know scientific truth, for it belongs to the nature of man to reach the truth in this way. It is to be remembered, however, that we are only concerned with truths necessary for salvation. Much of particular science, such as Mathematics and Physics, is not necessary knowledge in this regard.

Moral questions, and therefore the Natural Law, belong to practical knowledge. This Finnis separates out under the basic good of practical reasonableness. But he refuses to include as part of such practical reasoning the first practical principles, especially the very first one of synderesis, "go for good and against evil". This expresses the very nature of the intellectual appetite that is the will. As St. Thomas explains this principle follows from the very understanding of good just as the first principle of all understanding (of non-contradiction) follows upon the very understanding of being. The former is the first practical truth just as the latter is the first theoretical truth. Take away these and the whole structure of truth for human beings collapses.

Finnis's basic goods relate to the first act of apprehension from which issue concepts that relate to the essences of beings rather than the second act of judgment from which issues propositions that relate to existence; he misses the full import of these principles. In the practical order the relevant propositions are commands to do something. Finnis tends even to conceive them as indicative rather than imperative. They are of course expressions at the most universal level and are not effective immediately. But they are effective by the medium of less universal laws down to the last concrete acts of conscience and prudence. That they are not simply judgments of fact is evident in that the primary act of prudence, to which they are all related ultimately, is not simply a judgment but a command. That too is of the very nature of a practical principle or law, though the imperative nature of them is less evident the more universal they are.

Finnis thinks that morality begins at some lower level of laws where practical reasonableness involves reasoning. It is true that that is where most of us are most alive to the imperative force of laws. But this imperative force originates in the very first practical principles – that is what principle of practice means. There is an intimate connection between the first practical judgment of synderesis and the last practical judgment of conscience. Throughout that process the command is expressed as "you ought to do"; that is what you are bound to do from the will of the superior commanding: "I am ordering you to do". Prudence adds the perfect force of command to the subject's will: "do it". There is no division in the line of command between indicative or theoretical knowledge and imperative or practical knowledge. It is just a matter of a more universal scope at the beginning of the intellectual process. This process is not purely intellectual but it is entwined with the will, for it is ordered not simply to knowing but to doing.

The complex requirements of Finnis's sixth good may be allowed as elements of the process of reasoning in practical affairs, if listed in a rather disordered fashion. It is an ordering, it needs to be logical or coherent, it excludes arbitrariness, it respects ends (values), it takes consequences into account, secondarily as circumstances, it is not blind to reality (open-minded), it involves commitment to projects (if project is not taken in its usual sense of product, but of end), it pursues good as common, not self-interest, and finally it follows conscience, if we are equating the whole rational process with prudence. Conscience, however, as St. Thomas explains, is not so much another conclusion necessarily following from higher more universal principles but an application of the most specific conclusion/law to the concrete situation of the individual person, rather like how he describes the derivation of positive law from the natural law by way of "determination". It says: "I should here and now do this".

Prudence, as the last act in the whole reasoning process, carries out this order. Imprudence does the opposite.

Practical reasonableness, however, though it is a good for human beings, as the way of arriving at complete truth of things, is nonetheless not well characterised as a basic good in the sense of an end of human life. It is rather a useful or an instrumental good than a basic good or final end. The tendency of the modern philosophical mind is to regard reasoning as an end-good (for it holds to no other final truth or end-good). But logic is only an instrument of science (and wisdom) not a science for its own sake.

In Ethics it is the typical mistake of Utilitarianism, taking "practical reasoning", as formal logic, as the essence of moral science. This puts one's focus on logical consistency and validity of reasoning. But the proper focus of science should be on the truth of things. This truth is founded in the truth of the principles from or to which one argues. Finnis seems to have fallen into this modern trap, not willing to count principles as having the quality of morality, but only the working of "practical reasonableness". Prudence it is to be remembered is about means. The other cardinal virtues respect ends.

So Finnis has moral/practical principles or basic goods left suspended in the mind, on the one hand, with no metaphysical support and, on the other, with no essential connection with morality as "practical reasonableness". This badly affects his ability to deal with particular moral issues. A similar situation applies in regard to his understanding of law. This comes out in his treatment of unjust law, which amounts to an exercise in political prudence divorced from the principles of the Natural Law and from the virtue of justice.

Let us now, however, deal more particularly with the essential ideas connected with the discussion of Natural Law and Natural Rights according to their treatment by Finnis in various chapters but not necessarily in the same order that he deals with them.

Chapter 7

Natural Justice

The consideration of second error of Finnis with regard to his position on unjust laws enables us to look more closely at his understanding of law itself and also of justice. He has a chapter on each in his book. In this regard the title of his book, "Natural Law and Natural Rights", has a significance that he or his readers perhaps do not appreciate.

For the natural accompaniment of Natural Law and Natural Rights, Natural Justice, is left out. As St. Thomas explains, there are three things or goods that are essentially related, indeed, virtually the same thing or good in three different contexts. Law is it in the reason (*ratio*), justice is it in the will (*voluntas*) and right is in "thing" (*in rem*); two are within the soul, the other outside. Good as Aristotle says is "in things". So the just (*ius*) is primarily in the object of the other two, that is to say it is objective, just as good is. But this thing/good, like good itself, is necessarily considered as related to appetite or desire, i.e. of the will. As well as that it is a true good and as true is necessarily considered as related to intellect, i.e. the reason.

So we have the three subjects of this thing/good (*res/ius*) and we can see the relations of these subjects to each other.

The most basic is the thing outside, for in it is the object that defines and measures what is in the will and reason. (Finnis has made use of the principle that powers and habits take their nature from their formal objects – virtue is a habit and law is a quasi-habit)

What is this object? It is not a thing in the gross sense of a stone. It is in fact something or part of a thing seen as belonging to someone. It is such considered as due to that other person, the thing, such as an arm, not taken physically (as a thing in itself) but as the "property" of the person mutilated. That is the basic sense of natural equality needed if we understand *ius* as the equal. The "due" or "right" is what is owed to the subject/person affected on account of the unjust act. Essentially it is not an esoteric notion. If a thief steals your car he is obliged to render justice (give it back) to you. The "thing" therefore is not so much the car but the fact that the car is proper to you (property firstly signifies a right in you (as a part or possession of you) rather than the thing that belongs to you). Only an intellect can see that "thing" which is the right (*ius*) for it is a relation between you as a whole and some part or as some possession. Accordingly it is something that is owed to you from your very nature. St. Thomas explains that this notion of natural equality can be extended to what becomes yours from exchange or agreement, provided such is truly free. Like to natural law there may be added positive law, so as well as natural rights there may come into existence (by agreement) positive rights.

Ideally, the only justice that can be rendered to the victim of the mutilation is to restore his arm. (Perhaps this was the sense in the dictum "an eye for an eye") This could not be done, nor could the pain inflicted be measured in material terms, so some other means of equality had to be devised. The assailant had also to suffer for his unjust act. If "an eye for an eye" was taken to mean that he should suffer the same mutilation and pain this has been abandoned as a means of punishment. For one thing it in no way restored the victim's loss. But we need not go any further here into the question of punishment.

The virtue of justice therefore is the will made ready and constant so as to render to others what is their due. Such a habit makes the person just and the will a good will in this respect. Law (in the example that against assault) is but the same objective relation of right in the reason (of the law-maker first and secondarily in the citizen) as received in the understanding. However, because the human intellect is not intuitive there is a process of rational "construction" prior to the assimilation of the *ius* or right in the concrete. Accordingly, the law of assault may be expressed in the reason as a conclusion of more basic moral/legal principles.

That will give the impression that the wrongfulness of the unjust act is from the particular law to be applied. St. Thomas alludes to this in describing law as a measure of human behaviour. But we should not overlook the fact that ultimately the human intellect is a measured measure or rule. The rational structure of science including practical science has to be measured in the end (or beginning) by the way things are, including the relations between persons. That has to be remembered too when we are considering the will, for it is an appetite following good *as understood.* So the habit of justice in the will is from things but as mediated by the reason.

There are two errors therefore to be avoided here. The more gross is to make law and rights dependent on human will alone. That is the voluntarists' error and the one that Kant fell into. The other is to make justice and rights dependent upon human reason alone. That is the rationalists' error and the one that Finnis tends to fall into. Natural Law and natural justice are based in natural rights; their meaning is taken from the "nature of things", not crassly physically considered but intelligently and practically considered.

This does not mean that all (human) rights are natural rights, no more than all law is natural law or all justice is natural justice. There is room for positive rights based upon human agreement and social convention. But these may not supplant natural rights, as is the custom today. The danger then is that all rights are conceived in legally positivist terms as dependent upon the "will of Parliament assembled"; that is the road to totalitarianism not by violence and revolution but by stealth and evolution ("progress").

There is then some significance in the omission of natural justice from the title of the book, indicating some possible influence of positivist thinking. (It seems that the title was suggested by Finnis's mentor at Oxford). For it only takes a weakness in any one of the three integral aspects of the treatment of Law Justice and Right to affect the whole three.

An analogy drawn from an image of C.S. Lewis made in connection with modern education is an apt one. He saw the "project" of the modern education of youth as the production of "men without chests", that is to say the head joined directly to the belly. Staying fairly close to the points made by Lewis we can relate the head to Law or Reason, the belly to "base appetites" in immediate contact with the appearances of things and the chest to moral virtues. Modern education debunks the notion of virtues objectively based and without them the young are unable to resist the superficial attraction of their base appetites. Lewis makes the point that the modern theories are not put directly into the children's minds but are assumptions, which, later on, their origin forgotten, and they have become quasi-unconscious, condition the children, now grown up, to take one side of a manufactured "controversial" subject that never was controversial at all.

Legal positivists are uncomfortable with any linking of law and justice because the latter tends to limit the scope of the will of the legislator. They do not mind the word justice being used in a secondary sense where it is equated simply with the word law, such as in courts of law being called, by nominal analogy, courts of justice and the judges ruling on legal matters being called justices. For that accommodates the fact that the decisions of such law courts and their judges will be according to law regardless of whether the laws are just or unjust.

Finnis's position that unjust laws can still be called valid laws, if in a secondary sense, lends support for such a disconnection of law from justice. He would of course be mortified to realise this. But the logic of his distinction between "the focal meaning" and the secondary meanings of words, supported as he imagines by the authority of Aristotle, ensnares him in such a positivist error.

When it comes to his analysis in his chapter on Justice, Finnis bases it, with reservations, on Aristotle. But the weakness of the connection with law comes out in his short treatment of general justice, as opposed to particular justice. Aristotle's other name for general justice is "legal justice", in that it is meant to identify justice with the whole of the moral law in as much as all virtues can be considered in relation to the common good. Finnis comments: "we can discard the confusing term 'legal justice' …". (p. 165) The evident reason for this is his inability to see the necessary connection between law and justice in any general sense.

When he comes to treat of the two particular justices, distributive and commutative, Finnis tries to follow Aristotle's analysis but does not really come to grips with their strict notions, drawing all sorts of peripheral matters into the discussion. Because the same subject matters may have distributive and commutative aspects he says: "The distinction between distributive and commutative justice is no more than an analytical convenience." (p. 179) Since they have quite different definitions one might as well say that the difference between property and theft is no more than an analytical convenience. Commutative justice presupposes distributive justice but they are naturally distinct particular justices.

Finnis does not get the strict political notion of distributive justice, which can be explained in terms of the relations between wholes and parts, despite his criticism of Cajetan. But the whole that is relevant is the *polis* of Aristotle, the natural civil community whose principle organ (or part like the head) is the government (confusingly also called "State"), which can take six forms outlined by Aristotle – this principal part can be treated as a whole of which the offices are parts. Finnis has a vaguer concept of distributive justice, which applies wherever there are wholes and parts of organisations. He mixes up therefore the distribution of offices in government with the more basic problem of the distribution of common goods and evils within a political community (Latin *civitas*) to the citizen members as free individuals or independent organised parts of that community.

As St. Augustine noted, there can of course be theft on a grand scale through the abuse of the institution of property carried out by governments in the name of distributive justice.

> "Justice being taken away, then, what are kingdoms but great robberies? For what are robberies themselves, but little kingdoms? The band itself is made up of men; it is ruled by the authority of a prince, it is knit together by the pact of the confederacy; the booty is divided by the law agreed on. If, by the admittance of abandoned men, this evil increases to such a degree that it holds places, fixes abodes, takes possession of cities, and subdues peoples, it assumes the more plainly the name of a kingdom, because the reality is now manifestly conferred on it, not by the removal of covetousness, but by the addition of impunity."

The origins of such gross mal-distribution of wealth may be buried in history but its effects are all too evident in our own times. Let us just quote Vatican II and two addresses of Saint John Paul II.

> "While an immense mass of people still lack the absolute necessities of life, some, even is less advanced countries, live sumptuously or squander wealth. Luxury and misery rub shoulders. While the few enjoy very great freedom of choice, the many

are deprived of almost all possibility of acting on their own initiative and responsibility, and often subsist in living and working conditions unworthy of human beings." *Gaudium et spes*– 'Joy and Hope' (1965), paragraph 63.

"Absolute poverty is a condition in which life is so limited by lack of food, malnutrition, illiteracy, high infant mortality and low life expectancy as to be beneath any rational definition of human decency. The persistence of such degrading poverty, and especially the lack of the absolutely basic minimum of food, is a scandal of the modern world, in which one finds enormous contrasts of income and standards of living between rich countries and countries that are materially poor." (JP II to FAO, 13/11/1981)

"In the analyses which have accompanied the preparatory work for your meeting, it is recalled that more than 800 million people still suffer from malnutrition and that it is often difficult to find immediate solutions for improving these tragic situations. Nevertheless, we must seek them together so that we will no longer have, side by side, the starving and the wealthy, the very poor and the very rich, those who lack the necessary means and others who lavishly waste them. Such contrasts between poverty and wealth are intolerable for humanity." (JP II to FAO, 13/11/1996)

How anyone can discuss the matter of distributive justice without referring to the concrete situation of the world as scandalous and cause for shame on the part of those who are benefiting from undeserved legal privilege is hard to credit. Finnis notes the complexity of the question: "There is no one criterion universally applicable for resolving questions of distribution". There is one and that is to take seriously our obligations in distributive justice, starting from now. Our lawyers and politicians however will need a strong sense of justice to do that. That will not be found in those "educated" in legal positivism.

Finnis moves on to treat of commutative justice. Here he does immerse himself in the concrete situation, but of the mixed up state of English law. This is highly conditioned by the liberalist philosophy behind that law. There is no concept of natural justice and the notion of equality gives way to free agreement. St. Thomas has already allowed for an extension of the concept of justice or equality based on free agreement, but there must be no inequality in the nature of the things involved. The liberalist doctrine assumes that unless there is constraint or coercion the exchange must be considered free and therefore automatically "fair". The focus is of course on exchange of goods, or the "free market", i.e. the law of contract.

Aristotle and St. Thomas have an entirely different conception than this of justice in exchange, which though freely entered into, if meant as an exchange and not a gift, has to be governed by real objective equality, "of thing to thing". How this is achieved is discussed in terms of common need measured by common estimation – something explained in detail in my book "Economic Science and Saint Thomas Aquinas". Because the measures are practical there is room for some approximation in the assessment of the real exchange value. But the just exchange is based on equal value for equal value.

This is not understood in modern economic science, some even go to the absurd length of basing exchange on inequality of exchange value, and the modern law of trade suffers accordingly. According to English common law until more recent times so long as there was some "consideration" given by one of the parties to the exchange (it might be in theory a peppercorn for a mansion) the contract would be held as legally binding. If there was no deceit or coercion on the part of the person offering the manifestly unequal value, such a contract (despite deficiency of knowledge or duress from other sources on the part of the other) would be enforced. Roman law assumed that there was something wrong if the discrepancy was more than half the real value.

Why do you think there was this gross discrepancy between actual systems of law? Because Roman law had retained some sense of natural justice and English law virtually none. St. Thomas pointed out that the exchange is unjust unless there is some real equality (if it had not to be mathematically exact or, as he put it, *non punctualiter*). This is clearly set out in his reply to article 1 of Question 77 of the *Summa Theologiae*. He explained the failure of systems of law to ensure such equality to the weakness of human law to make subjects adhere to justice in all cases, as is clearly set out in the answer to the first objection that follows his answer to the question; "Whether it is lawful to sell a thing for more than it is worth?"

> "I answer that, It is altogether sinful to have recourse to deceit in order to sell a thing for more than its just price, because this is to deceive one's neighbor so as to injure him. Hence Tully says (De Offic. iii, 15): "Contracts should be entirely free from double-dealing: the seller must not impose upon the bidder, nor the buyer upon one that bids against him."
>
> "*But, apart from fraud*, we may speak of buying and selling in two ways. First, as considered in themselves, and from this point of view, buying and selling seem to be established for the common advantage of both parties, one of whom requires that which belongs to the other, and vice versa, as the Philosopher states (Polit. i, 3). Now whatever is established for the common advantage, should not be

more of a burden to one party than to another, and consequently all contracts between them should observe equality of thing and thing. Again, the quality of a thing that comes into human use is measured by the price given for it, for which purpose money was invented, as stated in Ethic. v, 5. Therefore if either the price exceed the quantity of the thing's worth, or, conversely, the thing exceed the price, there is no longer the equality of justice: and consequently, to sell a thing for more than its worth, or to buy it for less than its worth, is in itself unjust and unlawful."

"Secondly we may speak of buying and selling, considered as accidentally tending to the advantage of one party, and to the disadvantage of the other: for instance, when a man has great need of a certain thing, while an other man will suffer if he be without it. On such a case the just price will depend not only on the thing sold, but on the loss which the sale brings on the seller. And thus it will be lawful to sell a thing for more than it is worth in itself, though the price paid be not more than it is worth to the owner. Yet if the one man derive a great advantage by becoming possessed of the other man's property, and the seller be not at a loss through being without that thing, the latter ought not to raise the price, because the advantage accruing to the buyer, is not due to the seller, but to a circumstance affecting the buyer. Now no man should sell what is not his, though he may charge for the loss he suffers."

"Reply to Objection 1. As stated above (I-II:96:2) human law is given to the people among whom there are many lacking virtue, and it is not given to the virtuous alone. Hence human law was unable to forbid all that is contrary to virtue; and it suffices for it to prohibit whatever is destructive of human intercourse, while it treats other matters as though they were lawful, not by approving of them, but by not punishing them. Accordingly, if without employing deceit the seller disposes of his goods for more than their worth, or the buyer obtain them for less than their worth, the law looks upon this as licit, and provides no punishment for so doing, unless the excess be too great, because then even human law demands restitution to be made, for instance if a man be deceived [Lat. *deceptus* = lit. taken down] in regard to more than half the amount of the just price of a thing [Cod. IV, xliv, De Rescind. Vend. 2,8"

The English lawyers and legal philosophers simply do not understand this, let alone agree with it, for they are deeply indoctrinated in Positivism. There is however another aspect of Aristotle's and St. Thomas's understanding of commutative justice where exchange of goods is concerned that not only positivist philosophers have failed to understand but the whole tradition of modern Catholic and even Thomist moral philosophers and theologians have for some strange reason been blind to. That is the absolutely critical distinction between what Aristotle called natural and unnatural exchange, which St. Thomas preferred to call natural and artificial exchange with the second tending to become unnatural exchange.

Without this distinction one cannot make sense of the commercial and financial world in modern times. For it lies at the heart of the crises and commotions that plague modern economic life, no more evident than in these times of the "Global Financial Crisis". Without this distinction one cannot understand the role of money in exchange and the reason for the modern rejection of usury as an unnatural "exchange" in the lending of money. Indeed, without this distinction one cannot really understand Capitalism and the Marxian critique of it.

As this is fully dealt with in the chapter on "Commutative Justice and Unnatural Exchange" in our book "Economic Science and Saint Thomas Aquinas" we will not go into it here. Finnis, of course, makes no mention of this fundamental distinction of Aristotle in his treatment of commutative justice.

Finnis examines some of the intricacies of modern law related to the "dealings" of individuals. These are affected not only by moral deficiencies adverted to by St. Thomas but by all sorts of mental gymnastics required in trying to give some sort of consistency to the law overall. One needs to have qualified as a lawyer to hold together even part of this netted meshwork. The category of distributive justice is enmeshed with commutative justice in all sorts of ways, as in the modern law of negligence. "Tort" (French word for "wrong") is an English legal term adapted to resolve problems of culpability that are less than fully deliberate and malicious, as in modern motor car accidents. Initially, the law attempted to deal with them like involuntary* commutative justice (assault), as negligent rather than malicious, but the fact of there being in many cases accidental inadvertence rather than deliberate intention has shifted the law in this regard (via the contract of insurance) to a quasi-distributive kind, for it is part of distributive justice to distribute common evils as well as common goods. *(involuntary only on the part of the injured party.)

It is significant that these developments in the law have come out of a philosophy of individualistic liberalism, that treats all as equally free and so should be left to fend for themselves. Only gradually, as the enormous disparity in bargaining power has driven the poor to desperation, has the legal system bent to restore some sort of balance. Unfortunately, as usually happens, things are taken from one extreme error (Liberalist Capitalism) to the other extreme (Socialism or Statism). The politico-social scene then becomes a battleground in which the contending parties can only see the dangers of the other extreme, and they marshal their forces into parties such as Liberal and Labor in Australia and Republican and Democratic in the USA.

Conservatism is a deceptive political category, for it usually refers, as Chesterton noted, to conserving the interests of those who have profited from the kind of confederacy referred to by St. Augustine, that is to say to preserving the structural injustices that persist. In recent times this has been subtly equated with conserving the "values" of Western civilization itself, when it can be a cloak for preserving liberalism in politics and capitalism in economics. Unfortunately, Socialism and/or Communism are posed (by all parties) as the only alternative.

However, though very pertinent to the discussion of justice and its relation to law, these broader considerations need to be left to another time. None of the modern legal and moral philosophies pays respect to natural justice. They are all imbued with positivism and relativism. Finnis has tried to construct a theory of Law in which justice is not an essential and indispensible component. That is like trying to conceive of a human being without a heart, or as C. S. Lewis puts it to picture men without chests.

Besides his treatment of justice, however, Finnis deals with the related topics of right and obligation. We should comment shortly on his treatments of each of these before coming to law itself.

Chapter 8

Natural Right

Just as Aristotle divided law into natural and positive, and we may divide also justice into natural and positive, so right is divisible into natural and positive. Aristotle put the difference in that what is natural is from nature and what is positive is from will. St. Thomas distinguished the two kinds of justice in a similar way: the first is from nature and the second is from agreement. So too natural right is from nature and positive right is based upon agreement of wills.

Though a positive right may be from will it nonetheless is "in thing", in so far as it is now outside the will, but not as some natural relation, as the right to one's arm, but as an artificial order is in things, even though it is produced by a human being. It is not some mental unreal object of our understanding, if it is hard to visualise or even imagine. It is something intelligible made by human choice, but the result is something objective that now binds the will(s) concerned, as well as being measured by the reason that knows it (in the case of a natural right it is the human reason that is ultimately measured by the thing – the measure of the thing is the author of nature, God, according to his reason and will, the eternal law).

The primary division of law, justice and right into natural and positive can however be further divided so that we arrive at a fourfold division. (1) There is natural law most strictly taken. (2) Then there is the law of nations, which, as St. Thomas explains, is derived by reason (necessary conclusion) from natural first practical principles or laws. This makes for a division of natural law broadly taken into two.

(3) There is positive law strictly taken which is derived from the natural law not by way of necessary conclusions but by way of "determination", rather like the plan of an architect has to be adapted to the concrete conditions of an actual building. These laws come from the will of a particular political community expressed through its principal organ, the government. These laws constitute the general "laws of the land". It is to be noted however that law so taken remains general, for law strictly taken is "of the universal".

However, not so much applied to law, but to justice and right, which the law of the land will recognise, (4) there are positive rights arising from agreements arrived at by the members of the community. The pure cases of this are seen in gifts bestowed by one party upon another, immediately or by promise, meant to confer upon the recipient real rights in the things (or actions) concerned.

When St. Thomas comes to distinguish human law he applies the concept to (2) and (3), the former of which is included in natural law, and the latter in positive law:

"I answer that, As Augustine says (De Lib. Arb. i, 5) 'that which is not just seems to be no law at all': wherefore the force of a law depends on the extent of its justice. Now in human affairs a thing is said to be just, from being right, according to the rule of reason. But the first rule of reason is the law of nature, as is clear from what has been stated above (I-II:91:2 ad 2). Consequently every human law has just so much of the nature of law, as it is derived from the law of nature. But if in any point it deflects from the law of nature, it is no longer a law but a perversion of law." [By "law of nature" here St. Thomas means natural law]

"But it must be noted that something may be derived from the natural law in two ways: first, as a conclusion from premises, secondly, by way of determination of certain generalities. The first way is like to that by which, in sciences, demonstrated conclusions are drawn from the principles: while the second mode is likened to that whereby, in the arts, general forms are particularized as to details: thus the craftsman needs to determine the general form of a house to some particular shape. Some things are therefore derived from the general principles of the natural law, by way of conclusions; e.g. that "one must not kill' may be derived as a conclusion from the principle that "one should do harm to no man": while some are derived therefrom by way of determination; e.g. the law of nature has it that the evil-doer should be punished; but that he be punished in this or that way, is a determination of the law of nature."

Accordingly both modes of derivation are found in the human law. But those things which are derived in the first way, are contained in human law not as emanating therefrom exclusively, but have some force from the natural law also. But those things which are derived in the second way, have no other force than that of human law." (I-II, 95, 2 c)

In his reply to the second objection of this article St. Thomas clarifies the proposition that human law is the rule and measure of human conduct. What is from nature has to be extended to (2) so it is only of positive law that human law is the primary rule and measure.

"Reply to Objection 2. Human reason is not, of itself, the rule of things: but the principles impressed on it by nature, are general rules and measures of all things relating to human conduct, whereof the natural reason is the rule and measure, although it is not the measure of things that are from nature." (I-II, 91, 3 ad 2) "*Ad secundum dicendum quod ratio humana secundum se non est regula rerum, sed prin-*

cipia ei naturaliter indita, sunt quaedam regulae generales et mensurae omnium eorum quae sunt per hominem agenda, quorum ratio naturalis est regula et mensura, licet non sit mensura eorum quae sunt a natura."

Finnis simply equates human rights and natural rights. "I use the terms synonymously" (p. 198) Unfortunately this is what has happened generally in modern treatments of rights. It may be seen how this introduces confusion into the discussion of the difference between natural law and human law, natural justice and human justice and natural rights and human rights. It lends support to a positivist interpretation of law, justice and right, as if all rights are derived from human law as purely positive.

There is a refinement that may be added to the basing of positive law upon will alone. Human will does come into it but not to the exclusion of reason. But this is not only of reason concerned with abstract and universal laws and principles (i.e. immediate first principles) but rather of reason concerned with concrete and particular conditions which require determinations. It is reason acting like in art but it is as St. Augustine put it to do with "the art of living well and rightly". That is to say it is practical reason at the point of contact with the concrete and contingent; this is of the nature of prudence with which will as choice has to be coordinated. The third division of law then is not only a matter of political choice but also a matter of political prudence. However, it is not prudence taken to the ultimate particular, for it has to remain general, applying not just to this or that individual member of the civil community concerned but rather to all the members equally. This is evidently what Finnis is trying to bring out with his notion of "practical reasonableness". That is of the essence of the "determination" of natural law that is positive law (law No. 3).

Where the determination is totally indifferent from the point of view of reason, then will as pure choice does come into play, as in the example of determining the law of the road to be to keep to the left or right. But we need to be careful not to oppose nature and reason too simply to will and choice. There is interplay in different ways between nature, reason, will and choice in the two kinds of human law (2) and (3).

To take two important examples of laws in the former category (*ius gentium*), the natural institutions of marriage and property, the first is brought into existence by the free consents of the parties involved and the second is brought into existence through the free decision of government. But the nature of the relationships, the one between man and woman, the other between man and natural resources and materials is not merely a matter of will or choice, either of the parties concerned or of the government.

In the case of the institution of marriage the nature of the relationship is fixed by reason and nature in so far as the special requirements of human sexual union are a rational conclusion from the natural union of male and female at the bodily level in all animals (of which man is one species), which is plainly ordered to reproduction. In the case of the institution of property the distribution effected by the community through its government has to be according to that natural equality attaching to distributive justice, from which flow property rights in the members themselves to whom as St. Thomas points out the particular distribution is due naturally.

As all are aware today, most being unaware of the depravity and deceit involved, in both cases will has supplanted reason and nature. In the one case human beings have reduced themselves to the level of brute animals (or worse) and in the other subjected themselves to the arbitrary will of the State (or those who use the State to promote their own interests).

There is another natural institution (in the sense of pertaining to the *ius gentium*) that exemplifies this partially positive and partially natural character of human laws. That is the natural exchange system or market. St. Thomas refers to it as "just sales and purchases". This social institution he clearly places within the law of nations that practically all nations incorporate into their social orders. Here the parties to the exchange freely bring any exchange into existence but the nature of the exchange is governed by natural equality in commutative justice, which involves natural rights.

How this comes about has been discussed *longe et profunde* in other places by the writer. Yet not only modern economists but also moral philosophers and theologians, including Finnis, pay little attention to it. No attention is paid to the disorder of unnatural exchange that dominates modern economic life. Positivism or voluntarism reigns supreme not only in modern studies of law, ethics and politics but also in economics.

Though he asserts that his main aim here is to analyse natural or human rights, Finnis says: "The language and grammar of rights is derived from the language of lawyers and jurists, and is strongly influenced by its origins". (p.198) That language and grammar is plainly the language and grammar that is designed to express the concepts and principles of positive law, not those of natural law. He further says: "For the logic that we can uncover in legal uses of the term 'a right' and its cognates will be found largely applicable for an understanding of 'moral' rights-talk."(p. 198) "Moral' he equates with human and natural rights.

Though there is some value in considering positive rights first when they are consistent with the natural law, the actual situation of human law in the modern world is very much in contradiction of natural law. Hence, to begin in that way is to operate like a medical student having only pathological specimens to examine in the study of physiology (which as the name indicates is the natural way in which the human body functions). The "logic" that Finnis advocates is fundamentally flawed and can only end with a positivist vision of law.

In fact, Finnis goes on to use a "classic" work in positive law on the analysis of rights, that of the American Wesley Newcomb Hohfeld, who propounded his theory in 1913; he expanded the notion of right to include also privilege, power and immunity, thereby purporting to clarify the notion. There are some interesting observations in it but it is clearly based on a mistaken notion of right itself, which it reduces to a claim of right. But a claim is only a mere assertion of a right, it does not amount to a right, whether natural or positive, which has to be justified by reference to natural or positive law. There are plenty of "rights" argued for today that are no more than such claims that are asserted as "human rights". Much social pressure is then put on governments to "justify" them.

Hohfeld, then, has reduced the basic notion of right to a pure expression of will by some. Just how skewed his analysis was is seen by looking at his concept of privilege. It amounts to saying that to live in one's own home is a privilege.

Finnis spends the whole section examining Hohfeld's "analysis of rights" and commenting upon more recent disputes over the nature of rights, for example, whether right is individual benefit or individual choice. At the end of the section Finnis puts his own theory of rights in a kind of hohfeldian form. He sums up:

> " … we may safely speak of rights wherever a basis principle or requirement of practical reasonableness, or a rule derived therefrom, gives to A, and to each and every other member of a class to which A belongs, the benefit of (i) a positive or negative requirement (obligation) imposed upon B (including, inter alia, any requirement not to interfere with A's activity or with A's enjoyment of some other form of good), or (ii) the ability to bring it about that B is subject to such a requirement, or (iii) the immunity from being subjected by B to any such requirement."

It does illustrate Finnis's verbosity. As to its meaning make of that what you can. None of this is of much interest except to legal positivists. In the next section, however, Finnis does develop the notion of right in a way that is of historical and current interest to students of natural law. He does this under the sub-heading of a question: "Are duties prior to rights?"

In order to follow this, however, we need to refer to a distinction made by St. Thomas between a thing and its use. For when we have a right to certain things, whether naturally belonging to us, such as an arm, or consequent on some human production, such as a car, in many cases we can distinguish the thing from its use. Its use then naturally follows possession of the thing, so the right to the thing bestows on us the right to its use. We can then deal with each separately, as when instead of selling our car we hire out its use.

Now the right to use is often referred to as a freedom, for it pertains to the use of our free will where human conduct is concerned. We may even use the circumlocution "the right to freedom of" some kind of action. Thus, naturally speaking, we have a right to our tongue, and it would be a violation of that right to cut out our tongue unjustly (a surgeon may do it save our life). But, the tongue is the natural means to speaking our mind; and so we have a consequent right to speak the truth, i .e. to use our tongue (the same applies to other artificial means of communication of our thoughts, such as writing) to communicate in moral ways. Where society is involved then there are limits on such use from the needs of the common good. From these consequent rights of use we get the expressions, "freedom of speech" and "freedom of the press".

We should mention here the definition of freedom (attributed to St. Anselm): "power elective of means the due order to end being maintained". Typically, the modern liberalist misrepresents freedom, leaving out the second half of the definition. But we may notice that the relevant freedom is attached to the will, which is a power. This is where the notion that right may refer to power comes from. It is the power of the possessors of some thing to use it freely. But this is not disconnected from due order to natural ends and ultimately our ultimate natural end. So freedom is only verified if it is in accord with reason and morality, which fundamentally are in accord with nature and the divine reason and will (the eternal law). The modern liberalist philosophy would have the human will replace the divine.

However, we thus have to add to our notion of right to some thing the consequent right to its use. This may not be clear to one reading St. Thomas's simple analysis of *ius* as something to do with things. The point being made by St. Thomas is that right is something objective, outside the reason and will of human beings. The same applies to the use that follows possession of the "thing".

Finnis makes an historical examination of the notion of *ius* beginning in Roman Law. It looks very learned. He refers to St. Thomas's focus on *ius* as in things, in which indeed Finnis includes acts (implicitly uses). But, diverting the readers from any other secondary meanings, such as might be seen as freedoms, he refers to St. Thomas speaking of other analogous meanings as to courts of law as courts of justice even when they are not administering justice. This kind of nominal analogy we have already noticed. The right to use is a right by real analogy.

All in all it looks as if St. Thomas and his followers have not adverted to the notion of right as freedom. Finnis then proceeds: "If we now jump forward about 340 years to the treatise on law by the Spanish Jesuit Franscisco Suarez, written c. 1610, we find another analysis of the meaning of ius. Here the 'true, strict and proper meaning of *ius* is said to be 'a kind of moral power (*facultas*) which every man has, either over his own property or with respect to that which is due to him'".

If Finnis knew well his history of scholastic moral philosophy and theology he would have appreciated that Suarez was not a faithful interpreter of St. Thomas but rather tried to reconcile three scholastic streams of thought, that of St. Thomas, Scotus and Occam. Scotus was a partial voluntarist whilst Occam was a pure voluntarist, indeed more fundamentally the source of modern nominalism. Now what is Voluntarism in human psychology is Relativism in human morality, Positivism in law, Liberalism in political theory and Scepticism in general philosophy, or modern "Metaphysics". These are all the hallmarks of modern thought.

An elementary knowledge of the rise of modern thought would have made Finnis aware of the influence of Suarez, a Jesuit, upon the theoretical philosophy of Descartes. But we are more interested here on his influence upon practical philosophy, ethics and law. Unfortunately, the modern thinkers in reading Suarez's voluminous works thought they were representative of Scholasticism and even of Thomism. But just as Suarez distorted the Metaphysics of St. Thomas that came through Descartes so did he distort the Ethics that came through Hobbes.

Finnis notes the significant change with a quote from Hobbes: "*Ius* and *lex*, right and law ought to be distinguished because RIGHT, consisteth in liberty to do or to forbear, whereas *lex* determineth and bindeth to one of them, so that law and right differ as much as obligation and liberty which in one and the same matter are inconsistent." (p. 208) Here we have right opposed to law [and justice]. Why; because right as freedom is made absolved from the end, i.e. made absolute – the very soul of modern Liberalism.

Finnis further notes that the other pioneers of modern thought with regard to morality and law, such as Locke and Pufendorf, did not go all the way with Hobbes; "yet they did adopt the stipulation that 'a right (*ius*) is paradigmatically a liberty." (p. 208) That is to say they adopted the "watershed" event in the history of law that introduced the change in meaning of right wrought by Suarez.

There would not be any great significance in this change if it simply brought out what was implicit in St. Thomas, that right as it referred to use of what one possessed by right is also a right, to which is attached the notion of freedom. But the substitution of this notion for the more basic notion occurred with the rise of Liberalism, with a notion of liberty that was divorced from natural ends and goods, and, as logically deduced by Hobbes, divorced from law and moral obligation.

Finnis does not seem to be aware of this. So he says: "There should be no question of wanting to put the clock back". (p. 209) In the end, however, he tries to have it both ways. The modern development is a good development but we should keep the notion of duty tied to rights. It seems that the chariot of rights can still be driven forward even if one steed is loose from the reins.

Finnis moves then in this chapter on rights to consideration of certain apparently limiting factors such as the common good. But, we can move directly to his chapter on obligation, as this is the essential limiting principle in regard to the question of rights.

Chapter 9

Natural Obligation

The notion of obligation is at the heart of the understanding of law and morals. It is inherent in the notion of law. What would be the point of making a law if no one was obliged to obey it? It is inherent in the notion of justice. For to render to another what is his due means that one is in some way bound to do that, and obligation comes from the Latin *ligatum* which means bound.

This comes out more clearly in the other way of putting it as to render to others what is their own. "Own" is but another way of saying "owed", and "ought" is but an old English word for "owed". "Property" is but the same notion applied to human productions. Justice is concerned with our relations with others and the notion or right is but the word for what is owed to another. One's due and right are the same word in Latin (*ius*). Right is simply taken from a geometrical analogy, as many of our moral notions in justice, like equality itself, are taken from mathematical notions.

A natural obligation is reality based. Because our understanding of justice is mediated through reason, we can get the impression, as Finnis does, that our reason is the measure and source of moral and legal obligation. St. Thomas even says so. But he is careful to make the point that human reason is not the radical source and measure of natural or first principles, and accordingly of what follows necessarily from them (law 1 & 2 referred to above).

In this regard human reason is a measured measure. The way things (and their uses) are, that is the measuring measure, and even these are measured measures in relation to the divine reason. "Things stand between two intellects". It is only positive law, which also involves human will(s) that is the measure of "artificial" (moral and legal) things that are positive rights.

Finnis seems to want to treat all morality and legality as dependent upon human reason in the same way as positive law. He does not relate natural law directly to things (of nature), and is hesitant about bringing the divine reason and will (eternal law) into the picture. Even though (in Chapter XIII) he gives a serviceable argument for the existence of God, if couched in the obfuscating language of modern analytical philosophy ("states of affairs" etc.), in the end he desists from describing it as apodictic. He has not appreciated the short and clear proof given by St. Thomas in *De ente et essentia* (para. 80) The pull of modern thinking in this regard seems to have made him hesitate in following through the good natural bent of his mind.

Finnis, as is his wont, begins his treatment on obligation with the positive kind; indeed, he begins with the extreme of this kind that is based purely on agreement of wills, the promise of one will made to another. In positive law they are known, as he notes, as promissory obligations. As we have seen this purely voluntary action when put out of one's own mind and into circulation as it were, like a gift conferring rights, does bring into existence justice based in the social order between the two or more persons concerned. It is a real order, not natural but like the order produced by an artist. The subject(s) are natural bodies (human persons) and therefore able to be sensed but the moral order itself is intelligible, only detectible by an intellect.

Thus, an obligation is established by this voluntary act, as in the case of a gift. Moreover, involving at least two people within a social context, the promise made has a social character that makes it amenable to positive law and a matter of justice. However, the moral obligation established is not always backed up by positive law. To make it legally binding positive law often requires certain formalities such as it being under seal. In other cases there will need to be some "consideration", if it be only that the promisee has acted on it to his detriment.

In a way the promisor is freely binding himself by this sort of act. It is a nice case of the relation between freedom and obligation, which to modern minds indicates some sort of contradiction (as Hobbes felt). But this comes from a too materialist concept of being bound. A will that acts in accordance with its spiritual nature is perfectly free. A vow indeed, as Chesterton observed, is an exercise of the most perfect freedom. We have expressions as well like: "My word is my bond".

God spoke and the world was made. In creation God has as it were bound himself to respect the natures of the things created. St. Thomas says that governments should imitate the divine, which governs all things in accordance with their natures. Such natures (as our own) are divine gifts, and their natural inclinations are like divine promises, and there is none so trustworthy as God who will be bound by his word.

We will find that the obligations following from the Natural Moral Law do not contradict human freedom. They lie at its root. Who would wish to be free of one's nature, or of one's natural powers of reason and will? So it is that natural obligations are signs of human freedom no less than positive obligations constituted by human will itself. However, the latter will be so only if human reason and will are in accord (of the same heart) as natural law and the eternal law.

Finnis therefore does not go wrong in beginning with positive obligations of the purest kind. But he is faced with the same problem as before with rights. The positive obligations created by human free will have to be within the natural province of such freedom, "the due order to end being maintained". They are obligatory only if they are consonant with natural obligations, which are the basic moral obligations. Under present legal and political conditions of human law, human justice and human rights in the modern world there is much that is positively proposed that is very much in contradiction of natural law, natural justice and natural rights. In an atmosphere of positivism, little account is taken of such perversity and depravity.

Finnis moves from promissory obligation to the next level of obligations, which though they depend on human will or agreement for their existence depend on nature for their essence (equality). As we have seen these belong to what are called voluntary commutations, or commerce–type transactions, contracts in English law, or "sales and purchases" in St. Thomas's language (pertaining to human law in the sense of the *ius gentium*, or *ius naturale* in the second sense). These belong to human law, not to that part that has its force solely from human law but to that part that has some force from the natural law. These carry obligations that belong to natural justice (commutative justice).

Strangely enough, Finnis does not discuss natural obligation in the more basic senses. There are moral laws so close to the first principles of the Natural Law as to be commonly regarded as absolutely first principles, like those based upon the natural inclinations for life and bodily integrity, which found the moral laws against murder and bodily violence. One might say that the violent severing of one's arm by an aggressor is a rational deduction of the principle that we ought not to do harm, as St. Thomas uses murder, but its force (Lat. *vigor*) is so powerfully from nature that the person of virtue is naturally repulsed even by the thought.

Indeed, the principle "do no harm" is virtually the same as "shun evil" which is part of the very first principle of synderesis, so that the mental process from it to moral and legal prohibitions of murder and mutilation are hardly conclusions from a reasoning movement but rather insights of a purely intellectual nature under the immediate light of the very first principle. That is why such primary principles of the natural law are not proved by deduction but by *reductio ad impossibile.*

St. Thomas includes these kinds of natural obligations in involuntary commutations or "transactions", such as in our example of a vicious mutilation (severing of arm) of another. This is voluntary on the part of the wrongdoer but not voluntary on the part of the victim. In essence, it obliges the perpetrator to render to the victim what is his due, that is, the restoration of a healthy arm. That might even be possible today but in the past some alternative "compensation" needed to be found. That is very difficult to find. But it is very clear that the "transaction" is naturally unlawful, naturally unjust and a violation of one's natural right.

The killing of animals and plants below man is not strictly speaking a case of doing evil or harm, unless the actions go beyond what is necessary to obtain what is useful to human life and welfare. For the things of nature are obviously ordered to the good of humanity. Indeed there is a general natural principle that the lower is for the sake of the higher order of being, as we see animals "killing" plants for food.

Peter Singer and those pushing for "animal rights" are blind to this natural order of things.

On top of criminal-type "transactions" is the consideration of the effect of such an unjust action on the common good. Voluntary commutations (not involving deceit or fraud) may be confined to purely commutative justice, to compensating the particular members of society concerned. But involuntary "transactions" clearly go beyond that. So it is that there has to be provision in the law for the difference between civil and criminal injustice. The harm to the common good ("breaches of the peace") will require some sort of "compensation" in the form of a penalty or punishment, the most usual form being that of taking away the freedom of the criminal, by way of imprisonment. More severe punishments have been applied in the past, such as torture and even death. But these have come to be seen as uncivilised and even inhuman methods of human punishment.

We need to bring in here a more general point that is not well appreciated in regard to practical principles and conclusions. That is that laws depending on them are not a matter of knowledge and reason only but also of appetite and will. That means that the source of natural law is not to be found solely in intellectual insights and rational judgments but involves a close association with natural inclinations or desires. The fundamental laws of morality then can be translated into expressions of love which is ultimately traceable to the appetite for good understood, which is the will. In the natural order too there is the practical truth that the love of the supreme good, God, and love of neighbour, is the fulfilment of the law.

This has importance for our understanding of obligation. Understood at the proper spiritual level the moral obligations are but bonds of love. "If you love me, says the Lord, you will keep my word". God's word, i.e. his commandments, as we have noted above, is his bond. In the natural order they are to be seen as expressions of God's love, which, if we are faithful, we lovingly embrace.

However, Finnis goes on to focus rather on a peculiar problem discussed in both moral and legal circles to do with contractual obligations in law. What is the nature of the obligation in regard to contractual transactions; is it performance or compensation in the case of legal obligation; or is it performance or submission to penalty in the case of moral obligation? Oliver Wendell Holmes is the main figure in regard to the first issue; Francisco Suarez is the main figure in regard to the second.

The answers given are obviously connected with the belief that the laws concerned (in contract) depend solely upon human will, and in English-speaking legal and political terms, upon "the will of Parliament". We have already seen that this is a mistaken view of human law in regard to commutative justice. It is pure positivism in both the legal and moral contexts.

So the correct answer in each case is that the penalty or compensation in lieu of fulfilment of the obligation created is consequential to the essential natural obligation to "keep one's word". Finnis refers to Holmes's view: "'the test of legal principles' is 'the bad man's point of view'". (p. 322) That is to say, the law is supposedly indifferent to whether you keep your word in the context of a contract, but it merely enforces the contract by way of awarding compensation. That is clearly a cynical attitude but it was one explicitly espoused by Holmes, who aspired, as Finnis notes, "to wash with cynical acid [all] idealistic fancies about the law". (p. 322) Such cynicism is an occupational hazard for the legal positivist.

Finnis does not subscribe to this, but he finds he has to appeal to the remote principle of the common good to refute it. Whilst this is not wrong, the Thomist refutation relies rather more immediately on the very natural form of the commutation/contract. Just as the definition of law has four causes, so there are four ways in which an obligation may be seen, from the point of view of the end, agent, form or order and subject. In regard to contracts, the disorder may be seen immediately in one not fulfilling his or her side of the bargain. The unjust may prefer to pay "compensation" (especially if they are rich) but they are dishonourable in doing so. Where there is a criminal dimension to the injustice (as with deceit) and the law imposes only the penalty of a fine, the excessively wealthy can laugh at the law.

Finnis then goes on to examine the controversy from a moral point of view, which he notes anticipates the modern legal one. We should not be surprised that it is connected with Suarez, for his moral thought has been influenced by the voluntarism of Scotus and Occam. What if the legislator intends (specifically wills) contracts to be ruled by a "purely penal law", or makes the payment of a penalty (or monetary compensation) an alternative to performance of one's side of the bargain? Is it not the intent of the law that a party to the contract is not obliged to honour the terms of the contract, but may simply elect to pay the compensation awarded or the fine imposed?

This would be to involve the legislator in contradiction of the nature of the transaction and hence of the natural law. Positive law may provide for many conditions surrounding the coming into existence of contracts but it cannot change the nature of them. The posing of such a possibility comes from a flawed notion of law-making, thinking that the obligation arising is always from the pure will of the legislator. As we have seen such a kind of purely positive obligation does exist (as in regard to the rule of the road) but it is not applicable to the law of contract. For this is based upon the natural equality in the agreement between the parties. They can, of course, themselves make such a kind of arrangement, but the positive law's basic role is to see that the agreed terms of the contract are honoured by both parties.

There are, however, especially under modern conditions, situations where the human legislator is concerned only to manage the actions of people rather like the movements of cattle or sheep, for example in regard to the problems of transport and physical congestion in cities. Then regulations can be used rather like cattle prods to discourage the free movement and positioning of people by the imposition of fines and charges for parking and so on.

These fines may be raised so high as to work to allow only the relatively wealthy to use the public spaces – fines or charges being of little or no consequence to them; whereas they are such as to be prohibitive for the relatively poor. The moral significance is such cases lies rather in the structural injustice pertaining to the political system itself. On occasion these regulations may be perversely intended or used simply "to raise revenue", in which case there is no moral authority at all behind the measures.

In a socialist minded legal and political order all sorts of such measures may be adopted as a back-door way of redistributing wealth. But their arbitrariness defeats their purpose. There is no substitute for honestly facing the structural injustice and courageously taking the proper measures to address it. This is manifest from the fate of general taxation being so used. For the established beneficiaries of the long-standing mal-distribution in place easily find loopholes in the legislation to maintain their economic superiority.

The use of the term "penalty" itself confuses the distinction between the civil and criminal aspects of the law. The more appropriate penalty in criminal cases is imprisonment, rather then fine, especially where the fine means nothing to the offender. But, in a political constitution, which is in effect the rule of the rich (an oligarchy), the tendency is to make fines at least an alternative. For, such monetary forms of punishment have a great effect on the poor majority but little or no effect on the rich few.

However, these observations are put only to bring out the fact that the actual conditions in which the law has to operate under deep-seated socio-pathological conditions can be quite complex and the relation with morality often obscured. This is further complicated by a positivist leaning in the legal and moral philosophers (and some theologians) who consider the issues. It is clear, however, that the controversy around the idea of a law of contract being purely concerned with "paying the penalty" is an artificial one.

Finnis thinks that these modern "controversies" "force us to refine our conception of the role of the legislative will … in the imposition of legal and moral obligation". But he gives the questions an importance they do not deserve, for they occupy a large part only of the positivist tradition in both law and morals since the beginning of the modern era.

In the end Finnis says: "the lawgiver's acts of will have their significance for the practical reason of other people only because they can take their place in a normative framework *which is not of the lawgiver's making.*" (p. 335) That is to say he comes round to a natural obligation position in regard to the particular questions discussed.

But as noted above, he does this from the point of view of the common good, thereby missing the natural formality that attaches to contracts and agreements subject to the *ius gentium* as indicated. Neglecting that intrinsic formal reason leaves the matter open to a positivist position on contractual obligations. Thus, Finnis says near the end of this section of Chapter XI: "Nor does [my basic argument] entail or suggest that the legislator is confined to crystallizing obligations that are already 'there' (by virtue of 'natural law')". (336) In another part he refers to the expression "natural law" as an unhappy one. His overall position then is at best ambivalent.

In the next section of this chapter this ambivalence, at least from a Thomist point of view, is further demonstrated. For, whereas on the nature of right as freedom he saw Suarez's position as an advance on that of St. Thomas, here he comes down on the side of St. Thomas against Suarez on the question of *imperium*. But this question belongs more to the treatment of law itself to which Finnis has devoted a separate chapter. We therefore will treat it in our comments on that chapter to follow.

Chapter 10

Natural Law

Since the title of Finnis's book uses Natural Law one would think that in his chapter on Law he would highlight this notion of law. But the chapter is focused almost exclusively on what St. Thomas calls human law. Indeed, the first section, on "Law and Coercion", discusses a property of human law that arises because, as he notes, "in this world … justice may need to be secured by force …". (p. 260) Enforcement, however, is not a property of the moral or natural law as such in this world. Many offenders against the natural moral law seem to be able to get off scot-free for the most part, if there is in time the natural nemesis that follows injustice, and punishment in the next.

The need for physical force and the threat of force arises from the fact that, as St. Thomas notes generally of the human condition, "human law is framed for a number of human beings, the majority of whom are not perfect in virtue." (I-II, 96, 2 c) That is with reference to the limited power of human law to enforce all morality, but it also points to the need for force in relation to the regulation of human affairs in that most are not inclined to follow the directions of the law. This is no doubt a human condition much exacerbated by original sin.

But, the law-abiding citizen, though he still needs the direction of law, does not require the threat or exercise of force. That is why direction, or the ordinance of reason, and not coercion is stated in the essential form of law. [As we shall see directiveness as such is not quite the notion of ordinance – we can direct someone to a street address without it having the force of law] Finnis alludes to the directive mode in his discussion of the need for authority. Imagine what would happen without a ruling reason and will if half the community decided to drive on the left hand side of the road and the other half on the right.

Coercion does not appear in the definition of law given by St. Thomas, nor by Finnis in the "central case" notion of law that he puts at the very beginning of the first section: "the law and legal system of a complete community, purporting to have authority to provide comprehensive and supreme direction for human behaviour in that community …". (p. 260) [why "purporting"?]

Finnis objects nonsensically to Aristotle's "regrettable oversimplification of the relation between law and coercion", in that Aristotle put the need for coercion down to the selfish and brutish nature of many. Quite bizarrely Finnis thinks this inadequate because the need may be due to "high-minded conscientious opposition" to the law by people of conscience, such as "conscientious terrorists" – apparently to be considered not selfish and brutish. (cf. p. 260) This is a modern phenomenon, perhaps, but such conscientious objectors bent upon destruction, if acting according to their deluded conscience, are coerced (imprisoned) not for the sake of punishment, but by reason of civic self-defence (security).

Finnis paints a vivid picture of the effectiveness of the exercise of legal force and the threat of punishment in human systems of justice. This effectiveness is no doubt a major reason why legal positivists tend to see coercion as the defining characteristic of law. Unfortunately, it is in line with the view of law in tyrannical and oligarchical constitutions. The concepts of "law and order", "prison" and "police force" have an integral place in their thinking. The ethico-political thinking of Jeremy Bentham and the modern Utilitarians also comes to mind.

To reinforce the notion of coercion as essential to a legal system Finnis again brings in here the common good as the ruling principle: "sanctions are part of the enterprise of legally ordering society, an enterprise rationally required only by that complex good of individuals which we name the common good". (p. 264) But the same problem of ignoring the formal cause of law (as simply an ordinance of reason) exists here.

Finnis notes there is of course unjust punishment, but, applying his notion of analogy, it is called punishment only in a secondary or "non-focal" sense. (Finnis uses this linguistic device of his throughout the book)

Having dealt with coercion as a necessary mode of law: "law needs to be coercive" (p. 266), Finnis moves to the consideration of the directive mode of law. He introduces it by saying law needs to be coercive: "But other main features will come into view if we pursue the question: Would there be need for legal authority and regulation in a world in which there was no recalcitrance and hence no need for sanctions". Surprisingly, in view of his adoption of coercion as a main feature of law, Finnis comes down on the side of saying: "Yes".

He gives a list of features, where - in line with what he says about the need for authority - he says: "as a set … are distinctive of legal order. It will be evident from the list that the ways in which law shapes, supports and further patterns of coordination [sic] would be desirable even in a society free from recalcitrance". Indeed, he goes as far to say: "All this, then, stands as a sufficiently distinctive, self contained, intelligible, and practically significant social arrangement which would have a completely adequate rationale in a world of saints."

But, unable to abandon the positivist penchant for coercion, he ends by compromising what he has just argued for, by saying: "legal order has two broad characteristics, two characteristic modes of operation, two poles about which jurisprudence and 'definitions of law' [note the plural] tend to cluster". These are the coercive and directive modes. This is indicative of his overall effort to try to hold together two different definitions of law, one of which will accommodate the purely positivist position of modern jurisprudence in English-speaking countries.

Finnis then goes on to discuss the notion of the "Rule of Law". Without a clear and adequate definition of law that will expose its sources or causes, such a discussion goes nowhere, or rather around in circles. Where law is conceived as based purely on will, as is the positivist conception, it readily translates into the freedom of the few to oppress the many.

We need to move, therefore, to the core of this chapter, the section entitled: "A Definition of Law". This is rather a peculiar heading when one is attempting to define what is the basic subject matter of one's study. Would one propound a definition of sentence in grammar, or a definition of triangle in geometry, on the assumption there may be more than one?

We see here the influence of Finnis's notion of analogy. There may be more kinds of law than one, if we have to hold that one kind is primary, the focal sense or central case. The just, for instance, does not have one definite meaning but has one primary sense, just as in accord with natural right and another secondary sense, just as in accord with positive right. That is in fact the case with St. Thomas's definition of law.

But all the elements of the definition have to apply to both. Finnis wants to allow other secondary meanings where only some (even only one) component applies, where St. Thomas says that these alternative notions, especially one lacking "of reason" which in practical language is "of justice", are not law at all, even being species of violence, even though we may say they have an element of law. We have commented on the sort of analogy that will allow this contradictory situation to apply and have shown, we believe, that it is a logical or linguistic device rather than a real analogy. Finnis has been misled by a failure to note this distinction. Indeed, to compound his confusion, he has proposed what is a real primary analogate as univocal, so that his notion of (logical/linguistic) analogy is the only kind.

Finnis maintains that he has been using the term 'law' in this primary sense. Thus, he begins this section (x. 6): "Throughout this chapter, the term 'law' has been used with a focal meaning ...". (p. 276) It is a "multi-faceted conception of law" containing as we have seen at least two main characteristics. He insists: "Law in the focal sense of the term, is fully instantiated only when each of these component terms is fully instantiated." That is to say the primary sense of law must contain the coercive and directive modes. He continues to explain: " If one wishes to stress the empirical/historical importance, or the practical/rational desirability, of sanctions, one may say, dramatically, that an unsanctioned set of laws is 'not really law' [as a benthamite might say]. If one wishes to stress the empirical/historical importance, of the practical/rational desirability of determinate legislative and/or adjudicative institutions, one may say, dramatically, that a community without such institutions 'lacks a real legal system'". (p. 277/8)

Finnis's aim here is to point to the complex nature of the primary concept of law. This leads on to addressing the sticking point for legal positivists of St. Thomas saying that an unjust law is 'not really a law'. What Finnis says next is the most significant part of his treatment here on the nature or essence of law: "I have by now sufficiently stressed that one would be simply misunderstanding my conception of the nature and purpose of theoretical concepts if one supposed that my definition 'ruled out as non-laws' laws which failed to meet, or meet fully, one or other of the elements of the definition."

He obviously has in mind his way round what St. Augustine and St. Thomas have said about unjust laws within human legal systems. He is sensitive to the objection of his academic/legal colleague Raz that such a definition 'fails to explain correctly our ordinary concept of law which does allow for the possibility of laws of an objectionable kind' (p. 278). That, as we have noted already, only refers to the commonly used linguistic device in such expressions as someone being good at burglary, or a good counterfeiter. Finnis feels forced to allow such kinds of "analogous" meanings as "validly" applying to laws, if only in a secondary sense.

As for the notion of natural law, this is what Finnis has finally to offer: " 'Natural law' – the set of principles of practical reasonableness in ordering human life and human community – is only analogically law in relation to my present focal use of the term [law]: that is why the term [natural] has been avoided in this chapter on law ...". (p. 280) "But no synonyms are available for 'law' in our focal sense." (p. 281) The reason why no synonyms are available is that his focal sense is his own.

Finally, in this chapter Finnis considers the derivation of 'positive law' from 'natural law', with suitable inverted quotation marks applied. He outlines the well-known division of St. Thomas into laws derived by way of conclusions similar to scientific conclusions and into laws derived by way of "determinations" similar to artistic applications. As St. Thomas himself noted the former come under the notion of the law of nations (*ius gentium*) whilst the latter come under positive law (*ius positivum*) strictly taken.

Just anticipating a little (we deal with the imperative nature of law shortly) Finnis thinks that there is a difference in the manner of expression of moral law and positive law, the former as directives: "one ought not to do this", whilst the latter as simply statements: "It is an offense to do this". Where did he get the notion that to say something is an offense, i.e. that it is wrong to do, is simply a statement of fact?

After much convoluted explanation of the great deal of work needed by the positive lawmakers and judges to determine (or "define" more concretely) the principles and necessary conclusions of the moral law, Finnis concludes himself: "In sum: the derivation of law from the basic principles of practical reasoning has indeed the two principal modes identified and named by Aquinas; but these are not two streams flowing in separate channels." (p. 289) Murder, for instance, requires "countless elaborations" before it can be integrated into the criminal law. Aquinas is not suggesting otherwise.

Right at the end of this chapter Finnis comes to the defence of Natural Law or Morality as a necessary "guide" for positive law. It is equivalent to what he describes as objective reasonableness. The natural lawyers are only seeking "to determine what the requirements of practical reasonableness really are, so as to afford a rational basis for the activities of legislators, judges and citizens." (p. 290)

"Practical reasonableness" we may take as equivalent to St. Thomas's "ordinance of reason" in his definition of law. It is reason related not to further knowledge but to action. But, as reason, it is focused on means, not ends. Means that are acts are also the object of choice, which is the function of will, whose property in this regard is freedom. This is the heart of morality and as St. Thomas notes ordination and freedom are the definitive forms of the natural moral law. But there is more to the form of law than rational conclusions and determinations (choices). It is in what is presupposed to the operation of the human intellect as practical reason that Finnis's analysis tends to go astray.

Means cannot be understood divorced from ends; neither can rationality with regard to means be divorced from intellectual insight into such ends, nor free acts of choice from the will's intention of these same ends (freedom is defined as power elective of means, the due order to end being maintained).

So we have a deal of sorting out before we can simply say "act according to practical reasonableness". For practical reason so understood is but a kind of logic. We need to beware of identifying it with the formal part of logic, as Kant did. Formal logic is concerned only with reasoning, whether it is valid or not. Our reasoning needs to be supported by true premises if we are to arrive at true conclusions. Failure in this regard leads to false knowledge in theoretical matters and evil actions in practical ones (Singer's mistake is not in his "logic" but in his ethical "principles").

Finnis does not fall into Kant's formalistic error or make Singer's mistake. But, he disconnects moral (concepts and) principles from their sources outside the human mind (in nature, as St. Thomas and St. John XXIII, in *Pacem et terris*, insist). The (adequacy and) truth of such (first concepts and) principles is therefore held in mental suspense (somewhat like Kant does), and they are consequently unconvincing. He is furthermore not certain of the practical status of first moral principles, unable to distinguish them from theoretical principles, knowing in a way what practical reasonableness is, but not sure where it begins. It ends in prudence but its radical beginning is in synderesis.

This is where the question of *imperium*, dealt with by Finnis in the last section of Chapter XI (8), but which we have held over till this Chapter X, comes in. As St. Thomas explains, command (bid), which translates *imperium* in this context, is the principal part of the act of the virtue of prudence, which is the last moral act in the series of acts in the ordinance of reason to the doing (or deliberate omitting to do) of the human free act. It is where law, which is necessarily abstract to some degree comes in "contact" with the existential concrete situation of the individual person.

As noted before, St. Thomas has placed the act of command in the reason (or intellect) because it involves direction and order (to end) but he is careful to add that an act of will is presupposed. For movement to a practical end requires that the subject "appetize" the good as something desired. Practical human reason directs the human appetite (will) on the way to the end, and ultimately to the ultimate end. Both reason and will are then involved in the commands of the moral law. In the complete moral act therefore both rational direction and voluntary impelling are required. Prudence provides the former and Justice, Fortitude and Temperance provide the latter. A failure in any one of these will result in an immoral act. So one cannot be just if one is not prudent, nor prudent if one is not just.

Finnis notes well this interaction quoting St. Thomas: "the will is in the reason and is a rational appetite" (p. 338) The foundation of this is in the very definition of will as an appetite for good understood. Where the knowledge of good is concerned a psychic appetite ensues. So, absolutely speaking, the intellect is prior to the will. But, relatively speaking, all the acts of reason concerned with means presuppose the willing of the end. It is from this fundamental desire or attraction that the directions of reason obtain their motive "force".

We do not wish to get involved in the details of the arguments between the Thomists and the Suarezians with regard to whether we are finally moved to a particular action by will or reason. We simply need to be careful not to exclude either, as Suarez excludes St. Thomas's positing of the command in the reason as "unnecessary and indeed impossible, 'certainly a fiction'" (p. 339) To his credit Finnis does a good job in defending St. Thomas here. Suarez's position would reduce human behaviour to issuing immediately from a purely voluntary source, which is the very definition of arbitrariness. There is as we have seen a place for this in positive law, but it is of limited scope and secondary.

But, where Finnis goes astray is in not seeing that this element of command extends right up to the origin of the practical order of law and morality. Every law is a command to some degree. The combination of reason and will is present in the very first practical principle of synderesis, "seek good, shun evil". It is, as Kant says about moral rules, a categorical imperative. It does not say: "if you want to be happy, be good". It is an expression of the will's natural desire (inclination) for the ultimate good, happiness. It says direct all your actions to the pursuit of good; happiness is nothing other than the possession ultimately of goodness unlimited, and is not a matter of choice.

Command: "do this here and now", is a feature of prudence in the most concrete sense, and thus has the greatest force. This is to be taken in a spiritual meaning as an impetus from the reason and will upon the bodily powers and members under the control of the will. If capable the relevant parts of the body will move. The body may not respond, however, because of some physical or (sense) psychological disability but that is accidental to the state of the soul – it still is spiritually a good and moral act.

The law according to which one acts prudently is necessarily not in the concrete, where the action has to be, and so cannot move the person concerned immediately to do "this". The most proximate rule needs to be applied by the conscience, which is a concrete judgment of the morality of the act. But it has also the nature of a command one step removed from that of the command of prudence. It says: "you must do this here and now". The will, though, is still free not to. It is not till it is under the command of prudence that the will is bound to act, for it is an act that has engaged the free will.

Accordingly, as we go up the chain of command, the nature of the ordination becomes more general or universal and the "force" of the intellectual appetite appears weaker because less concentrated on a particular action. Nonetheless, the reason's ordination (law) retains the character of a command. For that is the very nature of the ordination of reason to human action. The practicality of reason reaches right to the beginning of thinking about how we should behave.

The point being made here is well explained by St. Thomas in answer to an objection with regard to the division of the theoretical sciences. The objector argues that Ethics should also be included because like medicine it has a theoretical part. The objection is: "Moreover, the science of medicine is most evidently a practical science, nonetheless it is divided into one part that is theoretical and another that is practical. For the same reason, therefore, there is a theoretical part in all other practical sciences, and so in this division [of the theoretical sciences] mention should also have been made of Ethics or Moral Science, although it is practical, on account of its theoretical part."

St. Thomas answers as follows:

> "To the fourth objection it must be said that, as Avicenna says in the beginning of his "Medicine", theory and practice are distinguished otherwise when philosophy is divided into the theoretical and

practical than when the arts [practical sciences] are so divided, as when the art of medicine is so divided. For when philosophy and other disciplines are distinguished according to theory and practice, it is necessary to take the distinction of them from end, so that the theoretical is said to be that which is order solely to the knowledge of truth, but the practical to operation ... But when medicine is divided into theory and practice, we are not concerned with a division according to end. For the whole of medicine is contained under the practical as ordered to operation. The aforesaid division [into theory and practice of medicine] is according to those things treated of in medicine that are proximate or remote from operation. For that part of medicine is called practical which teaches the manner of bringing about health as by such drugs one may be cured; [that part called] theoretical teaches the principles by which man [the doctor] is directed in regard to acting, but not proximately, as that there are three [kinds of curative] powers and the kinds of fevers are so many. Hence it is not necessary that when some part of a practical science is called theoretical that on this account it be called a theoretical science." ("On Boethius's *De trinitate*", Part 3, q. 5, art. 1, arg. 4) [translation ours]

This is precisely the mistake made by Finnis [and Grisez apparently] thinking that the highest principles of morality are "pre-moral". No; all the laws of morality, from the most general to the most specific are rational ordinations ordering human action. It is just that the most general are the most remote from operation and order our behaviour by the medium of more proximate laws (which are still removed from the concrete particular situation of the human agent) until we pass from the lowest level of legal and moral command to command concretized in the act of prudence.

Command (a combination of knowledge and appetite) is of the very essence of law, which we must remember is not a case of pure knowledge. All the work of reasoning in this practical order of things is ordered to action and suffused with the notion of "ought". In the art of medicine health is the good that we are directed to seek and ill-health the evil that we "ought" to avoid. There is no theoretical discussion about whether we ought to go for health.

This is also where Hume went wrong, thinking that in Morals we are making the mistake of arguing from "is" to "ought". He was so influenced by the theoretical science of Newton's mathematical physics that he thought of all reasoning as ordered to knowledge only. All reasoning for him then had to proceed from theoretical principles (if he thought more of the method of experimental side of Newtonian science than of the mathematical side). He had lost the notion of rational practical principles, asserting that moral science was ruled by "passion", not reason.

Though Finnis does not make this "naturalistic" mistake with regard to the understanding of the Natural Law generally, he is affected by the pre-moral/moral distinction referred to.

Law as we have seen is defined according to the four causes. Here we are concerned with the formal cause, "an ordinance of reason". It is not to be confined, as Finnis seems to do, to the level of laws most proximate to the concrete acts of prudence and free choice. It extends to the natural principles from which such practical conclusions and determinations are derived, even to the first and most universal practical principle of synderesis. They all order the way we behave. Moreover, the principles of the Natural Law are measured by the nature of reality or things, especially our own nature. That is why such laws of morality are called natural, a description that Finnis is not comfortable with. Finnis not only disconnects the primary practical principles or laws from being moral, but also disconnects them from the nature of things, and consequently from the divine measure of all human law.

Besides its formal cause law is defined also through its final and efficient causes, which are the common good and "the caretaker of the community". Finnis touches on these in his chapters on Community and Authority. So we should say something about them.

Chapter 11

Natural Common Good

The notion of common good is generally associated with the common good of civil society, Aristotle's *polis*. He listed two natural societies, the domestic or familial and the civic or political. The former, however, is seen as imperfect in that it only supplies for the immediate needs of daily life. The second is seen as perfect in that in principle at least it is able to supply for all the needs of humans in this life, that we call civilized. Ethics as personal ethics Aristotle saw as needing to be completed in political ethics, with domestic ethics somewhere in between.

However, St. Thomas draws attention to another dimension of the common good in relation to the human person, which is also natural, which though it pervades our earthly existence in some way transcends the temporal order of existence. This flows from the fact that man, though bodily and therefore belonging to the material world or physical universe, has a spiritual soul whose happiness consists in this life, as Aristotle even noted, in the contemplation so far as possible of things beyond the material, i.e. spiritual and even divine reality.

The implications of this are very profound and as we know from Revelation even this exalted concept of natural happiness is transcended again by supernatural happiness. The full nature of human happiness therefore escaped Aristotle. This elevation to the order of grace above nature complicates the discussion of moral matters but we will do our best to keep the natural order distinct from the supernatural.

The first thing to note even from the level of natural morality is that there are in fact three natural common goods, that indeed Ethics is not personal as if it were concerned with the individual human agent independent of the notion of community or society. That comes about because this third order of community is overlooked and the personal is opposed to the social. People, such as Maritain, touch on this in the use of the distinction between the person and the individual. But the notion of "society" or "community" still tends to be tied to civil society.

The third, or rather first, order of natural common good is that which pertains to the whole of creation, of which the common good is God himself. Every creature therefore is part of the most universal community of all. This has two great parts the material and the spiritual. Man belongs to both and though we tend to think first of the physical universe in fact, by reason of his spiritual soul, man belongs first and foremost to the spiritual part of the whole universe of created being.

In this view of things man is the highest being in the material order of things natural and the lowest in the spiritual. Accordingly, he would seem to have been assigned a special role of responsibility for the good of the physical universe. The highest of the angels it seems would be given a special responsibility for the good of the spiritual universe but the purely spiritual order of beings as a whole, one would think, would also have a delegated responsibility to care for man and the rest of material creation. There is a subtle significance in St. Thomas's description of the government of a community as being a "caretaker". He, or they, is the one, or ones, most interested in the good of all within the community.

Thus, though each thing and person is something (someone) unique and individual, it or he (or she) down to its very being is a part of a community. "No man is an island" as the saying goes. But neither is anything isolated is some imaginary ocean of being – a speck in infinite space. That is the vision of the crass materialist (so common today). This sense of community in nature is the truth perhaps latched onto by the modern environmentalist who, sadly, often does not wish to recognise God as the creator and caretaker of creation. In recent Theology it is perhaps the metaphysical truth that is behind the desire to make relation the very essence of persons. It is indeed a deeply natural property but only the Trinity has relation within its very divine substance.

Pope Francis has captured this love of the natural community of creatures in his important encyclical *Laudato Si.* This sense has virtually been destroyed by the exploitation of nature by or on behalf of the monied few, who, hiding behind the general innocence of the rest of humanity in this regard, have rallied their special pleaders (witting and unwitting) in the media and politics to ridicule any suggestion of human culpability for the pollution of the planet.

Saint Francis is the patron saint of this love of God's creation. But it is not generally appreciated that St. Thomas had the same deep sense of the goodness and beauty of nature. G. K. Chesterton, also with this sense, suggested that if St. Thomas were to be given an appropriate epithet it might be "Thomas of the Creator".

Even by the early part of the "Industrial Revolution", the pride of modern Capitalism, this sense of our connectedness with the rest of nature was fast disappearing. It is to be remembered that the new commercially and financially driven industrialism (the brain-child, as it were, of the scientific revolution put to use) was particularly in evidence in Scotland (as was the philosophy of the Enlightenment). The Scottish poet of nature, Robbie Burns, labelled, probably pejoratively, as a "romantic", penned this lament when he first saw the fire and smoke of the Carron Iron Works in 1787.

We cam na here to view your warks
In hopes to be mair wise

But only, lest we gang to Hell,
It may be nae surprise

He had already captured nostalgically the same sense of community behind the historical exploitation of nature in 1785 in his poem "To A Mouse":

"I'm truly sorry Man's dominion
Has broken Nature's social union
An' justifies that ill opinion
Which makes thee startle
At me, thy poor, earth born companion
An' fellow mortal!

Such exploitation of the earth and its resources for the benefit, not so much of the many poor but rather of the already excessively wealthy few, has proceeded relentlessly until now when alarm bells are starting to ring. We do not wish to enter into the environmental or ecological argument, which unfortunately is conducted along "party" lines. We only want to draw attention to the fact that humans are members not just of a family, or of a State, or even of a global human community, but also of the community of all creatures.

In this order the personal ethics of human beings relates not just to individual responsibility to God for one's conduct towards one's own individual nature but also to responsibility for one's conduct towards all other creatures below (and above) human nature. This is the primary community to which we all belong. This is personal ethics in all its amplitude. From this perspective, the family and civil societies, whilst natural are secondary. They are societies within a greater natural society. Contrary to the ancient Greek vision of the city (*polis*), even extended as in modern times to the whole of humanity, as the highest or most perfect society, it is only the community of men (and women) that serves a particular common good so far as the whole of creation is concerned.

The human person is subject to the common good of civil society only according to a part of himself. St. Thomas says that man is subject to civil society not according to his whole being. As a person his fundamental relationship is with God, not exclusive of his relationship with the community of creation of which he is part, but in co-ordination with it.

For the common good of this most universal community is God himself. He is also the caretaker, who governs all creatures immediately. This providential order is effected through the natures of things. God governs all things in accordance with their natures, St. Thomas says. But God also uses the other natural societies to achieve the ends he wills. This he does not out of any need on his part (he could achieve the same thing without them), but out of a generous will to give to creatures a share in his divine government.

This is the role of the family and civil society. They are natural communities but they are subordinate to the primary one.

That is how we should view the relationship of human persons to the communities of which they are part. As directly related to the common good of the whole creation, God, the human person is superior to the common good of the family and of the civil society to which he belongs. He is related to the universal common good according to his whole being. He is part of the family and civil society only in so far as the common goods of those communities serve his personal needs.

We need to adjust therefore Aristotle's notion of civil society as a perfect society. This is only to be taken relatively. Absolutely speaking it is not the most perfect society. That is why the individual human person's good transcends both common goods of family and civil society.

Moreover, the notion of Natural Law has to be applied beyond the limits of political rule. Also it has to be kept in mind that our usual notions of justice and right are relative to the relationships between human persons in a civil society, and to its common good. Thinking in terms of the common good of civil society as the ultimate common good results in all the problems of reconciling the relation between individual persons and civil society as a whole (the State in modern language). It will be seen that the good of persons consists primarily in a relationship with God. Accordingly the State has a natural obligation to promote the religious dimension of human life.

This is all at the level of natural reason. The notions of community and common good should not stop at civil society and its common good. Finnis, and many others, taking St. Thomas's commentaries on Aristotle's Ethics and Politics as the reference points for the study of the common good, miss (apart from indirect allusions that we will mention below) the qualifications on the notion of perfect community that Aquinas inserts in various places, and indeed to which Aristotle himself seems to have been sensitive.

The focus in current study of the common good is almost entirely on the common good of civil society, contrasted only with domestic society. "Others" for Finnis refers exclusively to other human beings. His notion of a complete community is equivalent to Aristotle's notion of civil society. Accordingly, St. Thomas's definition of law seems to fit only a civil community. Natural Law as a participation of the Eternal Law seems to apply only to our relations with other human beings. Yet such participation must extend to our awareness of the providence of God over all creation.

This is not to say that we may not focus on the more immediate common good of the humanly constituted community. It is something of great nobility in the natural order of things; "more divine" says Aristotle. But we should avoid falling into the error of regarding it as the highest community, even when extended globally to all humanity. That is the error of Humanism to which the error of Socialism is closely allied. Aristotle also comments: If man were the highest being then Politics, not Metaphysics, would be the highest science. The modern equivalent of what he refers to as politics is Sociology.

Both the family and civil society should be studied against the backdrop of the community of all creatures whose common good is God. That understood, we may proceed to examine the notion of common good as usually referring to that of the civil community or political society.

Before turning our attention to this, however, we should clarify the relation between civil society and the family, or domestic society. They are both natural associations and in a certain respect the common good of civil society is higher than that of the family in as much as the family is but a part of the whole that is civil society. That is how Aristotle saw things in his Social Ethics. But on closer examination it is seen that in another respect the family's good ranks higher than that of civil society's good.

For social organisation exists ultimately for the sake of the person, in that persons are the only substantial realities concerned and the two social orders, domestic and civil, are but accidental, if natural, relations between persons as individual substances. St. Thomas says that the person is what is most perfect in the whole of nature. Even the universal order of creation, whose common good is God himself, is in a strange way for the sake of our personal good. For the personal good of all beings of spiritual form, which is (subjective) happiness, merges with the (objective) common good of God in the possession of God.

Thus, when we come to consider the relation between the family and civil society we can see that the family is a more personal association, being closer to the good of the persons involved. More fundamentally therefore the common good of civil society is ordered to the good of the family rather than the other way round. Theologically, family is the closest analogy to the community of the divine persons in the Trinity. Pope Francis has drawn this out well in his apostolic exhortation *Amoris laetitiae.*

The modern movement to destroy the natural family is a more direct threat to the good of the person than was Communism, which is more directed to the destruction of the natural common good of civil society, in the mistaken belief of its being opposed to the freedom of the individual. Both movements are derived from the common error of Liberalism, which desires for the individual person absolute freedom from the ties of family, community and God. Even though Communism seems to be the same as Statism, its official stance on the State is that after it has done its hatchet job on Capitalism it is "to wither away" to usher in the true liberalist dream of the absolute freedom of the individual.

The natural family is now under attack within the Capitalist West more fiercely than it was under Soviet Communism. Neither ideology is a friend of the Catholic

Church, which today is practically the only institution prepared to defend the natural family. Pope Francis is seen in the West as a friend of Communism because he is such an outspoken critic of Capitalism. It is not an easy task today in Western "democracy" to negotiate the way between the rocks of Scylla (individualistic Liberalism) and the maelstrom of Charybdis (collectivist Socialism).

But the ugly face of modern liberalist Capitalism in the West is now being revealed. What Communism sought to do by violent means, liberalist Capitalism seeks to do by means of deceitful propaganda and a manipulated pseudo-democracy. In both ideologies a totalitarian-oriented government is enlisted to carry out the plans of the ideologues. The means of communication then tend to become propaganda agencies manned by those who have been duped by a compulsory education system.

The West has been committed to the free-thinking "values" conserved since the Enlightenment, of the freedom to offend (particularly the religious), to flout natural morality (particularly in regard to sexual activity) and for the people of property to use the "free market" to continue to hold the working poor in a state of servility.

The capitalist "Right", however, find that they have a battle on their hands, for the twin ideology of the Communist "Left", though discredited in recent times by the failure of the socialist "experiment" in Soviet Russia, has never been far from the surface in Western society. They are like two errant brothers fighting for exclusive control over the family estate. Those on the left deceitfully enlist the political muscle of the majority poor against the long-standing political power of the exploiting few and adopt with alacrity the "no holds barred" rules of the contest written into law by their opponents.

The "Conservatives" then find themselves on the defensive against the "Progressives", for they have no basis upon which to complain against the tactics of rank offence, gross immorality and abuse of economic power. Their plaintive cries of interference with "freedom of speech" are flung back in their faces, for are not the protestors only exercising their right to protest?

The securing of the legal legitimacy of "same sex marriage" has ominous social consequences that will quickly become evident. It makes actively "same sex", or homosexual, intercourse, as socially respectable as sexual intercourse within natural marriage. The religious institutions that regard such homosexual acts (not inclinations) as gravely immoral do not now have a legal leg to stand on. They cannot consistently accept such unions as legally constituted and exclude such "married couples" from being involved in all their organised social work, whether it be school, hospital or even purely religious functions.

They can still argue that sexual activity outside marriage, being also regarded as immoral or rather contrary to their "ethos" (cravenly avoiding the use of such "controversial" words as "ethics" and "morals"), is a reason for exclusion, but only if they apply it also to non same sex couples. It would seem that the religious institutions have already given ground on that score. Their defences are down; the progressives have got them where they want them; and they don't know where to go. The next few years in Western "civilization", starting with the immediate future, are going to be, as the Chinese curse has it, "interesting".

So much, however, for the natural common good of the family; let us move from these sombre thoughts back to our main subject, the common good of civil society. Finnis is rather vague about the notion of this common good even as dealt with by him specifically in the last section of his chapter VI. This is not surprising as he noted at the beginning of the section that the meaning of the word "social" is peculiarly vague. This would have to apply as well to the word "community", so he makes a point of including "communities" in the heading of this section.

Finnis begins by outlining what he calls "four basic ways in which human understanding stands to unifying relationships, and can show that human community involves relationships in all four orders". (p. 136) He states these orders as "of the ordered complexity of things" in connection with the basic principles of practical reasonableness. There is an acknowledged correspondence of this division to that made by St. Thomas in regard to the division of the sciences in his commentary on Aristotle's *Nichomachean Ethics* (not in the main text but in a short endnote). Finnis changes the order slightly, so that his subject comes last, but he tears the division out of its proper context.

The reader may compare what Finnis says with the text of St. Thomas:

> "Now order is related to reason in a fourfold way. There is one order that reason does not establish but only beholds, such as the order of things in nature. There is a second order that reason establishes in its own act of consideration, for example, when it arranges its concepts among themselves and the signs of concepts as well, because words express the meanings of concepts. There is a third order that reason in deliberating establishes in the operations of the will. There is a fourth order that reason in planning establishes in the external things which it causes, such as a chest and a house." (*In Ethic. I. lect. 1, n.1*)

> "The function of natural philosophy is to consider the order of things that human reason considers but does not establish – understand that with natural philosophy here we also include Metaphysics. The order that reason makes in its own act of consideration pertains to rational philosophy (logic), which properly considers the order of parts of

> verbal expression with one another and the order of principles to one another and to their conclusions. The order of voluntary actions pertains to the consideration of moral philosophy. The order that reason in planning establishes in external things arranged by human reason pertains to the mechanical arts." (*In Ethic I. lect. I, n. 2*)

Finnis is putting this fourfold division of orders of study (into the natural, logical, moral and technical) to his own use as if it were relevant to the study of "the complexity of human community". But the study of human community clearly falls into the study of "the order of voluntary actions [that] pertains to the consideration of moral philosophy". [St. Thomas's third and Finnis's fourth division] It is a practical as opposed to a theoretical study (of natural philosophy – which covers Metaphysics). Logic is classed as a theoretical study, so the only two studies of practical relevance are Ethics and Technics.

Finnis himself sees that the bringing in of the other orders is beside the point, for he says at the end: "Obviously, human community as we are concerned with it in this book's explanation of practical reasonableness is primarily a matter of community in the fourth order". (p. 138) All rather a display of learning that was unnecessary, and distracting.

Finnis makes passing mention of the modern distinction in Sociology between society and community, made classical by Ferdinand Tonnies, which brings out an important aspect of modern society (called in German *Gesellschaft*), namely its reduction of the notion of community that has many levels up to the highest cultural activities (called in German *Gemeinschaft*), to its crass economic level, understood in individualistic quasi-mechanical terms (called "rational") since the rise of modern economic science. Finnis sees "no advantage" in making use of that distinction, yet, despite its sociological context, in fact it has a moral lesson, perhaps unconscious, pointing up the reason why economics has been called "the dismal science" and its cultivation of the love of money has contributed to the corruption of business (politics and sport), not to speak of widespread depression among the young.

Allied to that is the degradation of the notion of common good to that of "the national interest" measured in terms of money and material wealth production ("GNP"). Moreover, this crassly economic concept makes it easy for the interests of the nation to be identified with those of the few rich, so that "the good of the economy" can mean no more than the furtherance of their special privileged position.

Finnis uses the word "common" in this context simply as opposed to what applies to one person. Two people, say playing a game, can be said to have a common good, just as any two can be called associates. That is the widest possible meaning of the words. No one would read Aristotle's treatment of the common good of the *polis* in such all too general sense. He is talking about the common good of an identifiable civil community, the city of Athens, for instance. Why discourse in these hopelessly general terms?

But, Finnis persists throughout the whole section in wandering all over the shop, only demonstrating the vagueness of his mind in this discussion. It is, however, rather typical of the positivist cast of mind which prides itself on its linguistic expertise. His subheadings are such as "'Business' Community'", "'Play Community'", and "Friendship", only coming close to the topic with "The Complete Community", which he has obviously taken from Aristotle's reference to civil society as the perfect society. He makes little treatment to the distinction between civil society and the other natural society, the domestic society, and then only under the subheading of "'Communism' and 'Subsidiarity'" [not sure what these half quotation marks are supposed to signify] and at the beginning of "Complete Community", as being a community that is "incomplete and inadequate". (p. 147)

He refers to the name "subsidiarity" as coming from "recent political writers" strangely (for a Catholic) only mentioning in an endnote Pope Pius XI's famous highlighting of it in *Quadragesimo anno* in 1931.The Church's strong line of social encyclicals gets only a cursory mention. Lenin gets a place in the Index at the back of the book, but not Leo XIII.

The perfect society for Aristotle was the city. This was not meant to exclude the country (and villages) surrounding it but it was the focal point (like the hearth of a home) around which a people were organised (or organised themselves). Its perfection lay rather in the notion of self-sufficiency, so that its citizens did not lack the capacity to produce and exchange all that was necessary for "the good life" at all natural human levels, agricultural, technological, economic, recreational, cultural and religious. The city is conceived of as living at all natural levels of human activity, the exchange system or market being like the circulation of the blood in an individual, supporting the higher levels of animal enjoyment (play) and even higher artistic levels (like "plays"), through to the highest levels of communication, science philosophy and religion.

The lowest, economic, level was meant to be quasi-automatic, quasi-unconscious like physical health. Civilized life existed principally at the highest most human level. For Aristotle (and Plato) the natural city was limited in physical size, territory and population. They would have regarded the size of modern cities as monstrous – akin to the modern health problem of gross obesity.

Why the tendency for modern cities especially to increase in size without limit? Just on two hundred years ago (1830) William Cobbett had an answer when he looked upon London, describing it as "the great wen", that is a swollen tumour, living on the destruction of life around it. But the answer has to be in the characteristic of a cancerous growth; that it is unlimited is a certain sign that it is unnatural. The inordinate increase in population is to be attributed not to the health and wealth of the community but to its poor health, or in economic terms, the poverty of its majority. For the poor will reproduce more in as much as an increase in people is a natural way out of poverty for a community, but the way is blocked if there is serious disorder in its constitution.

It is a well- known observation that as a people rise out of poverty their rate of reproduction decreases. The surest kind of population control then is simply to introduce and ensure a system of justice. The modern city will continue to grow as a kind of swollen thing as long as structural injustice within and without prevails. Growth of population will continue to put a strain on nations despite their persecution of the poor. And this disorder begins at the very lowest level of social life, the economic. It is significant that for the modern science of Economics unlimited growth is fancied to be the driving force of prosperity. Aristotle's idea of the city (*polis*) was a physiology; the modern idea is a pathology.

Finnis of course, like all schooled in a positivist academic atmosphere, has difficulty seeing the pathology; it is all "facts" to them, and so they cannot appreciate the natural in relation to political life. They are all unable to appreciate the concept of natural when applied to community and the common good, just as they do not understand it in relation to law.

One last but important consideration; the common good of the whole created universe from our point of view is to be put in spiritual terms, objectively it is God who is personal, and subjectively it is the knowledge (vision) of God in persons. That is common good seen as something really distinct. The common good however may be taken as a good of order; the intrinsic good of a community. The common good of the natural social orders of family and civil society, since they are secondary, is not immediately this separate thing or knowledge of it but nonetheless a spiritual good of order. It is a natural order but a moral order.

Even though it concerns material things or products at the socio-economic level, it is the order of justice in economic life that is the common good; it is not the material goods or products, though they be in abundance, that constitutes the common good; they are proper goods. Even lands and possessions of the Government are not to be thought of as part of the common good; they are public property. The greatest natural common good (of order) is peace, which cannot be had without justice (distributive and commutative) in the wills of the members of civil societies.

These common goods are spiritual "values", not material goods, not even the goods that are higher than wealth, such as "public" health and psychic equanimity ("peace of mind"). Anything material, even at the highest animal level, has to be possessed by individuals and proper to them. It is of the nature of a common good that it is not exclusive but diffusive; it is not diminished by others' possession of it; indeed, one's enjoyment of it enhances that of others. It is this intangibility that puzzles. You cannot sensibly observe it; you cannot measure it.

It is defined in Church documents as "the sum total of social conditions which allow people, either as groups or as individuals, to reach their fulfilment more fully and more easily". These social conditions in the natural order are principally justice and peace (charity is at the supernatural level). It is the States' (through their governments) duty to foster and ensure justice, something emphasised by previous Pope Benedict XVI. Preserving the Natural Law including, natural institutions like that of natural marriage and private property, belongs to the service by governments of the common good.

Finnis does not treat of the universal common good in his chapter on the common good and he seems at least initially to think of personal good as some sort of self-interest. However, in his final chapter (XIII) he does touch upon matters that belong to this order of divine providence. He discusses the argument for the existence of an uncaused cause or God (which he calls 'D' perhaps in deference to his expected readership), and he also treats of the relationship of law to the eternal law.

We have noted that his argument for the existence of God, though convoluted, has logical force, but that he draws back at the end from the conclusion: "The explanation that we have found warranted is, of course, incomplete". (p. 388) Moreover, he says in the last chapter, after discussing Plato's and Aristotle's belief in the existence of God: "This uncertainty of Plato and Aristotle corresponds to the objective inaccessibility to the argumentation and inference of rational inquiry". (p. 398)

The weakness of his appreciation of analogy comes out here. He views the Natural Law as only metaphorically related to the Eternal Law (instead of analogically): Quoting St. Thomas: 'The light of natural reason whereby we discern what is good and what is bad (which is what Natural Law concerns) is simply the impress in us of the divine light.' (I-II, 91, a. 2 c), he says: "This metaphorical language ..." (p. 402)

His discussion of Eternal Law and Natural Law's participation in it is confused by bringing back the division of the four orders. The Eternal Law, or divine providence, is only concerned with the practical order of things, not with Logic, as theoretical, nor with the technical order of human productions, as such. It is concerned with the natural order of all things, material and spiritual, which from our point of view is theoretical (as physics and metaphysics), but which from God's point of view is practical – the eternal law determining how all creatures should act. The difference is that creatures below man do not participate in the eternal law, but are moved to their ends without knowing them.

The natural law concerns our behaviour "towards" ourselves and towards others, domestically to our family, politically to our fellow citizens, but universally to all human beings and all creatures. It is a sort of delegated personal government under God in so far as we exercise some personal control of our actions. This aspect of the natural law is supplemented by the natural associations of the family and civil society in the manner described above. They have their own common goods, and their "caretakers" may be seen as exercising a (secondary) delegated role in the overall government of the universe.

But Finnis has only a tenuous notion of the most universal common good. He even questions the natural love that one has of God. He mixes up natural love here with supernatural love, of the friendship with God that is charity: "Without some revelation ... it is impossible to have sufficient assurance that the uncaused cause of all the good things of this world (including our ability to understand them) is itself a good that one could love ..." (p. 398)

His problem in seeing the practical nature of the fundamental principles of the Natural Law, which are founded equally on love of God and his creatures as on reason's reading of nature, appears again in this last chapter: "A few pages later Aquinas formulates one of the fundamental *theoretical* principles of the content of Natural Law" (p. 403) (italics added)

So far as the common good is concerned his focus is almost exclusively on the political common good. He has some sense of this being not material when at the end of his chapter on the common good he relates it to justice. But, political authority as such, which he infers at the end of the chapter is part of the common good, is not part of the common good; it is meant to serve it. It is proper to the caretaker of the community. The common good is of the nature of end, not means. Authority is not part of the final cause but of the efficient cause of law. It is the Government's proper role to care for the common good of the civil community. In this it is also its role, as Aristotle says, to lead the citizens to virtue (i.e. social virtue, which is to be just). We should then examine next what Finnis has to say in his chapter on Authority.

Chapter 12

Natural Authority

In his dealing with the notions of community and the common good we noted that Finnis brought in the division of orders into four, the natural, the logical, the practical and the technical, evidently taken from St. Thomas's commentary on Aristotle's *Nicomachean Ethics.* St. Thomas often used the term "natural" to cover the three main theoretical sciences, Physics, Mathematics and Metaphysics, specifically pointing out in this context that it included Metaphysics, so that there are three theoretical orders of human knowledge.

Finnis did not advert to this but took only from this the physical order. That is not surprising because modern thought has rejected Metaphysics and merged the other two as we have explained in other places into the modern science of physico-mathematics, now called Physics. Thus Finnis's general education would have been dominated by this equation of the study of a natural order that left Metaphysics out of account.

Logic is generally aligned with theoretical science. So the only two orders of human knowledge that are non-theoretical are the ethical and the technical. They can be included under the notion of practical orders, but practical is specially applied by St. Thomas to Ethics, which is subdivided into the personal, domestic and civic orders of human behaviour. Leaving aside Logic and Technics, we could divide the orders of study into four, three theoretical and one practical (or six if we use the subdivision of Ethics into three).

However, Finnis uses another fourfold division, which can be looked upon as made up of two theoretical, natural and logical, and two practical, ethical and technical. As we have seen he only uses this division to dismiss three, the natural, the logical and the technical, so as to concentrate upon the ethical/legal. St. Thomas did much the same with this division, for he was only concerned to identify the proper order for the study of Ethics.

Thus, Finnis did initially put aside the irrelevant attention on the theoretical study of things (reduced to the physical) and put the focus at least initially on the practical/ethical order in the study of Law. But we have already noted that he continued to insert this fourfold division into the discussion thereby confusing things and distracting readers from the proper consideration of the subject matter of his book.

We should remember that the difference between the theoretical and the practical is that the former is concerned with knowledge only as the end of the scientific endeavour, whilst the latter is concerned not with knowledge as such but with action as the end of the investigation. We saw how this means that the study is not a matter of reason alone but also a matter of moving/acting according to the desires of the will. The practical order, therefore, brings in notions not just of ordering of means to ends but also of loving the ends/goods and necessary means and of being "obliging" where the will of the true author of the law is known.

Obligation is not to be regarded (*a la* Hobbes & Co) in materialist/ mechanical terms as necessitating the (free) will of the subject of the law; for in the virtuous it is seen as a welcome direction to the natural end. It is only in things without understanding that the due (ought) signifies a physical necessity, evident in the movements of animals below man, plants and non-living bodies. The necessity signified by moral obligation is not only not opposed to freedom, it is a mark of human freedom. For the law-abiding subject freely accepts it.

Now Finnis gets off to a bad start in the discussion of authority by dealing with it as it applies in theoretical discussions, a totally irrelevant consideration of it in this practical context. This gets mixed up with the question of trusting the opinions of others, and leads to thinking that there is some kind of opposition between reason and authority. Thus he adopts the expression of his legal/academic colleague, Joseph Raz, of "exclusionary reason", that is accepting a proposition that is in some way not amenable to one's own reasoning power.

But this distorts the notion of authority even in regard to theoretical matters. We accept the authority of the scientist in regard to something beyond our particular experience, not because we cannot "otherwise see good reason for believing" what he says, or "cannot evaluate the reasons one can see", or "see some countervailing reason" (which are examples provided by Finnis). We believe the expert, precisely because we know he is experienced in the subject matter concerned. It is not a blind grasping at straws; it is a very practical/reasonable thing to do.

Such trust in authority is well founded. If the authority is known by objective evidence to be God, it is infinitely well founded. But the modern radical sceptic (the intellectual descendant of Descartes and Hume) does not even trust the evidence of his senses, treating their "authority" in much the same way as described. If he cannot believe his own eyes how can he believe anything or anyone? Such is the notion of authority that Finnis's analysis of "Authority" engenders – under the heading "The Meanings of 'Authority'". [there are those half quotation marks again]

We notice that Finnis says "meanings". But he straightaway says this notion of authority in matters theoretical is the "focal meaning". By this he means as we have seen that other meanings are secondary (in his special analogous sense). Then he enters on a discussion of "some linguistic complications" preparatory to dealing with authority in the context of practical matters (which include apparently matters of taste, practical experience and official duties).

The linguistic complication is explained as that we may use the notion of authoritative in three ways. "X has authority" may be said by someone "A", firstly so as to mean that it applies to others but also to "A"; secondly, so that it applies to others but not to "A"; thirdly, so that it applies to others, but "A" neither accepts no rejects it. Finnis labels the three kinds of meanings intended by the speaker ("A") as S1, S2 and S3.

Thus, to use an example not given by Finnis, "A" may say Einstein is an authority for a particular proposition in physics and mean some accept it, firstly, with "A" accepting also Einstein's authority; secondly, with "A" not accepting it and thirdly, with "A" suspending any acceptance or non-acceptance of it. All very interesting, but what is the point? The point, says Finnis, is that he will use this linguistic analysis in the dispute between himself, as an exponent of natural law, and positivists.

For they object: you say an authoritative rule exists (whether customary or otherwise). But such a statement only means that you ("A") regard such a rule ought to exist (S1). It is redundant then for you ("A") to say that an authoritative custom exists (S2 or S3), but that it is for the common good that it ought to exist (S1).

Finnis responds: "A" (like myself) could be meaning the statement that an authoritative rule exists simply in the senses of S2 or S3. Then, it would not be redundant to add my agreement or disagreement with it by arguing that it is for the common good. The discussion of my reasons could be subjected to the test of "practical reasonableness", as a distinct issue.

It seems a fair enough response, if he were talking theoretically. But in practical moral (legal and political) speaking you cannot separate the proposition from its ordination to human action (including your own). That is to say, an authoritative practical/moral proposition, which is what is meant here by "law", is a command, not a mere statement, as we have shown. That means the member of the community in which it applies cannot reject it or be neutral about it if it is truly authoritative; which a natural moral law is, as also is a positive law made in accordance with natural law. Finnis is making the same mistake here as he has done with treating an unjust law as a valid law. That is compounded in this case of the discussion of authority by his mixing up of theoretical and practical propositions. One can consider practical propositions (commands of the law) "theoretically", as St. Thomas says, only in the sense that they are remote principles so far as the action is concerned, but they remain obligatory first practical principles.

Theoretical propositions of a general nature, however, are either seen for oneself or are accepted on the authority of the "wise". That sort of authority it is wise to accept but Finnis evidently has in mind the modern kind of scientific laws, which are but propositions of a high level of generality (such as the Big Bang), but are for the most part hypotheses.

In this case there is no necessity on anyone, even scientists, to accede to them, not even if proposed by scientists of the greatest authority. They are regarded as only probable anyway. Finnis treats practical moral and legal propositions or laws as if they could be dissented from or treated as hypotheses. Then, he thinks he can prove their "practical reasonableness" by reference to the common good. But they already have necessary reference to the common good in being a valid/true law. The common good is already part of the definition of law!

Not only is the common good part of the definition of law, so too is the notion of authority connected with the true meaning of law. One may argue that the holder of supposed authority is a usurper. But this means he has no real authority. One cannot propose that he has authority for some and then argue he does or does not have real authority. Finnis has fallen for the use of nominal analogy where we refer to someone's purported authority as a false authority, just as we refer to a law as a bad law in the sense of intrinsically evil or unjust (a species of violence). A false friend is called a friend out of linguistic convenience but he is no real friend in any sense. The usurper or tyrant may have, as St. Thomas says, an element of law, namely, the power to subject (externally) people to his will, but something is not defined in terms of one of its elements.

In the last chapter of Part II Finnis discusses specifically the sense of "unjust law". It is clear that he is trying to agree with St. Thomas; he even says one may be obliged not to obey it. But he cannot get over the fact that we call it a LAW. The significance of this we have already commented upon. We also refer to the legal authority of tyrants, such as that of Hitler in Germany, but it is just as pointed to say that he had no authority at all, in any real sense, to do what he did to the Jewish people. Just because St. Thomas says that the express commands of a tyrant have an element of law does not mean it is to be regarded in any real sense as a valid law.

What Finnis misses is that a real law needs its four "elements" or causes, (1) ordinance of reason, (2) for the common good of a civil community, (3) by one who has the care of that community, and (4) promulgated. Even promulgation is an intrinsic part of the notion of law. Would Finnis hold that an ordinance of reason, for the common good, made by the caretaker of the community but never promulgated to those intended to be subject to the law, could nonetheless be regarded as in some sense a law? You can say it has three of the elements of law. But it fails to be a law at all. It is like a square table with three legs. Finnis is deceived by "linguistic complications". What is he trying to do; to placate his positivist colleagues who insist that we treat unjust laws as valid as law?

As well as that by treating legal and moral propositions as merely theoretical Finnis has the same problem with the traditional concept of law and morality that Hume had, thinking that it involved a passage from the theoretical ("is") to the practical ("ought"). Finnis thinks that his initial statement of the authoritative quality of a law or custom can be given practical/moral validity by bringing in the common good. But, he himself is indulging in the passage from the theoretical to the practical. That is the force of the positivist critique against him that he does not succeed in "deflecting".

Then, Finnis moves on to consider what is authoritative in moral and legal terms in that area of law that is the least authoritative, namely, international customary law and treaties between nations. That is an area of obligation that resembles the mutual agreements (express or implied) between citizens that need to be enforced by civil law. The problem here is that there is no effective world body to enforce such obligations.

The customs and treaties have moral force only, and they are regularly ignored by nations. There is true obligation of a positive kind from the implicit agreements in customary actions and the explicit agreements in treaties, but nations readily override them in the name of national sovereignty and "the national interest". And that is done even by nations who claim to have a respect for International Law!

The argument from sovereignty cannot be used to get lawfully out of international agreements: no more that in the case of "sovereign" individuals. For as seen before free persons do bind themselves and are honour bound to keep their agreements. The only way to get out of such agreements is to argue that they were made by governments without authority; that is to say by governments that had usurped power, either initially or by exceeding their authorised power subsequently.

Finnis begins his treatment of laws made through custom (which St. Thomas allows) by saying: "In this section I show how an authoritative rule can emerge … without being made by anyone with authority to make it …". (p. 238) This is as nonsensical as to say that an agreement was reached between two parties without it being made by anyone with a will to make it. He is making what is implicit of no consequence.

Finnis forgets two things here. Firstly, rulers or governments are but the living part (organ) of a civil community that makes laws on its behalf. The laws fundamentally are therefore like acts of prudence made to oneself by an individual person. The individual human being freely rules himself; so too, as Aristotle says, is a *polis* a system of self-government, which means that all the members of the community freely "make" the laws according to which they bind themselves, by consenting to the natural moral laws and by freely agreeing to the positive "legal" laws laid down.

This, of course, supposes that the citizens are not "unruly", a supposition that is not factual. Moreover, it supposes that the rulers are fully rational, a supposition also not factual. However, the fact that most people are not capable of perfect health, and medicos are not the best practitioners, does not make medicine not ordered to perfect health. It means that besides the primary end of medicine being to make people healthy it is also secondarily directed to reduce the level of sickness to as low a level as possible.

It is in this sense that Aristotle said that Politics is the art of the possible, or the expedient. He also said that it is the object of law to make citizens virtuous or just. That is not always possible; as St. Thomas says, human law has to deal with citizens who are for the most part lacking in virtue. Hence, there is the need for "compromise" in human laws, not to command or condone immorality (such as prostitution and some degree of dishonesty), but to permit it to avoid other social evils. The injustice and depravity present in a particular political society may reach such great proportions that law seems totally disconnected from morality. Legal positivist theory works best in such an "empirical" state of affairs.

This is pretty well the state of international affairs in modern times. Hence, the complete disdain in national governments for keeping to customs and treaties. They are followed as long as they are "in the national interest". This cynical attitude has been put into modern political philosophy under the name of Realpolitik. Hardly a modern politician or jurisprudent is unaffected by it, wanting to show their "hard-nosed" approach to political affairs. Even some Catholic politicians and academics fall for such "political realism".

The other thing is that custom to a community is what habitual behaviour is to an individual: it signifies an implicit willingness to do something or to agree with an arrangement involving itself and other civil communities (*poleis*). In principle, custom, whether national or international, originates in a consensus of wills, not explicitly engaged but able to be inferred from a course of behaviour. Just how general that custom becomes is a matter of degree. No custom arises as Finnis, not able to get over the vicissitudes with which such customs have to contend, asserts, "without being made by anyone with authority to make it".

The question of authority in regard to practical moral and legal matters (natural law and positive law) can be best considered by comparison with the other non-theoretical order, the technical or artistic. In artistic works the notion of authority is clearly linked with authorship. It signifies the person who has made or "created" the work. So too in the work of legislation we will attribute authority in this primary sense to the one (or few or many in agreement) who has made the political order or constitution.

The important difference between a technical order and a political order is that the technical product is usually thought of as made once and for all, being supported in existence by solid materials. But we could come closer to our practical situation if we compared the political order, which has to exist in a changing population, to a musical performance. There are two aspects there to the "authorship" of the work. There is first of all the composer (who may be dead) and the conductor (who needs to be alive); we can say that the conductor is the authority in regard to the present performance but he only brings into play the composer's "authority".

Primarily, then, authority comes from the originator of the work; so too does political and legal authority come from the persons or persons (in agreement of wills) responsible for the particular society's beginning. This may be lost in the mists of time, and it may be a case of various offshoots from an original community; but essentially someone has had to bring the political or civic order into existence, even if embryonic at the start. That is why particular civil communities are called "Fatherland" or "Motherland".

Over time of course various legends may arise, as the Greeks loved to attribute the origin of their cities to their gods. However, there is a peculiar characteristic of the "materials" in which such a social/political constitution arises. It has to be made, though it may be more appropriate to describe it as growing out of lesser organisations, such as villages and tribes. But it takes a conscious legislator or legislators to found "a republic" (Latin *res publica* for "public thing").

What is most characteristic, however, is that the order brought about is in human wills, which can only be individual. There is no universal will as Rousseau imagined. It is a real spiritual order of relationship between persons, formed according to the free directing will of the author. But the order (of justice) has also to be in the free wills of the persons ordered. So in a sense the community forms itself, with the assistance of the directing will of its author. The father of the state is not to be equated with the father (and mother) of a family, for they naturally generate the progeny. The comparison is analogous but no more than that.

In the case of human persons (and created persons generally) the legislator does not force the elements he has to work with, nor can he do so directly, for subject persons too have wills of their own, and they are created free. Indeed, in the crunch a created person can reject the authority of his author/creator and choose himself as the author of the (dis)order of his operations. That is at the root of the problem of authority in all legal matters, including those of the natural law. Anyone can adopt the attitude of Lucifer, and say *non serviam* ("I will not obey"). Modern liberalism has raised that to the level of a political slogan, though it puts it positively as "I will be (absolutely) free".

The work produced has to be freely acquiesced in by all (adult) members of the civil community right from the start. This applies to the continuance of the same community. Obviously over time not only the author dies but also the first members of the (fledgling) community. What happens then? That is where the notion of a conductor comes in. The work of the original author/composer can continue by a succession of conductors and descendants of the original members. That gives the particular community its ethnic character.

However, it is important to appreciate that this is not the most formal aspect of a civil society. That lies in the freedom of the wills of the members so that they remain in agreement with the leading idea of the original constitution. Accordingly, nothing prevents the ethnic character of the community changing over time. Naturally, of course, this has to be done sensitively, and gradually. Otherwise, as Aristotle noted, tensions will arise owing to the animal or tribal side of human nature. Australian multi-culturists take note.

Finnis attempts to deal with the notion of authority residing in one person (or few or more in agreement). But, like most, he tries to treat of this in terms of a conductor in mid performance. The question of authority is thus greatly diluted. No one knows where the political authority comes from. Indeed, translating the metaphor to the political order, the performance is disrupted by unwilling performers. Moreover, the conductor having no notion of the original ratio of the society's constitution, like a jazz player, has to *ad lib* throughout. Government under such conditions is hardly more than a cacophony.

Some wit has penned a name for the modern system of government, "Cacocracy": a system he says where the scum rises to the top. But, we must not be pessimistic. Despite the overwhelming presence of corruption, we (especially Christians) know that good will prevail, not just in the end, but even in the midst of (structural) sin.

Civil authority, or government, is a natural institution. Like marriage and the family, it comes not from the very first principles of the natural law but from the *ius gentium*, those rational conclusions that are derived necessarily from such first principles, which in this case may be seen as the (common) good that comes from human association.

As St. Robert Bellarmine said, the natural law tells us that government is a necessary institution but it does not tell us in whom such authority should in the present be placed (as conductor). It belongs rather to the community as a whole (in accordance with whose agreement such authority has to be exercised) to "determine" not just the mode of government (one, few or many) but also the person or persons in whom authority is to be entrusted. Political government and authority so understood, however, there must be for the sake of a good "performance".

Note that in this regard the quality in the rulers that counts is not theoretical intelligence or technical ability but moral virtue (political prudence and legal justice), if a certain experience in the actual condition of man and society is also required. St. Thomas observed that every government should have something of the three modes of good constitution, a head for unity, a council of wisest, "the best" (aristocracy), for assistance in practical wisdom, and the agreement of the multitude (ambiguously now called "democracy") to preserve the essential freedom of political rule.

The political ruler, in whatever mode, is not the main authority, not just with reference to the originator of the *polis*, but as he is bound by a law attributable to a ruler above him. That is in his subordination as well to the natural moral law, to which he is beholden according to membership, as a person, of the universal community discussed above. Accordingly, as St. Paul says: "all authority is from God". For God is the author of nature, including human nature. This it is that the ruler is equally bound to according to his or her conscience, which is the application of the natural law within each person's practical consciousness. Each person is aware of the force of obligation in this way, regardless of whether or not he sees it as from God's commanding reason and will. (even atheists will insist they have this moral sense!)

The civil ruler's role is not to substitute his own (reason and) will for that of the "authority" of the natural moral law but to apply it to the concrete circumstances of the particular community that he is elected to rule over. It is within the confines of natural law as understood by the ruler that the ruler can operate to make positive laws as "determinations" of the more general principles of the natural law, which extends to the "law of peoples" (*ius gentium*).

There do occur, of course, revolutions and *coups d'etat* whereby modes of constitutions are radically changed and rulers are overthrown. But we cannot enter here into the complications such events bring to the discussion of authority. Aristotle has dealt with them in his *Politics*.

The question of authority is related to that aspect of law that is from the angle of its efficient cause. The principal author is the lawmaker, originally the founder of the "city", subsequently the elected temporary "conductor". But the individual person subject to the law must be a willing cooperator, a co-efficient cause. There must be no contradictory opposition between authority and freedom. How is that possible? This is quite readily understood in the case of the natural law. This is the moral law that we apply in our conscience. We feel the obligatory "force" of the law, and the moral person feels it most forcibly. But we know that we are free not to follow it, even "should the heavens fall". So if we do follow it we follow it freely.

The ruler with authority does not coerce the subjects to follow the law if they are law-abiding (he does not need to) but coercion becomes necessary to protect the community from "outlaws", who are like an enemy within. The main manner in which this can be done is to take away their freedom of action. One point where Finnis departs from Aristotle's analysis of law, and accordingly of authority, as we have seen, is that he tends to make coercion a co-essential element of civil law. It is, however, but a consequential property.

The other point already fully discussed is that he allows for an unjust law to be counted in some real, if secondary, sense, as a valid law. This impacts on one's notion of legitimate authority.

That is perhaps sufficient for a commentary on Finnis's treatment of authority. The only remaining essential element of the definition of law is promulgation, which Finnis gives but minimal attention to, but which is a significant issue in a situation of mass production of modern laws and regulations, making it practically impossible for the ordinary citizen to know what the law applying to him is without having to hire a team of lawyers (and accountants). The rich do with, the poor do without. And then when one is "caught" breaking the law the inordinate cost of defending oneself in a court of "justice" is simply scandalous.

CONCLUSION

This book is a critique of the three most prominent Australian "authorities" on Law and Ethics of the present day. But, particularly in the case of the critique of the work of John Finnis, we have sought to bring to the fore the main lines of the philosophy of the Natural Law to be found in the works of Aristotle and St. Thomas Aquinas.

There is much in that tradition that we believe has been lost even in those who today claim to be its followers. How else to explain the high academic acclaim and great public respect accorded to those who deny or distort its thinking, even scornfully and disdainfully? If, as Aristotle says, truth is stronger than error, and yet error is at times more pervasive, then the real defenders of truth must be being silenced in some way or other.

One can only think that this is partly due to the fact that some of those who wish to be followers in that tradition rashly strive to be as innovative as great minds are, but as Saint Paul VI said in (*Lumen ecclesiae, 8*): "In thus involving themselves, men may be showing the kind of innovative daring St Thomas showed in his day, but they often lack the clear vision and balance which the great doctor possessed in a supreme degree."

Leading up to that conclusion the saintly pope had observed with regard to matters to do with the relation between Faith and Reason of particular relevance to our discussion: "At this point, however, a serious problem arises: that of finding a new way of conceiving the relationship between faith and reason, or, to state the problem in its most general form, the relationship between the whole created order and the order of religious truth and especially of the Christian message.

In this matter there is evident danger of falling into either of two opposite errors: a naturalism which completely eliminates God from the world and especially from Man's life, and a false *supernaturalism*, or *fideism*, which seeks to avoid any doctrinal or spiritual decline by using the principle of authority to suppress the legitimate demands of reason and the development of the natural order. In *fideism*, however, the principle of authority is extended beyond its proper sphere, namely, the truths of faith revealed by Christ which are the seeds in us of the life to come and which completely transcend the limits of the human intellect.

These two dangers have often arisen throughout the centuries, both before and after St Thomas's time. In our own day they wait, like Scylla and Charybdis, for those who incautiously involve themselves in the many problems raised by the relations between faith and reason."

One way the real defenders of truth may be being overshadowed is then that what is new is admired more than what is true. There are nonetheless powerful historical reasons why the truth is held captive in modern philosophy and science. We have endeavored to bring to the surface these "forces" of falsity, which are particularly influential in the moral and political spheres of human life. For it is evident that without an appreciation of them it is most difficult even to discuss the truth of things generally, let alone that of Natural Law.

Hence, we have divided our critique into four parts. Part I is devoted to an understanding of the background necessary for the examination of any philosophical problem in our times, with some preliminary observations regarding the discussion of law and ethics by Finnis and Singer.

Part II outlines the plan of approach to the critique of the three works of Rowland, Singer and Finnis. In respect of Rowland, we have taken advantage of a thoroughgoing critique already carried out by our colleague Frank Calneggia in his book: *Assertions and Refutations: An Assessment of Dr. Tracey Rowland's Natural Law: From Neo Thomism to Nuptial Mysticism.* (En Route Books & Media, 2022) This we have incorporated in part and placed in an appendix (Appendix A). In this part also we make some general preparatory observations regarding the works of Finnis and Singer that we have chosen to focus on.

Then in parts III and IV we make a detailed examination and critique of the principal work selected in regard to each author, firstly, of Singer in Part III and then of Finnis in Part IV. It will be noticed that the fullest critique is made of the latter, for the reason that in his work we are able to deal most directly with the question of Natural Law, with which we are primarily concerned.

We have added two further appendices, B and C, the first entitled": "Sexual Union, Procreation and Marriage" and the second: "Science, Religion and Growing Up." The first, apart from its position of centrality and supreme importance in the ethical and legal "controversies" of our times, is a good example for bringing the Natural Moral Law into the discussion, which must be done if there is to be any intelligent outcome. The second relates to the more general "controversy" about the relation between Religion and Science, which is at the core of our discussion in Part I.

It is aimed at the youth of today who suffer most from the loss, or rather throwing away, in the modern era of theoretical and practical wisdom (Metaphysics and Ethics) and are accordingly led by their "elders" (domestic and political), so deprived of mental and moral maturity, to believe there is some superiority in science and inferiority in religion, which is preached to them within a supposedly impartial "free secular, and compulsory" education system. In this precise philosophical respect, if not in respect of that modern meaning of science that we have allowed as useful, the modern world has produced perhaps the most successful work of deception ever devised.

Though this book is a work of criticism of three Australian authors, severe at times, it is not aimed at them most directly. Their works have rather provided the occasion for bringing back into focus some of the great truths of ethical and legal philosophy and for showing up, as best as one can from within, the diabolically perilous situation for our modern culture that has developed since the general breakdown of Christian civilization now so long ago as to be practically forgotten. Those we criticize are but the victims of this apparent "collapse of values", as are we all.

But again we do not wish to end on a sombre and pessimistic note. Our Faith assures us that the Christian religion never will be defeated, no matter how powerfully such demise might be wished for by some. The light of truth, even of natural truth, will continue to shine through the clouds, just as the barque of Peter, in Chesterton's wonderful description, will continue its course through the ages, "reeling but erect".

APPENDIX A

EXTRACTS FROM

ASSERTIONS AND REFUTATIONS

AN ASSESSMENT OF DR TRACEY ROWLAND'S

Natural Law: From Neo Thomism to Nuptial Mysticism

By Frank Calneggia (En Route Books & Media, 2022)

ACKNOWLEDGEMENT

I am both grateful and indebted to Dr Donald G Boland of the Centre for Thomistic Studies in Sydney, Australia, for reviewing my text and for suggesting a number of improvements that have been duly incorporated. His deep and thorough knowledge of St Thomas and Thomism has been especially valuable. Readers of my text can therefore be satisfied that it has been subjected to a critical Thomistic analysis, and has been enhanced thereby. I also thank Don for his encouragement and friendship.

PREFACE

Tracey Rowland asserts that "since it is christological, natural law cannot be understood apart from the spousal relationship of Christ with his Church", which means that both the Divine revelation of the New Testament and the supernatural virtue of Faith received at Baptism are necessary for anyone to understand the natural law: it cannot be understood by itself in the light of reason. To the contrary Pope Benedict XVI teaches that "Christianity has never proposed a revealed law to the State and to society, that is to say a juridical order derived from revelation. Instead, it has pointed to nature and reason as the true sources of law". [1] There could not be a clearer refutation of what Rowland says. What the pope is saying is that natural law can be understood by itself in the light of human reason alone, without Divine revelation and without the supernatural virtue of Faith received in Baptism.

To bring out the extent and implications of Rowland's contradiction of Papal Teaching a detailed examination of the paper in which she made the above quoted statement is in order. This exposition and analysis of her *Natural Law: From Neo Thomism to Nuptial Mysticism* will examine her statements about Natural Law, Faith and reason, grace and nature in the light of Thomism and the teaching of the Papal Magisterium, with particular emphasis on the teaching of Benedict XVI.

---

[1] *The Listening Heart: Reflections on the Foundations of Law.* Address of Pope Benedict XVI to the German Bundestag, at the Reichstag Building on September 22, 2011.

A GUIDING PRINCIPLE

To introduce the task at hand we take as a maxim for our work the guiding principle of the greatest philosopher and theologian God has raised up in his Holy Church. [2]

> The study of philosophy does not consist in knowing what others have thought but to know the truth of things.

St Thomas did heed to a remarkable degree what others have thought be they Christian writers, Muslims or pagans, living in cultures outside his own, and in many instances in ages long preceding his own time. In this activity he was always primarily concerned to find the truth of things, and he certainly did find much in the thought of others that expressed the truth of things. He was also concerned to find and expose the errors he found in the thought of others, which activity he saw as a necessity so that truth might be better understood and safeguarded. This twofold work of the true philosopher was well expressed by Pope Leo XIII. [3]

> For surely that is a worthy and most useful exercise of reason when men give their minds to disproving those things which are repugnant to faith and proving the things which

---

[2] St Thomas Aquinas, *Commentaria in Aristotelis De Caelo et Mundo* I, 22.

[3] Leo XIII, *Aeterni Patris*, No 9. August 4, 1879.

> conform to faith. In the first case they cut the ground from under the feet of error and expose the viciousness of the arguments on which error rests; while in the second case they make themselves masters of weighty reasons for the sound demonstration of truth and the satisfactory instruction of any reasonable person. Whoever denies that such study and practice tend to add to the resources and expand the faculties of the mind must necessarily and absurdly hold that the mind gains nothing from discriminating between the true and the false.

The extent of the vast enterprise that St Thomas carried out to a unique perfection, and the overwhelming harvest he reaped in return, were beautifully expressed by Pope Leo XIII.[4]

> Among the Scholastic Doctors, the chief and master of all towers Thomas Aquinas, who, as Cajetan observes, because "he most venerated the ancient Doctors of the Church, in a certain way seems to have inherited the intellect of all."[34] The doctrines of those illustrious

[4] Leo XIII, *Aeterni Patris*, Nos 17, 18, 21, 22, 23. References: [34] Cajetan's commentary on Sum. theol., IIa - IIae 148, 9. Art. 4; Leonine edit., Vol. 10, p. 174, n. 6. [36] Sermo de S. Thoma. [37] Bucer.

men, like the scattered members of a body, Thomas collected together and cemented, distributed in wonderful order, and so increased with important additions that he is rightly and deservedly esteemed the special bulwark and glory of the Catholic faith. With his spirit at once humble and swift, his memory ready and tenacious, his life spotless throughout, a lover of truth for its own sake, richly endowed with human and divine science, like the sun he heated the world with the ardor of his virtues and filled it with the splendor of his teaching. Philosophy has no part which he did not touch finely at once and thoroughly; on the laws of reasoning, on God and incorporeal substances, on man and other sensible things, on human actions and their principles, he reasoned in such a manner that in him there is wanting neither a full array of questions, nor an apt disposal of the various parts, nor the best method of proceeding, nor soundness of principles or strength of argument, nor clearness and elegance of style, nor a facility for explaining what is abstruse.

Moreover, the Angelic Doctor pushed his philosophic inquiry into the reasons and principles of things, which because they are most comprehensive and contain in their bosom, so to say, the seeds of almost infinite truths, were to be unfolded in good time by later masters and with a goodly yield. And as he also used this philosophic method in the refutation of error, he won this title to distinction for himself: that, single-handed, he victoriously combated the errors of former times, and supplied invincible arms to put those to rout which might in after-times spring up. Again, clearly distinguishing, as is fitting, reason from faith, while happily associating the one with the other, he both preserved the rights and had regard for the dignity of each; so much so, indeed, that reason borne on the wings of Thomas to its human height, can scarcely rise higher, while faith could scarcely expect more or stronger aids from reason than those which she has already obtained through Thomas.

.... while to these judgments of great Pontiffs on Thomas Aquinas comes the crowning testimony of Innocent VI: "His teaching above that of others, the canonical writings alone excepted, enjoys such a precision of language, an order of matters, a truth of conclusions, that those who hold to it are never found swerving from the path of truth, and he who dare assail it will always be suspected of error." [36]

> But the chief and special glory of Thomas, one which he has shared with none of the Catholic Doctors, is that the Fathers of Trent made it part of the order of conclave to lay upon the altar, together with sacred Scripture and the decrees of the supreme Pontiffs, the *Summa* of Thomas Aquinas, whence to seek counsel, reason, and inspiration.
>
> A last triumph was reserved for this incomparable man - namely, to compel the homage, praise, and admiration of even the very enemies of the Catholic name. For it has come to light that there were not lacking among the leaders of heretical sects some who openly declared that, if the teaching of Thomas Aquinas were only taken away, they could easily battle with all Catholic teachers, gain the victory, and abolish the Church. [37] A vain hope, indeed, but no vain testimony.
>
> ...

This exposition and assessment of Rowland's paper will concern itself with the truth of her own statements. It generally isolates her statements from the patchwork of opinions of others that she presents in her survey, so that her statements on her chosen subject stand alone and have to fend for themselves. The sentences extracted from her paper will be numbered R1, R2, R3 etc. After each of these sentences my comment C1, C2, C3 etc will be given so that the order of presentation will be R1, C1; R2, C2; R3, C3 etc. I have numbered the sentences in her paper, but not all will be reproduced herein. Consequently, there are some gaps in the numbering. Her subheadings in *italics* will be retained throughout.

EXPOSITION AND ASSESSMENT

1. Introduction: Toward a theological natural law

…

(R1) For decades now natural law has been presented to Catholic undergraduates as a kind of *lingua franca* for dialogue with non-believers, precisely because it was deemed possible to sever it from its theological roots.

(C1) Rowland's main mistake, manifested here, lies in thinking that the doctrine of Natural Law is somehow something in the nature of a *lingua franca* lately devised by Catholic scholars to "dialogue" with unbelievers. A *lingua franca* is a third language held in common by people who do not understand each other's mother tongue, and who are therefore only able to communicate with each other by means of this third and foreign language. She is all at sea here for natural law is not a language at all, but an ordered combination of concepts and propositions that can be expressed in any language.

This 'catholic' natural law project has failed in her view so we need to go beyond such a theologically neutered conception. There are two errors here: first the misuse of the phrase *lingua franca*. It assumes that "natural law" is a phrase foreign to Catholic theology. Has she not heard of St. Thomas? It further assumes that "natural law" is a phrase foreign to non-Catholic philosophy. Has she not read Aristotle?

From the outset a necessary distinction needs to be made, a distinction which Rowland fails to make anywhere in her paper. The distinction is between natural theology and supernatural theology. Natural theology is studied as a part of metaphysics in philosophy. The five ways or proofs of the existence of God that St Thomas formulated are studied in natural theology. The starting point for each of these proofs is with our sense experience of the world in which we live, with God's Creation. Supernatural theology infinitely transcends natural theology because the truths upon which it is based are those divinely revealed truths that are beyond the reach of the human intellect and which are concerned with God's Redemption revealed in Christ Our Lord. The truths of Supernatural theology are seen only in the light of infused Faith. Upon these truths supernatural theological science rests, and develops under the guidance of right reason or logic. When Rowland talks about 'theology' in her paper it is evident that she means 'theology' in the sense of supernatural theology, and not natural theology. In other words she refers persistently to that theology where principles are seen only in the supernatural light of infused Catholic Faith, and not to that theology where principles are seen in the natural light of Reason or philosophy and which are consequently accessible to anybody. The absence of the real distinction between natural theology and supernatural theology is the second of the two major errors of her paper.

Natural Law, according to Pope Leo XIII, is "written and engraved in the mind of every man; and this is nothing but our reason, commanding us to do right and forbidding sin" [5]. Its moral precepts are also revealed truths (so that they can be known easily and without error) in the form of the Ten Commandments. The precepts of Natural Law are studied in moral philosophy. The perfection of the Natural Law is part of God's Redemption revealed in Christ. The perfection of the Natural Law is studied in Moral Theology, which is part of Supernatural Theology. Moral philosophy has a common denominator with natural theology: both are philosophical studies, the principles of which, by definition, are seen in the light of reason.

The 'theological roots' that Rowland talks about in this sentence, and thereafter for the remainder of her paper, are the truths of supernatural theology that

---

[5] Leo XIII, *Libertas praestantissimum,* No 8. June 20, 1888.

became known to humanity at the Incarnation. Now it is a fact of biblical history that God spoke to Moses on Mt Sinai, and inscribed the Decalogue on tablets of stone for him without attaching the supernatural 'theological roots' in any essential way that Rowland thinks are attached to the natural law, and which she claims it is not possible to sever from the natural law. From this stark contrast between the Words and Action of God Who identified Himself to the same Moses on Mt Sinai as God discoverable also by Natural Theology "I Am Who Am" "He Who Is" and Rowland's opinions we are warned from the outset to be on our guard against ignorance and confusion, and the attendant falsehoods these intellectual maladies bring in their train.

(R2) This is notwithstanding the fact that Protestants have never really been all that keen on it, regarding it as something of Stoic, rather than biblical provenance, and notwithstanding the further fact that it depends on a conception of nature as something stable, and that this has been rejected by most contemporary post-moderns.

(C2) The Protestant aversion to reference to natural law or the necessity for good works is the practical equivalent of their denial of the value of reason.

...

(R8) It was perhaps for such reasons that Cardinal Ratzinger, as he was, described natural law as a "blunt instrument" in dialogues with secular society.

(C8) Now that "Cardinal Ratzinger as he was" has become Pope Benedict XVI (and has taught us that he defends Thomistic reason or logic against Cartesian / Kantian Rationalism) we find that he uses the "blunt instrument" of natural law extensively "in dialogues with secular society". Here listed in chronological order are seven examples: (i) *Address to The Participants in The International Congress on Natural Moral Law*, 12 Feb 2007; (ii) *Address to Members of the International Theological Commission*, 5 October, 2007; (iii) *Address to The General Assembly of the United Nations Organisation*, 18 April 2008; (iv) *Address to the Members of the Pontifical Academy for Life*, 13 Feb 2010; (v) *General Audience* "Saint Thomas Aquinas", Part 1, 2 June 2010; (vi) *General Audience* "Saint Thomas Aquinas", Part 2, 16 June 2010; (vii) "The Listening Heart: Reflections on the Foundations of Law". *Address to the German Bundestag*, at the Reichstag Building, 22 September 2011.

The first three of these Papal Addresses pre-date Rowland's paper, which was published in the Fall (northern) edition of *Communio*, 2008; the first Address, the *Address to the International Congress on Natural Moral Law*, pre-dates Rowland's paper by more than 18 months. This Address is entirely at the level of reason (philosophy) and is devoid of any supernatural theology.

....

(R11) Reason has been truncated to finding efficient ways of achieving ends and nature is now subject to scientific manipulation, so neither reason nor nature is a strong foundation upon which to build a bridge to the contemporary Liberal tradition.

(C11) Rowland notes that "reason has been truncated", but apparently has little understanding of the fullness of reason of which it is a truncation. To note the difference, refer to the Addresses of Benedict XVI quoted in (C7) [*General Audience* "Saint Thomas Aquinas", Part 2, 16 June 2010] and (C9) [*Address to The Participants in The International Congress on Natural Moral Law*, 12 Feb 2007] above.

...

Rowland asserts that "neither reason nor nature is a strong foundation upon which to build a bridge to the contemporary Liberal tradition". Pope Benedict XVI teaches the opposite[6] (*emphasis added*).

---

[6] *The Listening Heart: Reflections on the Foundations of Law.* Address of Pope Benedict XVI to the German Bundestag, at the Reichstag Building on 22 September, 2011.

> Christianity has never proposed a revealed law to the State and to society, that is to say a juridical order derived from revelation. *Instead, it has pointed to nature and reason as the true sources of law.*

There could not be a clearer refutation of what Rowland says. If one abandons the principles of "nature and reason": "the true sources of law" and replaces them with something else, then one is replacing them with entities that are not "the true sources of law" and one consequently falls into error.

(R12) Nonetheless, Catholic apologists for several decades have been attempting to defend a Catholic view of the good life in the forums of Liberal society using the vocabulary of natural law.

(C12) ...

Let us listen to the words of Benedict XVI.[7]

> The idea of natural law is today viewed as a specifically Catholic doctrine, not worth bringing into the discussion in a non-Catholic environment, so that one feels

---

[7] *The Listening Heart: Reflections on the Foundations of Law.* Address of Pope Benedict XVI to the German Bundestag, at the Reichstag Building on 22 September, 2011.

> almost ashamed even to mention the term. Let me outline briefly how this situation arose. Fundamentally it is because of the idea that an unbridgeable gulf exists between "is" and "ought". An "ought" can never follow from an "is", because the two are situated on completely different planes. The reason for this is that in the meantime, the positivist understanding of nature has come to be almost universally accepted.

So how is it that Rowland asserts that Maritain and those of a similar mind presented "a Catholic view of the good life in the forums of Liberal society using the vocabulary of natural law" when they did so, as she complains, without attaching the theological roots she thinks are attached to the natural law, and which would make such presentations identifiable as being Catholic? She has swallowed the positivist line because she has little comprehension of the Aristotelian metaphysics of being: the basis of the unity of "is" and "ought". Consequently, like the rationalists with whom she shuns argument on the basis of reason and nature, she sees natural law "as a specifically Catholic doctrine, not worth bringing into the discussion in a non-Catholic environment".

The only note of Catholicism in Maritain's presentations of natural law is the fact that his presentations were made by a Catholic. Therefore Maritain presented a Catholic doctrine in speaking about natural law! On this 'logic' we should conclude that the Catholic maths teacher who explains Euclidean Geometry to his students is teaching them Catholic geometry, and the Anglican maths teacher in the class room next door doing the same thing is teaching his students Anglican geometry.

(R13) Many have done so in an almost axiomatic belief that it is a *lingua franca* for dialogue with non-believers.

(C13) It is evident, as was explained above in (C5), that Rowland confuses the material signs of concepts (words) with the concepts themselves for she is the one who claims that natural law is (i) an unintelligible idiom of voice sounds or *lingua franca* (ii) invented for dialogue with non-believers. Maritain, Thomists and the Papacy have never held these ridiculous ideas.

...

Listen to the words of Benedict XVI.[8]

> With her long tradition of respect for the right relationship between faith and reason, the Church has a critical role to play in coun-

---

[8] *Address of His Holiness Benedict XVI to the Bishops of the United States of America on their "Ad Limina" Visit.* Consistory Hall. Thursday, 19 January 2012.

tering cultural currents which, on the basis of an extreme individualism, seek to promote notions of freedom detached from moral truth. Our tradition does not speak from blind faith, but from a rational perspective which links our commitment to building an authentically just, humane and prosperous society to our ultimate assurance that the cosmos is possessed of an inner logic accessible to human reasoning. The Church's defense of a moral reasoning based on the natural law is grounded on her conviction that this law is not a threat to our freedom, but rather a 'language' which enables us to understand ourselves and the truth of our being, and so to shape a more just and humane world. She thus proposes her moral teaching as a message not of constraint but of liberation, and as the basis for building a secure future.

The Church's witness, then, is of its nature public: she seeks to convince by proposing rational arguments in the public square. The legitimate separation of Church and State cannot be taken to mean that the Church must be silent on certain issues, nor that the State may choose not to engage, or be engaged by, the voices of committed believers in determining the values which will shape the future of the nation.

This first principle of the natural law is self evident and is intelligible to everyone before any external verbal expression is given to it in whatever language one might speak. Refer again to Pope Benedict XVI quoted above in (C9): "This law has as its first and general principle, 'to do good and to avoid evil'. This is a truth which by its very evidence immediately imposes itself on everyone" [9]. The communicability of the natural law is due to its fundamental intelligibility, which intelligibility is independent of all language. Benedict XVI says that the natural law is a 'language' because it is based on "our ultimate assurance that the cosmos is possessed of an inner logic accessible to human reasoning"; or, more specifically, as Leo XIII taught, natural law is "written and engraved in the mind of every man" [10]. It is a 'language' "written and engraved" by the Creator, and He does not engrave anything foreign like a *lingua franca* in the human intellect. Consequently, "the Church's witness, then, is of its nature public: she seeks to convince by proposing rational arguments in the public square."

(R14) They have been told that this was recognized at the Nuremberg trials and that it was a project promoted by the French Thomist and advisor of Paul VI, Jacques Maritain, who contributed to the drafting of the United Nations' *Universal Declaration on Hu-*

---

[9] Benedict XVI, *Address to the Participants in the International Congress on Natural Moral Law*, 12 Feb 2007.

[10] Leo XIII, *Libertas praestantissimum.* No 8, 20 June 1888.

man Rights (1948), which itself is upheld as the project's greatest achievement, or at least an example of what can be achieved.

(C14) "They have been told that this" meaning Catholics have been told natural law is not what Rowland means by *lingua franca*: Catholics have been wrongly told that natural law is not an unintelligible idiom foreign to both Catholic theology and non Catholic philosophy, but that it is a universally intelligible doctrine understood by everyone. Where has Rowland quoted Papal teaching to show that Catholics have been taught by the Popes the exact opposite of what the Popes have always taught?

The fundamental intelligibility of natural law, as we would expect, is at the basis of the "project promoted by the French Thomist and advisor of Paul VI, Jacques Maritain". It is with the truth of the fundamental intelligibility of the natural law that Rowland takes issue. Given what we have already heard Benedict XVI teach about the intelligibility to everyone of the natural law, it is clear that Rowland will be unable to provide substantial evidence to support her assertion to the contrary: that the natural law is unintelligible at the level of reason. So she will have to find another way to induce this conclusion in the minds of her readers, and that 'induction' is what she now launches into.

(R15) Nonetheless, between 1948 and the first decade of the twenty-first century, Western society underwent a cultural revolution.

(C15) Her focus shifts to the crafting of a dark pessimistic outlook that is being made to look invincible i.e. here begins the accumulation of 'evidence' or "sociological facts" to induce a *post hoc ergo propter hoc* 'conclusion' down the track at (R21).

The universal preparation for the "cultural revolution" to which Rowland arbitrarily assigns dates was clearly visible to a Pope and Saint long before 1948. In his Apostolic Letter of 1910 Pope St Pius X wrote to the French Bishops about a worldwide movement of apostasy from the Catholic Faith that he could clearly see operating in the world of his day[11] (*emphasis added*).

> And now overwhelmed with the deepest sadness, We ask Ourselves, Venerable Brethren, what has become of the Catholicism of the Sillon? (a social organisation composed of well-meaning Catholics in France) Alas, this organisation which formerly afforded such promising expectations, this limpid and impetuous stream, has been harnessed in its course

[11] Pius X, *Our Apostolic Mandate. 1910.*

> by the modern enemies of the Church, and is now no more than a miserable affluent, feeding the great movement of apostasy, *being organised in every country* for the establishment of a *One-World Church, which shall have neither dogmas nor hierarchy neither discipline of the mind nor curb for the passions, and which, under the pretext of freedom and human dignity, would bring back to the world (if such a Church could overcome) the reign of legalised cunning and brute force and of the oppression of the weak and of all those who toil and suffer* ... We know only too well the dark workshops in which are elaborated those mischievous doctrines *which ought not seduce clear thinking minds.*

One hundred years later Pope Benedict XVI said much the same [12] (*emphasis added*).

> The geography of Christianity has changed dramatically in recent times, and is in the process of changing further. Faced with a *new form of Christianity*, which is spreading with overpowering missionary dynamism, some-

[12] Benedict XVI, *Address at Erfurt.* Meeting with the Council of the Evangelical Church of Germany, 23 September, 2011.

> times in frightening ways, the mainstream Christian denominations often seem at a loss. *This is a form of Christianity with little institutional depth, little rationality and even less dogmatic content, and with little stability. This worldwide phenomenon* – that bishops from all over the world are constantly telling me about – poses a question to us all: what is this new form of Christianity saying to us, for better and for worse? In any event, it raises afresh the question about what has enduring validity and what can or must be changed – the question of our fundamental faith choice.

The distinguishing marks of this world wide 'church' are the same to two Popes separated in time by one hundred years, as can be readily seen when the words of St Pius X are inserted into the emphasised part of the Address of Benedict XVI as follows.

> This worldwide phenomenon [being organised in every country] is a form of Christianity [a One World Church] with little institutional depth [a church of no hierarchy], little rationality [a church with no discipline of the mind] and even less dogmatic content [a church of no dogma], and with little stability [no curb on the passions].

Who is there to argue that the emphasised words of the two Popes have not been realised in modern society, and who has understood and applied the remedy implied by the words of St Pius X: "ought not seduce clear thinking minds". Same problem identified by Benedict XVI in (C9) above, and same remedy: correct thinking based in true metaphysics, whether applied at the natural level (philosophy) or at the level of infused Faith (supernatural theology).

(R16) When Maritain was at the height of his academic career in the 1940s there were no contraceptive pills, no IVF babies, no embryo experimentations, no clonings, no internet and space satellites, to name but a few of the socially significant new factors.

(C16) Rowland should know that a change in "sociological facts" alters nothing of moral principle. However, we should note that artificial contraception was already condemned by Pope Pius XI in the Encyclical *Casti Connubii* of 1930; and that Pope Pius XII condemned artificial insemination in the 1950's. See his *Discourse to those taking part in the 26th Congress of the Italian Society of Urology*, 8 October 1953: AAS 45 (1953) 678; *Discourse to those taking part in the Second Naples World Congress on Fertility and Human Sterility*, 19 May 1956: AAS 48 (1956) 471-473; *Discourse to those taking part in the 7th International Congress of the International Society of Haematology*, 12 September 1958: AAS 50 (1958) 733.

Those interested to read philosophical exposition and teaching could do no better than read the Addresses of Pope Pius XII. What will become apparent when reading this Holy Father is that he was an outstanding Thomist. Here is a list, though not exhaustive, of the Addresses of Pope Pius XII which are at the level of reason, many of which are about the Natural Law.

1. *The Natural Law and the Divine Government of the World.* Feb. 8, 1948. (Address to the Pontifical Academy of Sciences)
2. *Address to the International Conference of Humanist Philosophers.* Sep. 25, 1949.
3. *Address to Midwives on the Nature of Their Profession.* Oct 29, 1951.
4. *Proofs of the Existence of God in the Light of Modern Natural Science.* Nov. 22, 1951. (Address to the Pontifical Academy of Sciences)
5. *Address to the participants of the World Congress of Astronomy.* Sep. 7, 1952.
6. *Address to the First International Congress on the Histopathology of the Nervous System.* Sep. 14, 1952.
7. *The Technical Age.* Christmas Message, Dec. 25, 1952.

8. *Address to the participants in the Fifth International Congress of Psychotherapy and Clinical Psychology*. April 19, 1953.

9. *Address to participants in the Primum Symposium Internationale Geneticae Medicae.* Sep. 7, 1953.

10. *Allocution to Congress of the Italian Association of Urology*. Oct. 8, 1953.

11. *The Technician.* Oct. 9, 1953.

12. *Television.* Jan. 1, 1954.

13. *Address to participants in the Eighth Assembly of the World Medical Association.* Sep. 30, 1954.

14. *Address to participants of the World Congress for the prevention of workplace accidents.* Apr. 3, 1955.

15. *Address to participants in the Sixth International Congress of the Latin Medical Union.* Apr. 7, 1955.

16. *Modern Science needs Philosophy.* Apr. 24, 1955. (Address to the Pontifical Academy of Sciences)

17. *Radio message on the occasion of the sixtieth anniversary of the discovery of Radiotelegraphy by Guglielmo Marconi.* Oct. 11, 1955.

18. *Address to the General Assembly of the European Union of Broadcasting in Rome.* Oct. 21, 1955.

19. *Address to workers in the field of cinematography participating in the International Congress in Rome.* Oct. 28, 1955.

20. *Address to participants of the Second World Congress on fertility and sterility.* May. 19, 1956.

21. *Space.* Sep. 21, 1956.

22. *Astronomy.* May, 1957.

23. *Automation.* June 7, 1957.

24. *Address to the Brazilian Association for the cure of leprosy.* June. 29, 1957.

25. *Address to members of the "Gregorio Mendel" Italian Institute of Genetics on reanimation and artificial respiration.* Nov. 24, 1957.

26. *Address to the participants in the 13th Congress of the International Association of Applied Psychology.* Apr. 10, 1958.

27. *Radio message to participants in the First World Conference on Health Care.* July. 27, 1958.

28. *Address to the International Society of Blood Transfusion.* Sep. 5, 1958.

29. *Address to the First General Assembly of the Collegium Internationale Neuro-Psycho-Pharmacologicum.* Sep. 9, 1958.

30. *Address to participants in the Seventh International Congress of Haematology.* Sep. 12, 1958.

Note that these Papal Addresses, written, to use Rowland's words, "when Maritain was at the height of his academic career", are not directed specifically to Catholics, but to groups of people who could be of any religion or of no religion; baptised or unbaptised. Consequently these Addresses are at the level of what their various recipients have in common: human reason and the Natural Law. The Addresses are philosophical in nature not theological.

...

(R18) By 1968, however, in Maritain's twilight years, the various alternative visions of what a human being is, and hence, what the meaning of life is, had captured the imaginations of the post-war generation, and with the expansion of higher education to the lower middle and working classes, an entire anti-Christian cultural revolution was effected.

(C18) The year 1968 seems to have some special significance in Rowland's mind. She notes two phenomena that for her by 1968 were visible as part of the "anti-Christian cultural revolution" or as part of what Pope St Pius X called "the great movement of apostasy being organised in every country" that was clearly visible to him in 1910 (see C15). The phenomena or "sociological facts" historically visible to Rowland by 1968 that she notes are: "various alternative visions of what a human being is" and "the expansion of higher education to the lower middle and working classes". A description of these same "sociological facts", of supposedly recent origin somewhere in her time frame of 1948 to 1968, was already given by Pope Leo XIII in 1879 [13] (*emphasis added*).

> Whoso turns his attention to the bitter strife of these days and seeks a reason for the troubles that vex public and private life must come to the conclusion that a fruitful cause of the evils which now afflict, as well as those which threaten us, lies in this: *that false conclusions concerning divine and human things, which origi-*

[13] Leo XIII, *Aeterni Patris,* No 2.

> *nated in the schools of philosophy, have now crept into all the orders of the State, and have been accepted by the common consent of the masses.*

The words "false conclusions concerning ... human things" readily cover what Rowland describes as "the various alternative visions of what a human being is". Apart from Rowland's historical short-sightedness, the major difference between the two statements concerns metaphysical first principles. Pope Leo XIII teaches as a Thomist who discerns between true and "false conclusions" whereas Rowland speaks like a relativist with her "alternative visions of what a human being is". Moreover, Leo XIII gives an answer to those who "seek a reason for the troubles that vex public life" i.e. he provides a reason for the "sociological facts" that are visible to him and to those who want to know the root cause of these facts. These visible phenomena or "sociological facts" are the visible effects of an identified cause: "false conclusions concerning human and divine things, which originated in the schools of philosophy".

The Holy Father notes these evils again later in the encyclical and teaches the whole Church where the remedy to both the cause and its effects is to be found [14] (*emphasis added*).

[14] Leo XIII, *Aeterni Patris,* Nos 27, 28, 29.

Many of those who, with minds alienated from the faith, hate Catholic institutions, claim reason as their sole mistress and guide. Now, We think that, apart from the supernatural help of God, nothing is better calculated to heal those minds and to bring them into favor with the Catholic faith than the solid doctrine of the Fathers and the Scholastics, who so clearly and forcibly demonstrate the firm foundations of the faith, its divine origin, its certain truth, the arguments that sustain it, the benefits it has conferred on the human race, and its perfect accord with reason, in a manner to satisfy completely minds open to persuasion, however unwilling and repugnant.

Domestic and civil society even, which, as all see, is exposed to great danger from this plague of perverse opinions, would certainly enjoy a far more peaceful and secure existence if a more wholesome doctrine were taught in the universities and high schools-one more in conformity with the teaching of the Church, such as is contained in the works of Thomas Aquinas.

For, the teachings of Thomas on the true meaning of liberty, which at this time is running into license, on the divine origin of all authority, on laws and their force, on the pa-

> ternal and just rule of princes, on obedience to the higher powers, on mutual charity one toward another-on all of these and kindred subjects-*have very great and invincible force to overturn those principles of the new order which are well known to be dangerous to the peaceful order of things and to public safety.*"

A Thomist will understand that those teachings of St Thomas to which the Holy Father refers in the last quoted paragraph have the natural law as their foundation. Those who have studied the United Nations' *Universal Declaration on Human Rights* (1948) will see that it very much upholds these teachings of St Thomas noted here by Leo XIII in 1879: teachings which are based on the natural law and which, according to the Holy Father, "have very great and invincible force to overturn those principles of the new order which are well known to be dangerous to the peaceful order of things and to public safety".

(R19) Meanwhile, within the great universities, the Enlightenment project of formulating a universally acceptable ethical framework with recourse to reason alone was of dwindling interest.

(C19) Rowland's sentence simply conveys an impression: "recourse to reason alone was (and apparently still is for many) of dwindling interest". Her reference to the loss in academia of interest in the "Enlightenment project", a product of Cartesian Rationalism, should not be allowed to evoke in the reader a bad impression of the 'Maritain project' which also has "recourse to reason alone", but reason based in sound metaphysics unlike Rationalism.

The 'Maritain project' and its rational basis in sound metaphysics is completely vindicated by the teaching of Popes Leo XIII, St Pius X, Pius XII and Benedict XVI as can be understood from the Papal Teaching either listed or quoted from above. Further vindication of the correct use of reason is provided by Pope Pius XII in what he taught Catholics. Here we quote from his 1950 Encyclical [15] (*emphasis added*).

> *It is well known how highly the Church regards human reason, for it falls to reason to demonstrate with certainty the existence of God, personal and one*; to prove beyond doubt from divine signs the very foundations of the Christian faith; *to express properly the law which the Creator has imprinted in the hearts of men*; and finally to attain to some notion, indeed a very fruitful notion, of mysteries. *But reason can perform these functions safely and well, only when properly trained, that is, when imbued with that sound philosophy which has long been, as it were, a patri-*

[15] Pius XII, *Humani Generis,* No 29.

> *mony handed down by earlier Christian ages, and which moreover possesses an authority of even higher order, since the Teaching Authority of the Church, in the light of divine revelation itself, has weighed its fundamental tenets, which have been elaborated and defined little by little by men of great genius. For this philosophy, acknowledged and accepted by the Church, safeguards the genuine validity of human knowledge, the unshakable metaphysical principles of sufficient reason, causality, and finality, and finally the mind's ability to attain certain and unchangeable truth.*

"It is well known how highly the Church regards human reason" ... apparently not as well known now as it was when the Holy Father wrote those words in 1950. ... Note that Catholics are here being taught in an encyclical that "It falls to reason (philosophy) to demonstrate with certainty the existence of God" and "to express properly the law (the Natural Law) which the Creator has imprinted in the hearts of men", but "reason can perform these functions safely and well only when properly trained, that is when imbued with that sound philosophy acknowledged and accepted by the Church, for this philosophy safeguards the genuine validity of human knowledge and the minds ability to attain certain and unchangeable truth".

The importance and moral obligation to use the God given gift of reason "to attain certain and unchangeable truth" is underscored by Pope Leo XIII. [16]

> For, since it is in the very nature of man to follow the guide of reason in his actions, if his intellect sins at all his will soon follows; and thus it happens that false opinions, whose seat is in the understanding, influence human actions and pervert them.

When one sins, one sins either by commission or omission. To neglect an investigation into the truth or falsehood of things, when it is within one's capacity to carry out such an investigation, is a sin of omission. The irrational acts of (i) assuming that such an investigation is a mental activity to be associated with rationalism, and (ii) that therefore one is 'absolved' from undertaking this study, and then (iii) recommending this state of mental stagnation to others for their imitation is best described by the words of St Paul. "The more they called themselves wise the more foolish they became." [17] To this warning we add the injunction of our Divine Saviour

---

[16] Leo XIII, *Aeterni Patris*, No 2.

[17] Romans 1:22.

"Thou shall love the Lord thy God with all thy heart, *with all thy mind*, and with all thy strength." [18]

...

(R21) By the 1990s at least some Catholic scholars were beginning to question whether the Maritainian project and its subsidiaries were still the most strategically viable options. Foremost among them was Alasdair MacIntyre.

(C21) ...

On a larger and well illuminated stage, in fact "from this very podium" that his "predecessors Paul VI and John Paul II" addressed the United Nations met in Assembly, Pope Benedict XVI stated the following about the United Nations' *Universal Declaration on Human Rights* (1948) and the Natural Law [19] (*emphasis added,* except for *Universal Declaration of Human Rights* and *De Doctrina Christiana*).

> This reference to human dignity, which is the foundation and goal of the responsibility to protect, leads us to the theme we are specifically focusing upon this year,

[18] Luke 10:27; Mark 12:30.

[19] Benedict XVI, *Address to the General Assembly of the United Nations Organisation*, 18 April 2008.

which marks the sixtieth anniversary of the *Universal Declaration of Human Rights. This document was the outcome of a convergence of different religious and cultural traditions, all of them motivated by the common desire to place the human person at the heart of institutions, laws and the workings of society, and to consider the human person essential for the world of culture, religion and science. Human rights are increasingly being presented as the common language and the ethical substratum of international relations. At the same time, the universality, indivisibility and interdependence of human rights all serve as guarantees safeguarding human dignity. It is evident, though, that the rights recognized and expounded in the Declaration apply to everyone by virtue of the common origin of the person, who remains the high-point of God's creative design for the world and for history. They are based on the natural law inscribed on human hearts and present in different cultures and civilizations. Removing human rights from this context would mean restricting their range and yielding to a relativistic conception, according to which the meaning and interpretation of rights could vary and their universality would be denied in the name of different cultural, political, social and even religious outlooks.* This great variety of viewpoints must not be allowed to obscure the fact that not only rights are universal, but so too is the human person, the subject of those rights.

The life of the community, both domestically and internationally, clearly demonstrates that respect for rights, and the guarantees that follow from them, are measures of the common good that serve to evaluate the relationship between justice and injustice, development and poverty, security and conflict. *The promotion of human rights remains the most effective strategy for eliminating inequalities between countries and social groups, and for increasing security.* Indeed, the victims of hardship and despair, whose human dignity is violated with impunity, become easy prey to the call to violence, and they can then become violators of peace. The common good that human rights help to accomplish cannot, however, be attained merely by applying correct procedures, nor even less by achieving a balance between competing rights. *The merit of the Universal Declaration is that it has enabled different cultures, juridical expres-*

sions and institutional models to converge around a fundamental nucleus of values, and hence of rights. Today, though, efforts need to be redoubled in the face of pressure to reinterpret the foundations of the *Declaration* and to compromise its inner unity so as to facilitate a move away from the protection of human dignity towards the satisfaction of simple interests, often particular interests. *The Declaration was adopted as a "common standard of achievement" (Preamble) and cannot be applied piecemeal,* according to trends or selective choices that merely run the risk of contradicting the unity of the human person and thus the indivisibility of human rights.

Experience shows that legality often prevails over justice when the insistence upon rights makes them appear as the exclusive result of legislative enactments or normative decisions taken by the various agencies of those in power. When presented purely in terms of legality, rights risk becoming weak propositions divorced from the ethical and rational dimension which is their foundation and their goal. *The Universal Declaration, rather, has reinforced the conviction that respect for human rights is principally rooted*

> *in unchanging justice, on which the binding force of international proclamations is also based.* This aspect is often overlooked when the attempt is made to deprive rights of their true function in the name of a narrowly utilitarian perspective. Since rights and the resulting duties follow naturally from human interaction, *it is easy to forget that they are the fruit of a commonly held sense of justice built primarily upon solidarity among the members of society, and hence valid at all times and for all peoples.* This intuition was expressed as early as the fifth century by Augustine of Hippo, one of the masters of our intellectual heritage. *He taught that the saying: Do not do to others what you would not want done to you "cannot in any way vary according to the different understandings that have arisen in the world"* (*De Doctrina Christiana*, III, 14). Human rights, then, must be respected as an expression of justice, and not merely because they are enforceable through the will of the legislators.

To any unbiased reader this Papal Address is a resounding endorsement of the United Nations' *Universal Declaration on Human Rights* (1948) and of the fundamental importance of the Natural Law to human rights, and simultaneously an exhortation to societies and nations of their obligations to protect such rights. Upon reading this Papal Address one can readily see that Rowland's paper self destructs.

APPENDIX B

SEXUAL UNION, PROCREATION AND MARRIAGE

How human sexual unions are connected with reproduction is a problem that has proved over time to be difficult to resolve from the mere observation of the activities of human beings. Below human nature it is quite clear that sexual union is but a mode of reproduction, something developed from a more basic asexual mode of reproduction. Even at the highest level of animal life below man the connection is quite evident. The male and female of the species engage in sexual union according to bodily urges and conditions that are plainly ordered naturally to the generation of offspring. On fulfilment of this vital function from time to time the adult males and females generally separate to perform the other animal functions appropriate to their natures. The sexual unions as such are temporary only.

This is in contrast to the practice of human couples, who generally continue to stay and act in sexual union even when it is clear that there is no possibility of the procreation of children. There is moreover no specific time of the year or season for mating. There normally remains in the human female indeed a naturally recurring monthly period (prior to menstruation) when reproduction can occur but this is not necessarily known very well. In fact it is mainly studied when the couple wish to avoid pregnancy.

From an observation of human behaviour in this regard we might conclude that if there is a connection between reproduction and sexual union it is the latter that is primary and the former secondary. Having a child almost seems to be a matter of choice in a sexual relationship had for its own sake, i.e. for the sake of the sexual union.

Indeed, we may say that this is the conclusion that has been arrived at in modern sexual ethics. Not all would take the next step and redefine sexual union to include that between two people of the same sex, i.e. between two males or two females. However, this is but a short step when the concept of sexual union has been totally disconnected from reproduction. A same sex union may appear to most to be an obviously unnatural union, one that contradicts the very notion of sexuality, but that is precisely because of the connection of the sexual parts involved with reproduction. They have always been and always will be named organs of generation.

Accordingly, even in the case of human sexual unions, despite the apparent loosening of the connection between sexual union and reproduction, so close in the case of animal sexual differences, the obviousness of the connection is never lost. The reason for this we may put in purely rational terms to derive from the fact that man, though possessed of a spiritual soul, is not a pure spirit. Man and woman are as much bodily as all other animals. It is evidently from the animal side of our nature that sexual union is tied necessarily to reproduction. Nor can we totally disconnect this tie, for bodilyness and animality belong to the very essence of human nature.

We may see clearly that the apparently great difference in the relationship between sexual union and reproduction in humans has to do with the union having to be spiritual as well as bodily. That first of all brings in free will so far as engaging in sexual activity is concerned. The sexual union itself and its connection with reproduction thus are not natural in the sense of unfree. They can only be natural in a moral sense. An understanding of them and their connection must therefore be from knowledge of the Natural (Moral) Law.

The human sexual union that involves the body (and animal levels of knowledge and desire) cannot be disconnected from the spiritual level of knowledge and love. The union is of body and soul, for the body does not exist without the soul. So far as the union is human it is true that it is the spiritual dimension that is superior. The bodily connection and its natural order to reproduction can be called primary or fundamental but not so as to suggest the inferiority of the spiritual. It is fundamental and primary only as in the same general way vegetative life is fundamental and primary in human bodily existence. In this life the spiritual level of human life very much depends not just on the animal level but also upon the lowest vital level.

We can thus understand that human sexual union in so far as it is bodily is just as much ordered to reproduction as plant and animal life are. Nonetheless, this ordination is not to be simply equated with what is in plant or animal life below man. The ordinations at the three levels of life are of different kinds or genera and thus one should expect there to be significant differences. We have seen that following Aristotle it may be said that plant life is virtually identified with reproduction. Animal life is not so identified but nonetheless the connection is extremely close.

In regard to human life the connection is not natural in the same way but mediated by reason. That is to say it is natural in the sense of morally necessary. Nonetheless, this morally natural ordination to reproduction is just as necessary to human life as the physically natural. Indeed, the moral necessity is taken from the physical side of human nature. From a spiritual point of view however it is secondary to the unitive significance of human sexual union. As a whole the union is clearly designed to promote the continuance of the human species, but at times the unitive function alone can be the reason for the union even at the bodily and animal level.

We will not go any further into showing the (moral) necessity of connecting human sexual union with reproduction. For, as we have noted, the practice of human beings in this regard very much clouds the reason and throughout history there has been a tendency to treat human sexual union as something only connected with reproduction from choice.

For the most part it has been recognised that natural sexual union means between male and female. But, despite its obviousness, the disconnection of sexual union from reproduction will weaken the appreciation of this basic truth; and a certain moral laxity in this respect has attended the practice if not the ethical theory of even the most civilized communities.

Indeed, we may say it is only with the advent of Christianity, where our practical reason has the benefit of the light of Faith, that the rational positions with regard to human sexual union and its natural connection with procreation have been clearly asserted and strongly defended.

But we need to bring into this discussion the question of the institution of marriage. For it is plain that people generally see that sexual union between man and woman needs to be confined within a stable relationship even before being confirmed by social laws. Here again, there is a degree of difficulty in determining what form this marital relationship should have.

It is only indeed with Christ that we have a definitive statement of the naturalness (moral necessity) of the institution of marriage ("from the beginning"). Even "the nation of

God" was permitted to divorce. So it is that human sexual union even of the natural kind was hardly ever held in practice to be life long. It is only in the Christian, indeed in the Catholic, moral code that the definition of marriage as "the exclusive union of one man and one woman for life" is still honoured in the full.

As this is held not just of the sacrament of marriage but even of marriage as a natural institution we should look more closely at the rational grounds for such a moral position. It is in this definition of course necessary that marriage be between a man and a woman. But the notion of marriage adds the necessity for the union to be exclusive and for life. Why should this be so?

Regarding it purely from the basic relationship of sexual union to reproduction a reason given is the specific need of human offspring. There is a deal of force in this reason since the parents' role is not finished until the child reaches maturity as a human being which includes a degree of intellectual and moral development.

That is to say there is to be considered the spiritual side of human nature on the part of the child. However, it seems to us that there is more to the union of the parents needing to be life long than the needs of the child. It is the compound union as spiritual and bodily on the part of the parents that founds the integrity of the marriage so that it cannot be broken while the bodily part exists. This lifelong integrity flows over into the relationship within the family as a whole, and its rupture by divorce causes deep wounds not only in the spouses (whether at fault or not) but also in the children.

This integrity or wholeness is what the unitive function of marriage means. It first of all applies to the spouses and we believe it is what founds the naturalness in human marital life of sexual union even when reproduction is naturally excluded. It also can explain the morality of regulating one's sexual union for a legitimate rational purpose. The spiritual aspect of marital union thus governs the bodily aspect though it cannot negate it.

But we should look at why this cannot be done outside marriage. Why is it that sexual union and reproduction in regard to human life requires the natural institution of marriage? This will require a close look at the rational structure of the Natural Moral Law, which, though it is drawn in some way from the human nature and its relation to others and the natural world, is also in a way constructed by the human intellect like theoretical science. For the Natural Law is but Ethical Science as a body of universal practical principles and conclusions that direct our actions to the point where conscience and prudence have to take over because of the concrete and particular situation in which all human behaviour takes place.

St. Thomas compares the process of the formation of the Natural Law or Moral Science (law being defined in this context as "an ordinance of reason") to the formation of principles and conclusions in the theoretical sciences. Since human nature spans not only the bodily or physical level of reality but also the spiritual or metaphysical, the Natural Law (Ethical Science) will be principally at the metaphysical level, but will also have to bear upon the bodily part of human life.

How this is may be can be seen in the consideration of the cardinal virtues of justice, fortitude and temperance. The first is subjected wholly in the will, which is a purely spiritual power; the other two are subjected in the sense appetites, the irascible and the concupiscible. The latter two are moral in so far as they are moved by the (free) will. Even justice is concerned with bodily things as in the case of theft, as well as purely spiritual things, such as religious liberty. The two essential parts of human nature are intimately related in human behaviour.

But, just as human theoretical science first understands propositions at the most universal level - the principle of non-contradiction - so the practical science of Ethics first understands practical propositions (which are commands or laws in principle) at the most universal level – the principle of synderesis. St. Thomas points out that just as the first theoretical principle is based upon the first concept of being so the first practical principle is based upon the first practical concept of good, which is only being considered in relation to appetite or desire (which at the intellectual level is will). These two first principles do not tell us what particular things are beings or goods but simply orientate us to the most fundamental character of existence considered theoretically and practically.

So, apart from the very first existential practical principle, there is an order of first principles focused on the essences or natures of good things, what is and what is not good. These are the most general principles from which we reason to more definite principles and necessary conclusions. The very first principles are the most self-evident – if we do not understand them we are simply not functioning with our power of understanding. The very first principle of "seek good and shun evil" is used in logical or scientific proof not directly but by way of *reductio ad absurdum*. Direct proof begins with the highest order of principles taken from the essences or natures of things, whose existence and goodness are taken for granted.

Thus the first principles of the Natural Law follow from human nature in itself and in its necessary relationship with the world in which we live, both spiritual and bodily. There is a twofold order that may be observed depending upon whether we begin with the body or with the soul, with man as animal or rational. St. Thomas uses the former which accords with the way our intellect has to begin with what is known to us through the senses, and the most basic universal or generic knowledge we have is of bodily substance. The first three natural laws in this regard correspond to the fifth, sixth and seventh of the Ten Commandments, concerning our obligations in justice in respect of human life, marriage and ownership of external goods.

What interests us here is how the two institutions of marriage and property fit into the Natural Moral Law. They are clearly not of the order of very first principles. Indeed it may be readily seen that they are dependent upon two more fundamental principles, in the case of property, the universal destination of earthly goods, in the case of marriage the reproduction of the species by the mating of man and woman. It is worth noting at this point that the human race has generally fallen down badly in respecting these two natural institutions. The right of property has been used even to deny access of others to the goods of the earth (to such an extent that the Fathers of the Church were prepared to equate such misappropriation in some instances with the crime of murder).

As may be appreciated from what we have noted so far the rights to sexual intercourse belonging to those within the institution of marriage have been used not just without any respect for their orientation to reproduction but also in deliberate frustration of such. It is by treating as absolute the dominion over their sexual organs and external possessions given by the institutions that the participants end up not only abusing their rights but also enslaving themselves to the unlimited pleasure and cupidity such imagined freedom delivers.

For marriage is evidently meant to provide a rational order for the reproductive needs of the human race through a union of the two human sexes. It does this in the context of a union of man and woman in the most complete way, body and soul. Without losing the supreme superiority of the spiritual soul over the material body the essential connection of human being with bodily reality is made to serve the needs of the continuation of the species, as with all other living bodies.

The institution of marriage, then, may be seen as a rational resolution of the subordination of individual human natures to the reproductive needs of the human species insofar as it is animal. For at the same time it has to be that one individual human spiritual soul is worth more than the whole material universe let alone the multiplicity of human bodies, though they may be the highest part of that whole. The spiritual relationship between two human persons therefore is to be held superior to the reproductive needs of the human race from a bodily point of view.

It is a bit more complex than that. But we may see the constitution of marriage as the perfect solution of this apparent twofold subordination. The first important thing to keep in mind is not to treat separately the two parts of human nature, spiritual and material. They are a perfect unity. The next thing to keep in mind is the relative priorities and nobilities belonging to each part.

But, our view is that by the use only of our reason unassisted by Faith it still is and probably always will be difficult to understand this sexual relationship as applied specifically to human nature and to appreciate fully the solution arrived at by the institution of marriage. We might also observe the same difficulty of appreciating the full meaning of the institution of property. In regard to both institutions, though mankind has seen their moral necessity a great number of individuals, backed up by political power in a lot of cases, have honoured them more in the breach than in the observance.

One might fairly say that at the present stage of human history these foundations of the sixth and seventh commandments, i.e. the universal destination of material goods and the ordination of human sexual activity to continuance of the human species, have never been held in such political and public contempt.

St. Thomas explains that the institution of property derives as a necessary rational conclusion from the primary principle of the universal destination of external goods, so much so that he puts it within the *Ius gentium,* which is that part of the Natural Moral Law that is adopted naturally by all nations prior to the institution of their own systems of positive law. This may be said also of the institution of marriage as the natural/rational conclusion applied to the human condition from the primary principle derived from the natural inclination (on the side of man as a living body) to reproduce one's kind.

It matches the needs of all with the proper desires of individuals to have control or a degree of personal responsibility for their sexual relations and the use of external goods. What is apparent, however, is that these natural institutions are not fully understood without the aid of Faith. This can be seen from the general distortion of their implementations within the legal systems of even civilized nations. This is especially evident in modern times, when the settled institutions inherited from Christendom have been more and more eroded as the secular state has more and more disdained the moral advice of the Catholic Church to the point now that it aggressively treats it with contempt.

Indeed, this reaction against religion and the morality that flows from it reaches to the depths of the foundations of these natural/rational institutions so as to cast aside first principles that are self-evident to all, such as the universal destination of material goods and the basic orientation of sexual activity to reproduction of the species.

Liberalist political thinkers and the politicians who subscribe to their philosophy now treat private property as a form of absolute sovereignty that would shut out others altogether from access to external goods regardless of the risk of perishing. Morally speaking, that is simply unthinkable, yet it is blithely promoted in the name of liberty.

Similarly, moralists and even theologians now treat sexual union as a form of absolute right to the use of one's organs of generation that shuts out any relation to reproduction. Indeed, they do so in the name of loving union.

The most clear rejection of these profoundly immoral attitudes has been given by the Church in two of the greatest popes of recent times, one John Paul II already declared a saint in heaven and the other Paul VI about to be so declared. It is indeed striking how both have been concerned to defend the natural institutions of property and marriage whilst at the same time condemn the distortion of their meaning in order to justify the very unnatural abuses of our fellow human beings that they are designed to correct.

Despite the efforts of the popes it seems that humanity is "hell bent" upon descending into the grossest depths of human injustice and depravity. One may read the present times as a last ditch effort of diabolical forces to prevent humanity from having recourse to the aid of Faith in the Church, particularly with regard to these two fundamental areas of natural morality. As noted they are expressed in the sixth and seventh commandments. But an attack is also well launched against the fifth commandment, which is not disconnected from the other two (and against the eighth commandment as is evident in the fact that the attacker is not only a murderer from the beginning but also the father of lies).

There can be no other time in the history of humanity that so many innocent poor are done to death daily by the luxury of the rich in the name of property and so many abuse their organs of reproduction in the name of sexual union modelled on marriage. Such is the degree of deceit employed that many of those suffering as a result are persuaded to attribute their misery to nature or God, and join in the railing against religion and morality led by the leaders of academic and political life. A certain blindness and hardness of heart seems to have penetrated deep into modern society. One shudders at the retribution that naturally follows from such a generalized condition of social injustice and personal depravity.

If it were not for the principle of resurrection observed by Chesterton to be in any society in which Christianity survives to some extent, one would lose all hope of recovery from such a spiritually mortal condition. So there is no cause for despair, despite the desperate situation. Certainly, some particular nations and even civilizations may fall but we have Faith that the Church and human society (the supernatural and natural bodies) will not perish but will survive unto the end of the age, and beyond.

It is evident that the institutions of property and marriage will not be needed in the next life, having fulfilled their natural ends. But they will not be destroyed in this world.

APPENDIX C

+++

dgboland © 2018

Human beings (apart from the first) do not come into existence as "grown ups". The very phrase indicates that there is a process in the life of every human being beginning with generation and proceeding through a period of growth to a known end; this characteristic human beings have in common with every other kind of bodily life. Such "evolution" is sometimes fast sometimes slow. In the case of humanity it is notably slow and gradual, taking up many years of man's allotted life span before one is called a "man", or "woman".

Now what applies to the lower bodily (or biological) part of human life has a parallel in the psychic (or animal) part of human life. For example, it takes some time for the senses of babies to operate perfectly. As a general rule, the full operation of the higher senses of an animal depends upon the development of the brain to its mature state, and the higher levels still of humans depends upon the prior maturation of the higher internal senses such as the imagination and the memory.

Thus, more specifically in the case of humans, even the higher rational operations, once the physical organ of the brain is fully developed, show a gradual process of maturation in spiritual terms. Here we have to be clear that by spiritual we do not mean religious, let alone pertaining to revealed religion. We simply refer to the higher intelligent life of humans compared to brute animals. For Plato and Aristotle, doing Mathematics is a spiritual and rational activity. Intellectual activity is what specifies human beings, the essential difference that marks them off from the rest of nature.

So we already have to connect science with human spiritual and rational life and note it is involved also in a process of perfection, which in a certain respect never is finished in this life. It is in the nature of human intellectual development that it transcends human bodily existence; so "growing up" in this regard is never fully achieved in this life. However, we will have to consider shortly the various levels of science and note their different kinds of development.

We usually associate science with what Aristotle called theoretical science. But he pointed us to another important part of the intellectual and rational life of human beings that is called practical science. For, this great thinker (St. Thomas Aquinas followed him in this regard) it is with this department of science that religion is normally associated. It is in fact within ethical science.

Here, in modern times, in which Aristotle's fine distinctions and definitions are lost, along with the meanings of words that were used for hundreds of years afterwards with Aristotle's sense, we encounter much intellectual confusion, and consequent difficulty of communication. Religion from a rational point of view is a matter of morals. It is a matter of science, but not science as theoretical like geometry, not even physical science like cosmology.

As may be appreciated at this point, growing up in the full human way has to involve both Mathematics and Morals. Science in the theoretical sense cannot in any way be opposed to science in the practical sense. There cannot be any conflict between Science and Religion according to the true notion of science and religion as understood by the most rational of pagan thinkers. You might as well say that a belief in the sacredness of human life contradicts a fact of biology or that holding to the wrongfulness of theft contradicts a scientific finding in chemistry.

More pointedly, a natural desire to pay homage to the Creator for the gift of life and existence (a moral debt in justice confirmed by the first three of the Ten Commandments) does not contradict one's scientific knowledge, as is evident from the fact that many if not most eminent scientists in history have been religious in the sense of worshipping God.

So where can this modern belief in the conflict between science and religion have come from? It has to be in a change in the meaning of science and/or religion. Our contention is that it consists in a subtle change in both which is a radical change in the meanings of science and philosophy introduced into modern thought with the rejection of Aristotle.

Religion, as a practical duty to give due worship to the Creator came to be confused with the theoretical question of the existence of God, which is not an ethical matter but a metaphysical one. Then science came to be contracted so that it was seen to deal only with questions wholly within the limits of the particular sciences of Mathematics and Physics, (merged since Newton) necessarily excluding from the notion of science any questions of ultimate or first causes, i.e. of Metaphysics. Mixed up with this was the rejection of the old Physics, whose deficiencies were unjustly loaded upon Aristotle so as to reject all his theoretical philosophy and science from Metaphysics down.

Within such a truncated understanding of the range of science it was inevitable that religion and science would be seen as incompatible, and " a consummation devoutly to be wished" by the practical proponents of a new philosophy of absolute freedom from morality. Looked at more closely the new scientific atheism has more to do with the push from the modern "religion/morality/politics" of liberalism than with any antipathy in genuine scientists against the practice of religion or belief in God.

In the result then philosophy, which used to be considered as respectable an intellectual exercise as science, and, as

Metaphysics, even more to be honoured, has been downgraded to mere opinion; whilst religion, and morals generally, have been treated as part of a pseudo-theoretical Metaphysics, a purported rival to science.

Religion has become treated as a matter of theoretical science, consigned to that part of Metaphysics called Natural Theology, the theoretical investigation of the existence and nature of God, which, by the way, Plato and Aristotle were prepared to find rationally conclusive. It is the subtle exclusion of Metaphysics from the modern notion of science that has sidelined the rational status of religion. It has not been realised that at the same time the whole of moral philosophy or ethical science has been undermined. In such a confusion of mind it is not to be wondered at that revealed religion, or divine Faith, has been surreptitiously reduced in the process to mere human faith or opinion.

But first let us return to looking briefly at the "history of the human mind" considered both in the individual, or personally, and in human civilization, or historically. We find a close parallel between these two aspects of human life, individual and social, so that we can relate one to the other quite freely. It is convenient, however, to start with the social or historical viewpoint. So let us first look in a summary fashion at the history of philosophy and science, with particular reference to the relation between Metaphysics and Physics (For this purpose we may take Mathematics as part of Physics).

Just as in regard to Faith we find that there are two levels, or stages of revelation, as it were, the propaedeutic and the mature, which can be looked at historically, identifying them with Judaeism and Christianity; so there are two levels of reason, or stages in the historical development of philosophy.

In terms of education, the word "propaedeutic" has the same root as "pedagogy". St. Thomas alludes to this in his advice on study: "You should choose to enter not immediately into the ocean depths, but rather through small streams, for one should reach more difficult matters by going through the easier ones first."

The two levels of reason, or intellectual understanding, are the physical and the metaphysical. St. Thomas points out that Physics or Natural Philosophy should be studied before Metaphysics. For the former is not so deep or difficult, being close to sense. Nonetheless, we are not meant to stay at that level, as the child is meant to grow up intellectually.

Physics, taken with Mathematics, confined as it is to the physical world available to us through our sense life (through the imagination in the case of Mathematics), is the field of theoretical reason that we need to focus on first. This is the way of pedagogy of the human mind. Yet this is not the field of reason that satisfies our wonder ultimately. It is suitable rather to the childhood and adolescence of the human mind. Just as wisdom comes with age so should we come to consider questions in Metaphysics as we go beyond the physical (and mathematical).

This we see applies individually. Hence, St. Thomas explains the order of theoretical study as beginning with logical and mathematical questions, progressing through the natural sciences and ending with Ethics and Metaphysics. But we can see it also in a general way in the history of human civilization or culture.

Even prior to such theoretical or scientific investigations there was a period of "infancy", where the imagination (fancy) founds the reason in the modes of literature and poetry. It is still an activity of the human mind, i.e. rational, but in its most concrete manner, with abstract ideas kept to a minimum. In the individual it marks the beginning of the movement of the child from mere animal imagining to the most elementary understanding.

This earliest stage of human wondering finds a parallel in the history of humanity's exploration of reality. For, as Aristotle himself noted, before natural philosophy or natural science arose in Greek society there was the period of the "poets"; the period of earliest science came after the period of myths, both having in common a sense of wonder. Right from the start we have an interest in seeing things in concrete terms of the spiritual and personal. However, these are "made up" in our imagination, producing stories of gods and heroes, in the case of early mankind, and of fairies and talking animals, in the case of children.

We have thus in the earliest stage of the human mind's encounter with the outside world the predominance of the creative imagination, representing things in a fanciful way. This is not to be taken as a necessarily false representation, but rather looking at reality in a metaphorical fashion, indeed the work of reason grasping in an elementary way the truth of things at a deep and intuitive level. It is immersed in the concrete, attributing spiritual and personal traits to material things and non-persons. What is grasped here is the distinction between good and evil, rather than being and non-being. The struggle of the human spirit with the forces of evil is transferred to reality as a whole. G. K. Chesterton is one who has presented the deep realism of this world of the child in a marvellous way.

So we should not see this early opening of the human mind to the world as irrational (but as "romantic"). It is deeply rational but not in the strict sense of seeking the abstract reasons of things, or natural causes, but as the more primitive intellectual insight ("intuition") operating like a sense, with the trappings of sense. It is the deep childlike mode of the spirit that should stay with us as our abstract reason develops, and it comes again in full strength in the lives of saints and sages. This storytelling mode may be seen in the history of literary studies that develop along with scientific studies. It is prominent at the early stage of the education of each individual human being. (In modern thought it is deceptively presented as irrational – mistakenly identifying reason with modern rationalism - this "romantic" view of things is what attracts many to the work of Nietzsche, who it is to be remembered was enamoured of the Greek dramatic and poetic genius, but who re-acted too strongly against the rationalism of his age)

Just as the infant moves on from this fanciful stage of looking at the world so did humanity, particularly in the genius of the Greeks, move to consider things in a more abstract and logical way, what Aristotle called scientific. It seeks the intermediate natural causes of things and events without our needing to posit the ultimate cause until we reach the mature level of natural wisdom in Metaphysics, which comes into our mind at the summit of our study of Physics, or Natural Science.

This accordingly second more explicitly and definitively rational and logical stage began in history with those who Aristotle called natural philosophers, though significantly they were also referred to as the first natural scientists, beginning with Thales of Miletus (c. 624 – c. 546 BC). The early connection of science with Mathematics, which becomes more significant later, can be seen already in Thales.

Aristotle indicated that in the beginning of Greek philosophy and science, that is, in the first stirrings of abstract rational investigation of things, the thinkers tried to find a general cause of things or explanation of reality. They thought though only in terms of physical reality and looked to a common material cause. This was a first attempt at scientific explanation.

However, Aristotle noted that this attempt was deficient from a rational point of view. For causality, signifying that which has influence unto the existence of anything, can be seen in three other modes, the formal, efficient and final. What is needed to fully explain the existence of a house, for instance, is not just the materials out of which it is made, but also the builder (efficient cause), the plan (formal cause) and the purpose it is made for – to "house" human occupants (the final cause). Take away any one of these four causal influences and the house would not have come to be.

Aristotle showed that this has to apply to all natural existing things, since, being contingent (meaning not necessarily existing) they can be all seen as having come into existence (as they can go out of existence). However, in terms of seeking the efficient and final cause, it is necessary to go outside the order of natural things and causes in order to provide a full explanation; for even extrinsic causes within the order of creation cannot be the very first and last final causes, since they themselves exist contingently.

Indeed, though the formal cause is within the natural thing, as part of its essence, its existence has to be attributed to an extrinsic formal or exemplary cause, just like the plan of the house must first exist in the mind of the builder or his architect. Thus the search for an explanation of nature as it exists has to end up with positing a Maker who is extrinsic to the natural order and indeed has an intelligence capable of creating all forms of things and providing their ultimate final cause. We should not, then, overlook the truth that the Maker must also love the final cause as the good for which things come into existence.

Aristotle traces the history of science in terms of the human mind coming to recognise these other causal influences. After a focus on the material cause there was a turn to formal causality, but this began with explanation in terms of mathematical forms or formulas, with Pythagoras. He greatly influenced Plato but Plato was able to move to the metaphysical level with his theory of Ideas. However, Plato did not explicitly connect these formative causes with the efficient cause so that his theory of the connection between the ideas and the forms of individual things came to be expressed in terms of participation, a sort of exemplary causality.

The final cause seems to have come into consideration through Socrates, but rather in ethical terms. This did not bring out the full metaphysical significance of final causality, paralleling a downplaying of efficient causality in the metaphysics of Plato. For Socrates seems to have focused on the formal cause in ethical matters, such as the moral virtues, particularly justice, seeking their definitions. That happiness was the final cause necessarily tied to them was simply taken for granted. It was left to Aristotle, then, to free the human mind completely from being tied to the mathematical and physical, and to point to the full significance of extrinsic causality. He assigned Mathematics to the physical field of reason, for it did not rise above the quantitative aspect of bodies.

The study of Metaphysics was therefore the pinnacle for Aristotle of scientific study in the fullest sense, which we call wisdom. This, as he pointed out, is a level of thought that is in a way above us (though he refuted the contention by the poet Simonides that it was not appropriate for man, for God would be jealous – quite the contrary, argues Aristotle: "But it is impossible for the Deity to be jealous (indeed, as the proverb says, "poets tell many a lie"), nor must we suppose that any other form of knowledge is more precious than this; for what is most divine is most precious. Now there are two ways only in which it can be divine. A science is divine if it is peculiarly the possession of God, or if it is concerned with divine matters". (*Meta. 983a*)

Put in Christian terms, Metaphysics, or natural wisdom, may be said to belong to that part of our life of the spirit that is just a little lower than the angels. Moreover, St. Thomas points out that it is only in this highest kind of knowledge that man is truly free, for the reason given by Aristotle: "Here he proves the second attribute, namely, that wisdom is free; and he uses the following argument: that man is properly said to be free who does not exist for someone else but for himself. For slaves exist for their masters, work for them, and acquire for them whatever they acquire. But free men exist for themselves inasmuch as they acquire things for themselves and work for themselves. But only this science exists for itself; and therefore among all the sciences only this science is free." (*In Meta. I, lectio 3, n. 58*)

However, as happens in individual human life, it is a level of exalted rational life that is difficult to sustain and many opt for an easy (and servile) life. Historically, too, after Aristotle people fell back into dealing with the more immediate concerns of practical life. This manifested itself in the rise of different ethical and political theories, such as that of the Stoics, who came into prominence in the study of philosophy.

The metaphysical/spiritual focus did not completely fall out of the picture as can be seen in the history of Neo-Platonism. It was however only a partial continuation of Aristotle's great work, if from a spiritual point of view the better part. It was the balanced core of his Metaphysics (Ontology) that came to be neglected, the notion of being that included as well material and bodily reality.

This platonic bias development in Socratic philosophy coincided with the beginning of Christianity. The continued study of Metaphysics then showed a preference for Plato's idealist/realism and this extended well into the period of Christendom, virtually until the time of St. Thomas Aquinas, who, most importantly, revived Aristotle's correction of Plato's Metaphysics.

Unfortunately, the focus of the philosophers/scientists thereafter, outside that of a few like St. Thomas, was more on the lower level of scientific work with which was associated the neglect of the empirical side of physical science. This scientific deficiency (unjustly attributed to Aristotle himself) was used to discredit the whole of Aristotle's philosophy/science, not just the physical but also the metaphysical.

As it turned out the physical sciences benefited from this but it also involved a tendency not to accord rational status to the spiritual and the theological, shunting such studies into the exclusive province of Sacred Theology as connected with Christian Faith. This happened gradually and the study of Metaphysics in some partial form continued until Kant. Nor did the spiritualist philosophy of Plato completely disappear from modern philosophical studies. But as we shall see the focus shifted away from the theological to the epistemological part of Metaphysics.

For science became disconnected from philosophy and with this went the foundations of science. When it came to the crunch of ascertaining the truth of modern science it was discovered that it could not be done within science. Thus, along with the aversion to the consideration of theology as a science, went the fall into radical scepticism and inevitably the atheism that characterises modern secularist thinking.

It is in this context that we need to understand the apparent conflict between religion and science. It is more properly to be seen as a conflict between religion, understood as a metaphysical question to do with God's existence as Creator, and science understood so as to exclude natural wisdom, which obliges us to acknowledge the world as created. With that necessarily goes the exclusion of natural morality. This, however, is most congenial to the vision of humanity as possessed of a god-like freedom to make all things in its own image, the very heaven of the modern liberalist visionary.

Ironically, this individualistic philosophy finds itself trapped into promoting socialistic/collectivism because the vision of humanity has to be realised in political terms. Thus, as may be seen proved again and again historically in modern times this exaltation of false freedom, where it has managed to dominate the minds of those who gain political control, has resulted in regimes that have subjected whole communities to the most degrading slavery not to speak of wholesale death and destruction. That some modern societies have avoided this civilization-ending catastrophe must be attributed to a section of the population holding onto religion (if diminishing in influence) and such societies maintaining some semblance of respect for natural morality.

All this is traceable, at the level of nature and reason, to the rejection of Aristotelian Metaphysics and Ethics as science or true human knowledge able to be arrived at rationally. This is the part of Aristotle's corpus that was of most interest to St. Thomas, for it was integral to the study of Sacred

Theology, having to do with reality and man's place in the world.

It is important to note though, that by the work of St. Thomas Aristotle's thought was "transfigured" by being brought under the higher light of Christian wisdom had from Revelation. This does not mean that natural wisdom was "transformed" into something other than the work of natural human reason. Like Christ's transfiguration whilst still on earth, the Christian's human figure will shine with a beatific splendour when perfectly infused with sanctifying grace, but it is still human nature. That nature is distinct from the divine quality given to human beings, which is the life of grace.

Faith enlightens reason operating as it must in this life. It enables human reason in the graced Christian to function most perfectly, not weakening natural certitudes but further strengthening them, not only in theoretical/metaphysical terms but also in practical/ethical terms. Unfortunately, at the beginning of the modern era of human thought a lower level of theoretical scientific knowledge, the physico-mathematical, was embraced as the true and only science. This meant the rejection of the use of reason at the higher metaphysical level, resulting in fact in a sort of second childhood of the human mind.

Mathematics (strong in adolescents) came back into pre-eminence with the modern rejection of Metaphysics. At this stage what we wish to note is the contrast between science in the narrow sense as Physics and science in the wider and deeper sense as Metaphysics. But the story is a bit more complex than that simple opposition. What complicates it is the peculiarly modern marriage of Mathematics and Physics (or Natural Science), which has come to be virtually equated with Science itself.

We have wished to highlight the move in ancient times from the physical to the metaphysical level of human theoretical reason and the move back in modern times from the metaphysical to the physical, or natural science in the stricter narrower sense. This was accounted justifiable, as we have noted in other places, by the neglect of the material cause or inductive method, called empirical, in the period of Christendom, dominated as it was by theology. This led to a stagnation of the natural sciences, which was only overcome in the modern scientific revolution.

As noted above the interest in Metaphysics continued into the modern era but mainly as Epistemology or the problem of the certainty of our knowledge. For the general result of the rejection of Metaphysics proper was a philosophy of scepticism.

We need to be clear about the two levels of human theoretical knowledge seen as the two stages in the development of human thought considered not only individually, but also worked out historically. We have seen a parallel of this relationship between the propaedeutic and the mature at the supernatural level. Reason as Philosophy (and science) reached its early maturity in Aristotle. But the human mind could not sustain this level of natural wisdom and Metaphysics fell back into various partial and distorted speculations, as explained above.

It is a mistake then to treat religion and science as understood in modern times as not in conflict, and indeed as not in mortal conflict. It should be clear that there is no true conflict between them properly understood as we have explained above. But that is not the way they are understood today. There needs, then, to be a new revolution in our understanding of religion and science if we are to get out of the war to the death that is presently being waged between religion and science.

The difficulty consists in correcting the notion of science so as to be able to show not only the lack of any conflict or opposition to religion but also to show their perfect harmony and co-operation. This will be clear if we simply substitute the notion of wisdom (within which religion and theology are to be found even at a natural rational level) for religion.

It is not necessary to say that science, even as understood today, is not science in a true sense, just as science for Aristotle was used in a sense distinguished from wisdom. It is not necessary to deny that modern science is a great advance on pre-modern science, including that as presented by Aristotle, and this in two important respects. The first is the recovery of the necessary empirical side of the natural sciences or what was generally called Physics (including the study of the bodily side of human nature). The previous neglect, as we have noted, is not to be attributed to Aristotle's influence but to various accidental factors, such as the radical disruption of the Greco-Roman civilization and the shift of intellectual concerns in the emerging Christian civilization away from the things of this world towards higher things.

The second is the great expansion of the mixed or medial sciences, and the increased power over natural processes brought about by the combination of mathematical analysis with empirical observations and measurements. Though Aristotle and Greek science generally were familiar with this mathematical formalization of empirical knowledge their familiarity was partial and limited. They had an awareness of it in ancient Astronomy and Mechanics, Optics and Harmonics, but it took the likes of Galileo and Newton to realise the depth of the quantitative character of material nature and to demonstrate the possibility of the quasi-universal application of the science of quantity to the study of the physical world.

Newton became the universal genius of the new mixed science. Corresponding to it was a new mixed scientific method, combining empirical observations and measurements with mathematical laws and deductions. Such was the success of this mixed method that it was thought to be the unique method of science itself, the one way for human reason to discover the secrets of all nature, including human nature.

The experience in recent times that certain of Newton's universal laws did not quite match up with more detailed observations and more accurate measurements made possible by advanced technology has not basically altered the faith in the modern scientific method. It has rather given rise to a felt need to adjust our view of the physical nature of matter and of the formal character of mathematics, from an absolutist one to a relativist one, from a determinist one towards an indeterminist one. It is still a mixed science of Mathematics and Physics that is the paradigm, but with some justice called a new Mathematics and a new Physics.

With little account taken of the metaphysical implications all sorts of contradictions and nonsense that have been introduced into the language of science at the most basic level, though that is not to say that there is no real basis for the conceptual changes needed to be constructed to account for the new empirical evidence uncovered. The felt need for the accommodation of contradiction is but a consequence of the ignorance of Metaphysics from which flows a failure to understand the nature even of Logic.

Nonetheless, the magnitude of the discoveries of the workings of material nature by the application of the new scientific method is not to be denied, nor the almost miraculous control over all physical nature that it has delivered to humanity. In this regard, the work of Aristotle and pre-modern science can be made to look juvenile, even though it remains the historical basis of all science.

Yet, that version of the development of the human mind is only half, and indeed less than half of the story – for in a real way it is to do with a superficial view of things. The modern era shows a side that is bright and shiny compared to the past. But the other side of the picture is dark and disturbing – for it shows what has been lost; what belongs not to the physical but to the metaphysical "dimension" of nature, and, where human nature is concerned, what belongs not to the body but to the soul that is spiritual, upon which more directly depends morality.

We do not wish to go into this breakdown in the practical/moral/political order of human affairs though it is quite evidently closely connected with the change in the understanding of reality that occurred in the theoretical sciences. What we wish to bring out are the implications of this radical change purely from the point of view of science considered as theoretical knowledge of reality. It is to do with human intellectual maturity before any consideration of the practical consequences that follow quasi-inevitably from this failure of intellect.

The two, the theoretical and the practical, of course interact and though we are not here concerned with priorities in this regard, we may say that in all human affairs, including the exercise of our understanding, human (free) will fails first. But let us confine our consideration to the purely intellectual failure, and from a natural point of view. The main fact that we wish to point to is that in the early history of the human mind the Greek genius stands out in a multitude of ways but here we focus on the work of reason in philosophy and science, taken firstly and rightly as wisdom or human intellectual knowledge in its widest range of reason and at its deepest level of natural insight into reality.

The most vulnerable victims of this failure of maturity are the young who depend so much on their elders' wisdom, i.e. Metaphysics, much more than on their science, i.e. Mathematics and Physics, in order to become themselves maturely wise. From a social point of view with this lack of theoretical wisdom has historically gone a loss of practical wisdom, i.e. Natural Morality. The evil forces that arise to dominate in this state of human affairs easily reduce whole populations to conditions of servitude, manipulating the education system and means of communication so as to cleverly deceive the young into blaming their servile condition and mental misery upon religion and morality.

Our focus here is not, as already stated, on the practical consequences of the manufactured opposition between religion and science, but upon the pretence that identifies the range of human reason with the truncated notion of science so as to exclude natural wisdom. It is this equivocation with regard to the meaning of science that has succeeded in presenting religion as something unscientific and accordingly irrational.

Then, to bolster the supposed superiority of science so understood, religion as an integral part of human wisdom is lampooned as belonging to the earliest (infantile) stage of human mental development as described above. But it may be readily appreciated that though science in its narrow sense can be in some ways regarded as an advance in human thinking it is but an intermediate stage, to be equated more with adolescence in the individual. The adult stage, where human life reaches its maturity, is marked by a wisdom that goes beyond the particular sciences and is their intellectual foundation. This is where religion properly understood belongs.

The truly wise do not preen themselves with an air of superiority over the childhood and adolescence of the human mind, for they have come through those stages and appreciate their necessity and value. Religion does not therefore oppose science that is distinct from wisdom. As the highest part of either theoretical or practical wisdom religion is the most loving support of both poetry and science. Science, like an adolescent who thinks he knows everything, rebels against true religion at a most terrible cost to itself and humanity.

Made in the USA
Monee, IL
30 October 2024

68999974R00197